History and Culture Series

ESSAYS ON INDIAN FREEDOM MOVEMENT

Edited by
Dr. Raj Kumar

D P H

DISCOVERY PUBLISHING HOUSE
NEW DELHI-110002

First Published-2003
Reprinted-2010

ISBN 81-7141-705-1

Published by

DISCOVERY PUBLISHING HOUSE
4831/24, Ansari Road, Prahlad Street,
Darya Ganj, New Delhi-110002 (India)
Phone: 23279245 • Fax: 91-11-23253475
E-mail:dphtemp@indiatimes.com

Printed at Mehra Offset Press, Delhi.

Preface

Struggle for freedom of India was an epic phenomena. In this collection of essays we have made an attempt to collect some of the important works which could interest, inform and enlighten our readers.

Aim is to understand the main landmarks of the struggle which should enable the reader to analyse the topic in proper perspectives. It is likely to be of use to the general reader as well as those working on the subject.

Raj Kumar

Acknowledgements

In preparing this work we have incurred indebtness of those eminent scholars who have worked on the above subject. I am grateful to Professors S. Gopal, Ravinder Kumar, Bimla Prasad, A.C. Bose, S. Kadival, A.L. Basham, David Dilks, B. Sheikh Ali, A.R. Kulkarni, S. Bhattacharya and V.N. Dutta for their love and kindness.

Some of the universities and research institutions their librarians and staff members have been good and helpful, I am thankful to them all,

My publisher Sri Tilak Wasan has worked hard to bring it out in its present form. He deserves full patronage of the readers.

Raj Kumar

Acknowledgements

Contents

1.	Introduction	1
2.	The Nationalist Ideas Behind the Revolt of 1857	14
3.	Nationalism Takes Root : The Moderates	16
4.	The Indian Struggle for Independence—1885 to 1909	62
5.	Politics of Indian Revolutionaries—1905-1910	74
6.	Armed Struggle from the South-East	83
7.	The Indian Self-Government as Advocated by Annie Besant	97
8.	Quit India Movement	104
9.	Tribals and Freedom Struggle	110
10.	Muslim Nationalism and Freedom Struggle	124
11.	Subhash Chandra Bose—His Role in India's Freedom Struggle	162
12.	Shyama Prasad Mookerji and Freedom Struggle	172
13.	The Last Phase of the Freedom Struggle—The R.I.N. Mutiny	179
	Appendix I	*191*
	Appendix II	*198*
	Appendix III	*200*
	Appendix IV	*202*

1

Introduction

Resistance to the British rule in India started almost from its inception. In 1857 impression of patriotism and nationalism manifested in various forms. The struggle for freedom in India was broadbased. But organised movement no doubt began with the establishment of the Congress in 1885. With the Swadeshi movement and boycott in 1905 the movement gained momentum. Surat split of 1907 divided the congress movement into moderate and extremist groups. The early call for complete independence came from the Ghadar Party.

Early Calls for Complete Independence : The Emergence of the Ghadar Party

The first Indian political organization to call for complete independence from British rule was the Ghadar (or Gadar) Party, organized in 1913 by Indian immigrants in California. The *Ghadar* movement was remarkable for many reasons. Although Sikhs from Punjab made up the majority of its founding members, the movement was completely devoid of any trace of regional or religious chauvinism. Its platform was uncompromisingly secular and called for a total rejection of any form of caste discrimination. And unlike the Congress, its membership was primarily drawn from the working class and poor peasantry. Sikhs, Muslims, and Hindus of all castes (including Dalits) were welcomed in the movement without bias or discrimination.

The *literature* of the Ghadar Party was also the clearest in describing the depth of misery that the common people of India experienced under British rule. They were also amongst the first to anticipate the outbreak of the First World War. Correctly sensing that it was an opportunity for the Indian people to liberate themselves from the yolk of colonial rule, they called for a mass movement for total independence. In their widely distributed poster, "*Jang Da Hoka*" (Declaration of War) they warned of the danger of Indian soldiers being drawn into the British war effort in the First World War.

Unfortunately, the Congress failed to take advantage of this tremendous opportunity and leaders like Gandhi went as far as campaigning for the British war effort, calling upon Indians to enrol in the British Army. This treacherous and sycophantic policy of the young Gandhi not only drew biting criticism from Ghadar activists, but opposition from other quarters also emerged.

At a time when Gandhi was still addressing "War Recruitment Melas", Dr. Tuljaram Khilnani of Nawabsha publicly campaigned against War Loan Bonds. Sindh was then part of Bombay Presidency and the Sindh Congress, part of Bombay Provincial Congress Committee. When Gandhi sought election to the AICC from Bombay PCC, the delegate from Sindh opposed his election in view of his support to the British war effort.

Nevertheless, by and large, the Congress was a relatively conservative organization at this time and drew stinging *criticism* from the Ghadarites. Rejecting the notion that freedom could be won by participating in the oppressive bureaucracy of the British or by pleading with the British for reforms or self-rule, the Ghadarites believed that only a militant mass movement that involved workers and peasants and all other sections of Indian society on a non-sectarian basis could succeed. They envisaged an India that would not only be free from exploitation by the British but would also be free from hunger, homelessness and disease. In their vision of India there would be no place for religious superstition or any socially sanctioned inequities.

Although the Ghadar movement started in California, chapters were established all over the world and by 1916, a million copies of their weekly pamphlet were published and circulated. As the movement grew in strength, there were plans to set up cells of the

Ghadar party all over India and thousands of young volunteers attempted to return home and initiate local chapters wherever they could. The British, realizing the dangers posed by this extremely radical movement, moved quickly and closed in on the revolutionaries. Hundreds were charged for sedition in the five Lahore Conspiracy Cases. According to one estimate, a total of 145 Ghadarites were hanged, and 308 were given sentences longer than 14 years. Several were sentenced to hard labour in the notorious prison known as Kala Pani in the Andamans.

The Ghadarites were especially successful in winning over Indian soldiers in the British Army and enticing them to revolt. Soldiers in the Hongkong regiments were arrested and court-martialed for distributing Ghadar and sent back to India and imprisoned. Two Singapore regiments rebelled in Penang, but the rebellion was brutally crushed. In Rangoon in January 1915, the 130th Baluch regiment revolved. 200 soldiers of this regiment were court-martialed. Four soldiers were hanged, 69 were given life imprisonment and 126 were given rigorous imprisonment for varying terms. Pandit Sohan Lal Pathak, one of the outstanding leaders of the Ghadar Party, was hanged on February 10, 1916 in Mandalay jail for inciting rebellion against the British rule. The party was also active amongst Indian soldiers in Iraq and Iran. As a result of their work the 15th Lancers, stationed in Basra, revolted and 64 soldiers were court-martialed. Similarly, the 24th Punjabi and 22nd Pahari regiments also revolted. But in spite of the tremendous repression unleashed by the British against the Ghadarites, the British were unable to stop a mass wave of revolutionary unrest in 1919. The closing months of 1918 and the first months of 1919 saw the opening of a strike movement on a scale never seen before. The Bombay mill strike extended to 125,000 workers. In spite of the Rowlatt Act of 1919 that sought to extend the provisions of martial law, a wave of mass demonstrations, strikes, and civil unrest confronted the British authorities. The British rulers were taken by surprise by the courageous resistance of the workers and the official Government Report for the year noted with alarmed amazement how Hindus and Muslims had resisted their power unitedly. Unsurprisingly, the British responded with extraordinary measures of repression.

General Dyer's Jallianwala Bagh massacre followed the strike wave, when an unarmed crowd of 10,000 Baisakhi celebrators was mercilessly attacked with over 1600 rounds of ammunition. Yet, Gandhi continued to advocate cooperation with the British in December 1919, even as the resistance of ordinary Indians continued. The first six months of 1920 saw an even greater level of mass resistance, with no less than 200 strikes taking place involving 1.5 million workers. It was in response to this rising mass revolutionary tide that the leadership of the Congress was forced to confront its conservatism and give a somewhat more militant face to its programme. The "non-violent non–cooperation" movement was thus launched under the stewardship of Congress leaders like Lajpat Rai, Motilal Nehru and Gandhi.

Other Radical Forces

But in contrast to the foot-dragging of the Congress, other far more radical forces were already coalescing. The Communist Party of India was formed in 1920 who, while demanding complete independence, also stressed the need for giving a radical content to the slogan of swaraj through a definite programme for social and economic change by including such vital questions as abolition of landlordism, end to feudal domination and elimination of caste oppression.

While participating in the freedom struggle, they devoted their energies to the task of organising workers in trade unions, peasants in the Kisan Sabhas, and students in their unions. It was due to these efforts that the national organisations like the All-India Kisan Sabha and the All-India Student's Federation were founded and the All-India Trade Union Congress strengthened. The Communists also took the initiative in founding progressive, cultural and literary organisations like the Progressive Writers' Association and the Indian People's Theatre Association.

But the British rulers were determined to stamp out communism in India. Just as they had repressed the Ghadarites, they unleashed brutal repression on the fledgling Communist groups and banned communist literature to prevent the spread of revolutionary ideas. They conducted a series of conspiracy cases against the young leadership of the communist movement – Peshawar (1922); Kanpur

(1924) and Meerut (1929). The party was declared illegal soon after its formation in the 1920s and had to work in conditions of illegality for over two decades.

The Conservatism of the Congress

In many respects, the analysis of Indian conditions by the Ghadar Party and of the Indian Communists was very similar, and in spite of the repression they faced, their message continued to draw followers. But the Ghadarites were far more critical of the Congress and were a good deal more skeptical of the Congress leadership than were the Communists who thought that the pressure of the mass movements would force the Congress to act more decisively against the British. But they had perhaps underestimated the depth of conservatism that held back the Congress leadership. In 1921, Republican Muslim leader Hasrat Mohani wanted to move a resolution defining Swaraj as complete independence, free from all foreign control. Much to the relief of the British, Gandhi led the opposition against the resolution and secured its rejection. In 1921, there was seething anger against the high taxes imposed by the British. Delegations from numerous districts approached Gandhi to lead a No-Tax campaign. In Guntur, the no-tax campaign began without the permission of the national leadership, but Gandhi responded by calling for all taxes to be paid by the due date. However, he agreed to lead a No-Tax campaign in the single district of Bardoli, but even that was withdrawn when he heard news of a peasant rebellion in Chauri Chaura village in UP.

Gandhi's Bardoli decision created deep consternation in Congress circles. Subhas Chandra Bose wrote: "To sound the order of retreat just when public enthusiasm was reaching the boiling point was nothing short of a national calamity. The principal lieutenants of the Mahatma, Deshbandhu Das, Pandit Motilal Nehru and Lala Lajpat Rai, who were all in prison, shared the popular resentment. I was with the Deshbandhu at the time, and I could see that he was beside himself with anger and sorrow" (quoted from *The Indian Struggle,* p. 90). Motilal Nehru, Lajpat Rai and others sent from prison long and indignant letters to Gandhi protesting at his decision to which Gandhi replied that men in prison were "civilly dead" and had no claim to any say in policy. Following this deeply unpopular decision, the popularity of the Congress slipped dramatically, with Gandhi himself having to admit that in place of the proclaimed aim of the Congress reaching ten million members, it could barely count 200,000 in its favour. It was thus inevitable that young revolutionaries would seek inspiration from other and more radical forces. Some like M.N. Roy were attracted by the idea of organizing a revolutionary armed struggle against the British and joined hands with Rash Behari Bose in trying to seek support for such a campaign abroad. For others, the message of the Ghadar Party struck a chord. The influence of the Gadharites was particularly notable in Punjab. The young and charismatic martyr, Shaheed Bhagat Singh, was born into a family of Ghadar supporters and was deeply inspired by their message. The Naujawan Bharat Sabha (1925) was initiated by Shaheed Bhagat Singh who also coined the widely popular slogan '*Inquilab Zindabad*' (long live the revolution). Also in 1925, Ghadar supporters established a Workers and Peasants Party (Kirti Kisan Party) in the Punjab. The Kirti Party also worked amongst youth and enjoyed close relations with the Naujawan Bharat Sabha, with Bhagat Singh working on the Kirti Urdu edition. Like the Ghadarites, the Kirti party also drew its membership from all ranks of society – cutting across religious barriers, with leaders drawn from all communities: Sikh, Hindu and Muslim.

With the Congress unable to initiate mass movements of any significance in the late 1920s, the opposition to British rule came largely from organizations such as the Worker's and Peasant's Party and militant unions like the Girni Kamgar Union or Red Flag Union of the Bombay textile workers. The Congress held on to its conservatism by once again rejecting a vote for complete independence at its 1928 session. (Gandhi prevailed over the more radical demands of Subhash Chandra Bose and Jawahar Lal Nehru). Nevertheless, 1929 was a year of significant peasant uprisings and strikes. It was also a year when small groups of underground revolutionaries organized attacks on police stations, British Army camps and other British controlled centres of repressions. Most were caught and either hanged or sentenced to hard labour in Kala Pani.

Emergence of the armed revolutionaries

Virtually all the armed revolutionaries had participated enthusiastically in the non-violent non-cooperation movement earlier.

But when the non-cooperation movement was suddenly suspended by Gandhi, the more radically minded of the young leaders looked to other leaders for inspiration. In 1904, V.D. Savarkar had organized Abhinav Bharat as a secret society of revolutionaries. Anushilan Samiti and Yugantar were two other such societies. Ideas of arm ed resistance to British rule were propagated and international centres were established with Madame Cama and Ajit Singh representing the struggle in Europe, and Shyamji Krishnaverma and others organizing chapters in London.

Frustrated and disillusioned by the inaction of the Congress, the revolutionaries in northern India were the first to reorganize under the leadership of the older veterans, Ramprasad Bismil, Jogesh Chatterjea and Sachindranath Sanyal whose Bandi Jiwan served as a textbook for the revolutionary movement. They met in Kanpur in October 1924 and founded the Hindustan Republican Association (or Army) to organize armed revolution to overthrow colonial rule.

The advance of the armed struggle required bold and risky actions. Volunteers had to be recruited and trained and arms had to be procured, requiring money—hence raids on the British treasury. On 9 August 1925, ten men held up the 8-Down train at Kakori (a village near Lucknow), to get access to its railway cash. British reaction was quick and hard. Ashfaqulla Khan, Ramprasad Bismil, Roshan Singh and Rajendra Lahiri were hanged, four others were sent to the Andamans for life and seventeen others were sentenced to long terms of imprisonment. The Kakori case was a major setback to the revolutionaries of northern India; but it was not a fatal blow. Younger men such as Bejoy Kumar Sinha, Shiv Varma and Jaidev Kapur in U.P., Bhagat Singh, Bhagawati Charan Vohra and Sukhdev in Punjab set out to reorganize the HRA under the overall leadership of Chandrashekhar Azad. At this time, they were also strongly influenced by socialist ideas. At a Delhi meeting on September 1928, a new collective leadership adopted socialism as their official goal and changed their party's name to the Hindustan Socialist Republican Association (Army).

On 8 April 1929, HSRA embarked on a plan to throw a bomb in the Central Legislative Assembly against the passage of two new repressive bills – the Public Safety Bill and the Trade Disputes Bill. The aim was not to cause any loss of life, but to use the daring action to awaken and energize the Indian masses. It was intended to 'make the deaf hear'. The objective was to get arrested and to use the trial court as a vehicle to disseminate their dreams and ideas for a new and liberated India.

Bhagat Singh and B.K. Dutt were tried in the Assembly Bomb Case. Later Sukhdev, Rajguru and tens of other revolutionaries were also tried in a series of famous conspiracy cases. Their fearless and unswerving attitudes in court became legendary. Everyday they entered the court-room chanting slogans *'Inquilab Zindabad,' 'Down, Down with Imperialism,'* singing songs like Sarfaroshi ki tamanna hai (our heart is filled with the desire of martyrdom) and Mere rang de basanti chola (dyemy clothes in saffron, the colour, of courage and sacrifice).

In March 1931, Rajguru, Sukhdev, and Bhagat Singh were hanged by the British in spite of tremendous popular opposition to their hanging. Bhagat Singh became a household hero, and his hanging led to an outpouring of grief and sorrow all over the nation. Although the Congress could have utilized the mood of popular anger to accelerate the mass struggle, its response to the Bhagat Singh trial was tepid. In his private negotiations with the British, it appears that Gandhi did not press the issue of Bhagat Singh's impending death sentence. Supporters of Bhagat Singh became particularly bitter when Gandhi failed to fight hard on their behalf.

In Bengal too, armed revolutionary groups started reorganizing and developing underground activities even as some of the leaders maintained their links with the Congress. One of their planned actions was to assassinate Charles Tegart – the much hated Police Commissioner of Calcutta. The attempt failed and Gopinath Saha was arrested and hanged for the attempt despite massive popular protest. Despite the setback, attempts at armed revolt were not abandoned. Among the new 'Revolt Groups,' the most active and famous was the Chittagong group led by Surya Sen.

Surya Sen had actively participated in the Non–Cooperation Movement and had become a teacher in a national school in Chittagong. He had also been closely associated with Congress work in Chittagong. Along with other colleagues in the local Congress committees, and several young recruits, Surya Sen and his compatriots decided to organize a rebellion, on however small a scale, to demonstrate that it was possible to challenge the armed might of the British empire in India. Their action plan was to include occupation of the two main armouries in Chittagong and the seizing of their arms with which four large band of revolutionaries could be formed into an armed detachment. In a fierce fight (April, 1930) eighty British troops and twelve revolutionaries died, but Chittagong could not be held by the revolutionaries. When the armed revolutionaries dispersed into the Chittagong countryside, most of the Muslim villagers gave food and shelter to the revolutionaries in hiding, enabling them to survive for three years. The Chittagong Armoury Raid had a tremendous impact on the people of Bengal and inspired numerous other acts of armed resistance. But Surya Sen was eventually caught and hanged in 1934. Many of his co-fighters were also caught and sentenced to long terms of imprisonment. Just as it seemed that the national movement was completely slipping away from the influence of the Congress, Gandhi returned to the mode of non-violent struggle and launched the salt satyagraha (1930-31). Campaigns to boycott imported goods were also launched. With the masses energized once again, a series of anti–British action took place, of which most notable were the raid on the Chittagong Armoury and a mutiny by Garhwali soldiers in Peshawar. For ten days, British authority in Peshawar collapsed. But the brave soldiers of Peshawar who had resisted British orders to shoot at their civilian brethren during a mass demonstration received little sympathy from Gandhi.

Trade Union Resistance

In addition, a wave of strikes confronted the British authorities once again. Although the communists were officially outlawed, communist and socialist sympathizers remained active in the trade union movement. The industrial workers of Bombay offered the most heroic resistance, refusing to be daunted by lathi charges, beatings and indiscriminate firings. In response to such growing opposition, the British resorted to massive armed retaliation even calling in bombers from its Royal Air Force to bomb striking or protesting workers.

These actions by Bombay's militant workers also had an impact on British businessmen in Bombay, who joined with Indian businessmen and the Bombay Chamber of Commerce in demanding immediate self-government for India on a dominion basis. Working class resistance continued throughout the 30s, but overall (barring minor and cosmetic concessions obtained from the British) the national movement made insufficient progress, hamstrung as it was by the conservatism of Gandhi and his followers in the Congress on one hand, and pushed back by the brutal repression of the British colonial overlords on the other.

Building up to the Quit India Movement

Subhas Chandra Bose attempted to lead a radical revival of the Congress and tried to steer it in a more radical and socialist direction. In 1939, he defeated Gandhi's nominee Pattabhi Sitaramayya to be re-elected Congress president. But he was ill-prepared to deal with a campaign of non-cooperation launched against him by Gandhi, and resigned a few months later to launch an alternative and more radical platform that eventually became the Forward Bloc in independent India.

The outbreak of the Second World War opened up a new and more determined phase of the struggle against British rule. In 1939 and 1940, strikes and peasant uprisings reached a fever pitch. In 1941, the Indian National Army (INA) was launched by General Mohan Singh in Malaya with the help of the Japanese. He belonged to Sialkot (Punjab) and had been greatly influenced by the killings of Jallianwala Bagh and hangings of the Ghadar Party members during his younger years. In 1943, Netaji Subhas Chandra Bose (who had always been close to the armed revolutionaries of Bengal) took over the Indian National Army and it was renamed as the Azad Hind Fauj. More than two million Indian civilians living in South-East Asia responded to his call for "total mobilization". In his army of liberation Punjabi, Muslim, Sikh and Pathan professional soldiers fought side by side with Tamil and Malayalee rubber plantation workers. In his Azad Hind Movement Netaji was able to demonstrate by example how to achieve Hindu-Muslim unity and amity and enable women to get their rightful role in public affairs.

By 1942, the Congress too was compelled to act boldly, and issued the Quit India call in August. The Quit India Movement of 1942 swept across the length and breadth of the country like a mighty tidal wave bringing in its fold people from all walks of life, arousing in them tremendous patriotic fervour and an irresistible urge to act. Volunteers from groups like the Hindu Mahasabha who had all this while remained aloof from the mass struggle joined in as well. Individual industrialists were emboldened too and encouraged strike actions against the British.

The Role of Women

One of the important facets of India's freedom movement was the growing participation of women. Women played an especially crucial role in the economic boycott campaigns and often participated in the non-cooperation movement with as much or even greater enthusiasm than their husbands or male relatives. In rallies organized by the Congress, women attended in large numbers often with little children in tow. Particularly notable was the participation of women in the armed struggle of Bengal. In the group led by Surya Sen, they provided shelter, acted as messengers and custodians of arms, and fought, guns in hand. Pritilata Waddedar died while conducting a raid, while Kalpana Dutt (now Joshi) was arrested and tried along with Surya Sen and given a life sentence. In December 1931, two schoolgirls of Comilla, Santi Ghosh and Suniti Chowdhury, shot dead the District Magistrate. In February 1932, Bina Das fired point blank at the Governor while receiving her degree at the convocation. When the entire Congress leadership was put in jail in 1942, women leaders like Aruna Asaf Ali and Sucheta Kripalani emerged with Achyut Patwardhan and Ram Manohar Lohia and others to lead the underground resistance. Usha Mehta ran the Congress radio. Congress socialists, Forward Bloc members, and other armed resistance factions were active in this period, working through underground cells in Mumbai, Pune, Satara, Baroda, and other parts of Gujarat, Karnataka, Kerala, Andhra Paradesh, UP, Bihar and Delhi.

The Revolutionary Peasantry, Adivasis and Dalits

The final phase of the Indian freedom struggle also saw peasant struggles rising to new heights of militancy. Throughout the country, Kisan Sabhas had been active in the 1930s. After the Quit-India call, peasants of all classes joined in the freedom struggle in Eastern UP, Bihar, Midnapur in Bengal, Satara in Maharashtra, and also in Andhra, Gujarat and Kerala. Even some of the Zamindars (landlords) joined in. The Raja of Darbhanga was one of the most supportive of the resisting peasants. Adivasis and landless peasants were particularly heroic in their struggles. Crushed by the inhumane demands of the Zamindri system, they had to fight a dual war–one against the British and the other against the Indian landlords who collaborated with British rule. Amongst the most significant of these struggles were those of Tebhaga, Punnapra Vayalar, the Worli adivasis and above all the historic Telangana peasant's armed struggle which was directed against the Nizam of Hyderabad who had collaborated with the British.

During the course of the freedom struggle, the issue of equality for Adivasis and Dalits came up again and again. Phule, Periyar and Ambedkar emerged as amongst the most prominent of the Dalit leaders. The Ghadar movement, the HSRA and later the INA led the way in breaking down caste and communal barriers. The Congress, while open to some reforms, often did not go far enough – leading to well-deserved criticism from the more radical of the Dalit and Adivasi leaders. Nevertheless, virtually all the advanced sections of the freedom struggle came to the conclusion that for India to succeed as a modern nation, the issue of equality for Dalits and Adivasis could not be dismissed.

Final Push towards Freedom

After the Second World War, the momentum created by the Quit India Movement led to growing militant actions that weakened British authority in an irreparable way. The World War had compelled the British into setting up Indian Navy units that recruited officers from various parts of India. The Indian naval men were mistreated and discriminated against, leading to a strike call in February 1946. It quickly drew support from the Indian crews of all the 20 vessels anchored in Bombay port. 20,000 naval ratings went on strike. 'Victory to India', 'Long live the Revolution', and 'Hindus and Muslims Unite' were some of their slogans. The struggle soon spread to barracks in Thane and Delhi, and also to ships anchored in Karachi, Calcutta and Vishakapatnam. 200,000 workers in Bombay's factories downed their tools in solidarity. But leaders of the Congress including Gandhi and Maulana Azad were critical of the strike as was Jinnah of the Muslim League. Patel attempted to assuage the strikers by promising that they would not be victimized. But the assurances of Patel did not prevent mass arrests or police actions that led to a death toll of 1700.

Nevertheless, the strike in the Indian Navy played an important role in energizing and emboldening the Indian masses. Militant acts of resistance accelerated. The British realized that they could no longer hold on to India and instead turned their attentions on partitioning India. The Muslim League was more than willing to play an active role in these dangerous and divisive maneuvers. In a bizarre interpretation of the '*right to self-determination*', the then legal Communist Party of India (who in their many years of being underground played a vital role in energizing the trade unions and Kisan Sabhas) endorsed the idea that India's Muslims constituted a separate nation, thus providing ideological cover for the Muslim League's incendiary propaganda. This led to a split with the Ghadarites and other communist organizations who fought vehemently against the ideology of the *two-nation theory*. Hindu and Muslim unity had been almost exemplary in the trade union and radical peasant movements. Yet, in a blunder of monumental proportions, the leaders of the Communist Party appeared to endorse the divisive message of the Muslim League.

The Congress although reluctant to accept partition put up a feeble fight. Decades of conservatism prevented it from moving the Indian masses into a struggle against the terror tactics of the Muslim League. The Indian Navy strike had shown that Hindus and Muslims were more than willing to unite against the British. In the Indian National Army of Subhas Chandra Bose, they were willing to take up arms together. But the Congress leadership remained wedded to non-violence even as the Muslim League was arming its separatist volunteers.

Independence was won but at a heavy price that continues to torment the people of the sub-continent through the creation of Pakistan, a state based on the thoroughly reactionary foundation of religious separatism and intolerance.

2

The Nationalist Ideas Behind the Revolt of 1857

Historians hold different views about the nature and character of the revolt of 1857. Radical Indians describe it as a national war of independence. Savarkar's work on the subject forms the historical background for the Indian revolutionaries. The ideas which moved the rebels were Swadharma and Swaraj.

"It was a combination, whether due to the growth of deliberate design and long preparation, or the sudden birth of chance and unexpected opportunity—a combination of military grievance, national hatred, and religious fanaticism, against the English occupiers' of India" (p 2, Buch)

Soldiers, princes, Mohammedans, Hindus joined to oust the foreign rulers. Greased cartridges served as the chance spark flung in among all the combustible material.

"They had found in one moment a leader, a flag, and a cause, and the mutiny was transfigured into a revolutionary war". Thus they had all "unconsciously seized one of the great moments of history, and converted a military mutiny into a national and religious war." Contemporary literature reveals a stir for a long time in the minds of both Hindus and Mohammedans that their religion was seriously threatened by the growing influence of Christianity.

The whole Indian history is a long record of fights for Swadharma for the defence or the aggressive assertion of one's own faith. The religion of the people, therefore, has always been the most tender point of their systems, and any danger to it stirs up violent convulsions in society. Various activities of the missionaries and the government support to them inspired the Indians to die for the faith of their fathers.

The literatures of proclamations and placards of the time show clearly that the people were led on to fight by the usual cries of their country and their faith being in danger. There was a strong patriotic or national feeling among both Hindus and Mohammedans showing their attachment to their soil, their culture, and their own native rulers. Thus all the native pride of the population asserted itself in a violent way, and called upon all true believers to rise against the English inifidels, and drive them from India.

Hindus and Mohammedans of India Arise! Brethren! of all the gifts of God, the most gracious is that of Swaraj. Will the oppressive Demon who has robbed us of it by deceit be able to keep it away from us forever? At the back of the hatred there was a strong instinctive attachment to native culture, native religions and native policy.

The rulers realised that it was possible to have a revolution in which Brahmans and Sudras, Hindus and Mohammedans could be united against them. It was a rising in defence of faith. The cries which were repeated were "Din! Din! "Har, Har Mahadev", the religious cries.

The revolt illustrated the close connection between religions and nationalism in India. It was essentially a movement for Swadharma and Swaraj. It was assertion of the Indigenous culture against the alien invasion, both political and cultural.

3

Nationalism Takes Root : The Moderates

Before the British conquest, the concept of membership in a permanent political order embracing and involving them all seem to have been unknown to the inhabitants of India. Dynasties rather than nations were the centres of political power and the foci of personal loyalties. Powerful rulers like Ashoka, Samudragupta, and Harsha had indeed succeeded in bringing large parts of the subcontinent under their sway, but their empires dissolved with the death of the last strong ruler in each reigning line. Thanks largely to the genius of Akbar (1542 – 1605), the Mughal empire created a somewhat more durable administrative order, but internal dissensions and Persian-Afghan invasions led to the empire's dismemberment after the passing of the militant Aurangzeb (1619 – 1707). For a time the Mārāthas gave promise of re-establishing Hindu dominion, but again their rule could not even unite all of Hindudom around their standard, let alone bridge the gap between India's two major religious traditions.

A new chapter opened when British arms and diplomacy placed the whole of the subcontinent under one paramount power for the first time in history. They imposed not only peace and unity on India, but a relatively efficient administrative machinery as well. Gradually the sinews of a new nation were strengthened by the introduction of printing and journalism, railroads, a postal and telegraph system, and by the growth of an all-India economy centering in large modern cities accessible to ocean-going ships.

The new political and economic order attracted able Indians anxious to improve their status and increase their wealth by entering its service. A new class emerged to mediate between the foreign rulers or traders and the mass of the people. Using their knowledge of English as the key to advancement, Indian clerks and functionaries found employment in government posts; Indian lawyers pleaded in British-style courts; Indian businessmen dealt with foreign firms; and Indian teachers imparted to their countrymen the language and culture of the conquerors. This rising middle class demonstrated a loyalty to the British which outweighed the angry discontent of the old elite–both Muslim and Hindu. The suppression of the latter in the Mutiny and Rebellion of 1857-58 only confirmed the entrenched position of their parvenu successors.

But the English education which provided so many willing collaborators for the British in India eventually proved the undoing of their empire. For one thing, the members of the new middle class—whether from the South or the North, from Bengal or from Mahārāshtra—could all communicate with each other through the medium of a common language. Equally important, their reading of the English classics instilled in them the Western ideals of justice, freedom, and love of country. As their numbers grew they found the good government jobs too few, with the best ones reserved for Europeans. To economic frustration was added the bitter sting of racial discrimination, for "the Mutiny" of 1857 had sharpened British suspicions of Indian loyalty, while the late nineteenth century doctrines of social Darwinism and aggressive imperialism compounded to increase the white man's feeling of inherent superiority over his darker-skinned subjects. Ignoring the sympathetic statements made in Parliament and the conciliatory proclamation of Queen Victoria in 1858, Britishers in India saw little reason to grant Indians a greater measure of control over their own affairs.

Under these circumstances, it was not long before the seed-idea of nationalism implanted by their reading of Western books began to take root in the minds of intelligent and energetic Indians. A.O. Hume, a Scotsman sympathetic to their aspirations, made possible the first meeting (in 1885) of the Indian National Congress, which was intended to serve as a forum for the discussion of political reforms and patriotic projects. From this beginning as a safety-valve through which the upper classes could air their grievances, the Congress quickly transformed itself into an all-India nationalist organization.

The Moderates, the first men to come forward as leaders of the nationalist movement, shared a great many assumptions with those liberal Englishmen who advised and encouraged them. They believed in the providential character of British rule and in the gradual evolution of India toward enlightenment and self-government under that rule. They regretted the backwardness of Hindu society and worked to bring about the reform of its grosser evils. The poverty of the people depressed them, and they therefore concerned themselves with plans for India's economic improvement. Although they were not men devoid of religious faith, they accepted the divorce of religion from government and maintained a secular view of politics which contrasted markedly with the religious outlook of the Extremists, who later posed a serious challenge to their leadership.

Having become, as Macaulay proposed, "English in taste, in opinions, in morals, and in intellect," the Indian Moderates gained certain advantages but at the same time ran certain risks in guiding the nationalist movement. Their familiarity with British culture enabled them to appeal to the best instincts of their rulers, from whom they demanded the same rights and liberties which all Britons took for granted. Their knowledge of the gradual rise of democratic government in English history furnished them with useful ammunition, and they repeatedly harked back to the assurances given by Parliament and Queen Victoria that Indians would be allowed to compete freely with Europeans for positions in the Indian Civil Service.

In relation to their rivals the Extremists, however, the position of the Moderates was bound to be a somewhat shaky one for several reasons. Their heavy reliance on British good faith embarrassed them whenever the concessions they asked for were refused or postponed. Moreover, the more anglicized they became in their thinking, the further they removed themselves from emotional rapport with the bulk of the population—the illiterate, poverty-stricken, and devoutly Hindu peasantry.

In one respect the Moderates did yeoman's service in tending to the needs of the peasantry. Unwilling to attack British rule for the political and social reforms it had introduced, they focused their attention on the obvious disparity between Britain's prosperity and India's poverty. Dādābhāi Naoroji, and Indian businessman resident in London, placed the blame for his country's plight on foreign rule, and in doing so was seconded by English socialist theoreticians. The Bengali leader Surendranath Banerjea accepted Dādābhāi's thesis, while M.G. Rānade (pronounced Rānadé) sough a constructive solution in rapid industrialization under government auspices. Rānade's disciple G.K. Gokhale (pronounced Gokhalé) left the theorizing to others, and bent his efforts to reducing the load of taxation burdening the Indian people.

These four men were probably the most outstanding moderate leaders in the opening decades of the nationalist movement. It is significant that all were scholarly in temperament, and spent part of the early careers as teachers in colleges imparting English education to Indian students. Each possessed a flawless command of the English language and was able to hold his own in debates with Englishmen. Three of them–Naoroji, Banerjea, and Gokhale—made speaking tours in Great Britain to impress the British electorate with the importance of greater self-government for India. The same three were also elected presidents of the Congress, and all four were deeply involved in its work.

Although the Extremist leaders could muster far greater support through their appeal to Hindu symbols and traditions, it is doubtful that they could have succeeded in freeing India without the patient, more diplomatic efforts of the Moderates. Their greater willingness to cooperate with the British in instituting administrative reforms kept the nationalist movement from "going off the rails" into senseless violence, which could only lead to severe reprisals and political deadlock. Their contribution to the achievement of self-government has largely been forgotten by subsequent generations, but independent India's dedication to parliamentary democracy, economic development, and social progress stands as mute testimony to their farsighted wisdom.

Dādābhāi Naoroji: Architect of Indian Nationalism

Inevitable as the rise of Indian nationalism may seem to have been under the conditions created by British rule, its emergence would have been impossible without the strenuous efforts of devoted national leaders. The first of a long series of such men, Dādābhāi Naoroji drew the plans and laid the foundations for India's self-government.

This architect of Indian nationalism was neither Hindu nor Muslim, but a descendant of the followers of Zoroaster who had fled Persia after the Muslim conquest of that country. Settling as refugees along the western coast of India the Zoroastrians became known as Parsīs (Persians). When the British came to trade they emerged as the group most willing to do business, for they were bound neither by caste rules nor by prejudice against taking interest on loans, and as a minority group they had little to lose and much to gain by dealing with the Europeans. As a result of their trading contacts, the Parsīs became the most Westernized and the wealthiest single community in India.

Dādābhāi Naoroji was born in Bombay in 1825, the son of a Zoroastrian priest. His family name, Dordi, was little used; but the original meaning of the word (twisted rope made of coconut husk) had a symbolic significance for Dādābhāi, who was absolutely inflexible once he had made up his mind. "You may burn a *dordi*," he once said, "but you can never take the twist out of it. So it is with me. When once I form a decision, nothing will dislodge me from it."[1]

Tenacity of purpose was indeed his chief characteristic. He so distinguished himself in his studies at the Elphinstone Institution (Bombay's leading college) that he became at twenty-seven its Professor of Mathematics—the first Indian to attain such an academic rank. At thirty he left India to become a partner in the first Indian firm to do business in England. His aim in moving permanently to London, the heart of the empire, was not to gain wealth, but to enable himself to appeal directly to the British public for a better understanding of India's problems. For fifty years Dādābhāi delivered papers on Indian subjects to numerous learned societies, submitted memoranda and petitions to British officials concerned with India, and agitated both privately and publicly—all in the service of one cause: that Indians should be granted the same rights and privileges as other British subjects.

With his famous theory of "the drain" of India's wealth to Britain, Dādābhāi Naoroji sounded the keynote of Indian economic nationalism. But for all his bitter condemnation of the costliness of foreign government to his country, he never advocated violent action as a solution. His loyalty to the parliamentary system of government was rewarded in 1892 with his election to the British House of Commons on the Liberal ticket. The first Indian member of Parliament, he served both his London constituency and the interests of India for three years, succeeding in his attempt to have a parliamentary commission investigate the financial administration of British India.

Dādābhāi punctuated his long residence in England with frequent visits to India. In 1873–74 he served as chief minister to the Indian state of Baroda to prevent it from being annexed by the British crown (the usual penalty for misgovernment in the princely states). He took a prominent part in the first session of the Indian National Congress in 1885, and was thrice elected its president—in 1886, 1893, and 1906. The younger generation of nationalist leaders all looked up to the patriarchal patriot for advice, and Gāndhi especially revered him. He died in Bombay in 1917, but to this day the affectionate title "the Grand Old Man of India" is associated with his name.

Dādābhāi Naoroji

The Pros and Cons of British Rule

In the discussion following the presentation of a paper on India to a learned society in London in 1817, Dādābhāi drew up an impromptu account of the advantages and disadvantages of British rule to India. It shows both his fairness in recognizing the good the British had done, and his persistent criticism of the crushing cost to India of their rule.

[From *Essays, Speeches, Addresses, and Writings of the Hon'ble Dādābhāi Naoroji*, pp. 131-36]

Credit—*In the Cause of Humanity:* Abolition of suttee and infanticide.

Destruction of Dacoits, Thugs, Pindarees,[2] and other such pests of Indian society.

Remarriage of Hindu widows, and charitable aid in time of famine.

Glorious work all this, of which any nation may well be proud, and such as has not fallen to the lot of any people in the history of mankind.

In the Cause of Civilization: Education, both male and female.

Though yet only partial, an inestimable blessing as far as it has gone, and leading gradually to the destruction of superstition, and many moral and social evils. Resuscitation of India's own noble literature, modified and refined by the enlightenment of the West.

The only pity is that as much has not been done as might have been in this noble work; but still India must be, and is, deeply grateful.

Politically: Peace and order. Freedom of speech and liberty of the press. Higher political knowledge and aspirations. Improvement of government in the native States. Security of life and property. Freedom from oppression caused by the caprice of avarice of despotic rulers, and from devastation by war. Equal justice between man and man (sometimes vitiated by partiality to Europeans). Services of highly educated administrators, who have achieved the above-mentioned good results.

Materially: Loans for railways and irrigation. (I have been particularly charged with ignoring this , but I consider it one of the greatest benefits you have conferred upon India, inasmuch as it has enabled us to produce more than we could before, though there is not yet enough for all India's ordinary wants, and I have said this in may paper.) I cannot ascertain the exact amount of investments in irrigation works, but I take them to be about £ 10,000,000 making the total £ 110,000,000. The development of a few valuable products, such as indigo, tea, coffee, silk, &c. Increase of exports. Telegraphs.

Generally: A slowly growing desire of late to treat India equitably, and as a country held in trust. Good intentions.

No nation on the face of the earth has ever had the opportunity of achieving such a glorious work as this. I hope in this credit side of the account I have done no injustice, and if I have omitted any item which anyone may think of importance, I shall have the greatest pleasure in inserting it. I appreciate, and so do my countrymen, what England has done for India, and I know that it is only in British hands that her regeneration can be accomplished. Now for the debit side.

Debit—*In the Cause of Humanity:* Nothing. Everything, therefore, is in your favour under this head.

In the Cause of Civilization: As I have said already, there has been a failure to do as much as might have been done, but I put nothing to the debit. Much has been done or I should not be standing here this evening.

Politically: Repeated breach of pledges to give the natives a fair and reasonable share in the higher administration of their own country, which has much shaken confidence in the good faith of the British word. Political aspirations and the legitimate claim to have a reasonable voice in the legislation and the imposition and disbursement of taxes, met to a very slight degree, thus treating the natives of India not as British subjects, to whom representation is a birthright.

(I stop here a moment to say a word as to a mistake into which my friend, Mr. Hyde Clarke, fell, in supposing that I desired the government of India to be at once transferred to the natives. In my belief a greater calamity could not befall India than for England to go away and leave her to herself.)

Consequent on the above, an utter disregard of the feelings and views of the natives. The great moral evil of the drain of the wisdom and practical administration and statesmanship, leaving none to guide the rising generation. (Here, again, have I been misunderstood. I complain not of Englishmen returning to their own country, but of the whole administration being kept entirely in English hands, so that none of the natives are brought up to and taught the responsibilities and duties of office, so that we have none amongst ourselves to guide us as our elders and to teach us our duties as citizens and as moral beings. A foster mother or nurse will never supply the place of the real mother, and the natives will therefore naturally follow their own leaders, unless you prove more kind, humane, and considerate. Draw these leaders on your side.) The indifference to India, even of a large portion of those who have had an Indian career, and who are living on Indian pensions. The culpable indifference of a large portion of the people, the public press, and Parliament of this country to the interests of India: therefore periodical committees of inquiry are absolutely necessary, for the knowledge that such will take place would be a check on careless administration. With regard to the native states, though their system is improving, it is most unjust that their cases should be decided in secret. The frequent change of officials is a constant source of disturbance in policy, and though it may be unavoidable, it is none the less hard upon India.

Financially: All attention is engrossed in devising new modes of taxation, without any adequate effort to increase the means of the people to pay; and the consequent vexation and oppressiveness of the taxes imposed, imperial and local. Inequitable financial relations between England and India, i.e., the political debt of £100,000,000 clapped on India's shoulders, and all home charges also, though the British exchequer contributes nearly £3,000,000 to the expenses of the colonies. The crushing and economically rude and unintelligent policy of making the present generation pay the whole cost of public works for the benefit of the future, instead of making the political like all other machinery, and distributing the weight so as to make a small power lift a large weight by the aid of time. The results of trying to produce something out of nothing, of the want of intelligent adaptation of financial machinery, and of much reckless expenditure; in financial embarrassments, and deep discontent of the people.

Materially: The political drain,[3] up to this time, from India to England, of above £500,000,000, at the lowest computation, in principal alone, which with interest would be some thousands of millions. The further continuation of this drain at the rate, at present, of above £12,000,000, with a tendency to increase. (I do not mean this as a complaint; you must have a return for the services rendered to India, but let us have the means of paying. If I have a manager to whom I pay £1,000 a year, and he only makes the business produce £400, so that £600 a year must be paid him out of capital, any man of business can see what will be the result. Peace and order will soon be completely established by the closing of the concern).

The consequent continuous impoverishment and exhaustion of the country, except so far as it has been very partially relieved and replenished by the railway and irrigation loans, and the windfall of the consequences of the American war, since 1850. Even with this relief, the material condition of India is such that the great mass of the poor people have hardly 2*d* a day and a few rags, or a scanty subsistence.

The famines that were in their power to prevent, if they had done their duty, as a good and intelligent government. The policy adopted during the last fifteen years of building railways, irrigation works, etc., is hopeful, has already resulted in much good to your credit, and if persevered in, gratitude and contentment will follow.

[An] increase of exports [without adequate compensation]; [a] loss of manufacturing industry and skill. Here I end the debit side. ...

To sum up the whole, the British rule has been—morally, a

great blessing; politically peace and order on one hand, blunders on the other, materially, impoverishments (relieved as far as the railway and other loans go). The natives call the British system "Sakar ki Churi," the knife of sugar. That is to say there is no oppression, it is all smooth and sweet, but it is the knife, notwithstanding. I mention this that you should know these feelings. Our great misfortune is that you do not know our wants. When you will know our real wishes, I have not the least doubt that you would do justice. The geniuses and spirit of the British people is fair play and justice. The great problems before the English statesmen are two: (1) To make the foreign rule self-supporting, either by returning to India, in some shape or other, the wealth that has been, and is being, drawn from it, or by stopping that drain in some way till India is so far improved in its material condition as to be able to produce enough for its own ordinary wants and the extraordinary ones of a costly distant rule. If you cannot feel yourself actuated by the high and noble ambition of the amelioration of 200,000,000 of human beings, let your self-interest suggest to you to take care of the bird that gives the golden egg of £12,000,000 a year to your nation, and provisions to thousands of your people of all classes. In the name of humanity, I implore our rulers to make up their minds not to prevent the restoration of the equilibrium, after the continuous exhaustion by drain and by horrible famines. I do not in the least grudge any legitimate benefit England may derive for its rule in India. On the contrary, I am thankful for its invaluable moral benefits; but it is the further duty of England to give us such a government, and all the benefit of its power and credit, as to enable us to pay, without starving or dying by famine, the tribute or price for the rule; (2) How to satisfy reasonably the growing political aspirations and just rights of a people called British subjects to have a fair share in the administration and legislation of their own country. If the Select Committee solve these two problems, before which all other difficulties, financial or others, are as nothing, the will deserve the blessings of 200,000,000 of the human race.

The Blessings of British Rule

Dādābhāi's presidential address at the second session of the Congress in 1886 rings with protestations of loyalty and gratitude to British rule for the unity, peace, civil liberties and education it brought to the Indian people.

[From *Essays, Speeches, Addresses, and Writings of the Hon'ble Dādābhāi Naoroji*, pp.332-33]

The assemblage of such a Congress is an event of the utmost importance in Indian history. I ask whether in the most glorious days of Hindu rule, in the days of Rajahs like the great Vikram,[4] you could imagine the possibility of a meeting of this kind, where even Hindus of all different provinces of the kingdom could have collected and spoken as one nation. Coming down to the later empire of our friends, the Mahomedans, who probably ruled over a larger territory at one time than any Hindu monarch, would it have been, even in the days of the great Akbar himself, possible for a meeting like this to assemble composed of all classes and communities, all speaking one language, and all having uniform and high aspirations of their own?

Well, then, what is it for which we have now met on this occasion? We have assembled to consider questions upon which depend our future, whether glorious or inglorious. It is our good fortune that we are under a rule which makes it possible for us to meet in this manner. [Cheers.] It is under the civilizing rule of the Queen and people of England that we meet here together, hindered by none, and are freely allowed to speak our minds without the least fear and without the least hesitation. Such a thing is possible under British rule and British rule only. [Loud cheers.] Then I put the *question* plainly: Is this congress a nursery for sedition and rebellion against the British Government [cries of "no, no"]; or is it another stone in the foundation of the stability of that Government [cries of "yes, yes"]? There could be but one answer, and that you have already given, because we are thoroughly sensible of the numberless blessings conferred upon us, of which the very existence of this Congress is a proof in a nutshell. [Cheers.] Were it not for these blessings of British rule I could not have come here, as I have done, without the least hesitation and without the least fear that my children might be robbed and killed in my absence; nor could you have come from every corner of the land, having performed, within a few days, journeys which in former days would have occupied as many months. [Cheers.] These simple facts bring home to all of us at once some of those great and numberless blessings which British rule has conferred upon us. But there remain even greater blessings for which we have to be grateful.

It is to British rule that we owe the education we possess; the people of England were sincere in the declarations made more than half a century ago that India was a sacred charge entrusted to their care by Providence, and that they were bound to administer it for the good of India, to the glory of their own name, and the satisfaction of God. [Prolonged cheering.] When we have to acknowledge so many blessings as flowing from British rule—and I could descant on them for hours, because it would simply be recounting to you the history of the British empire in India—is it possible that an assembly like this, every one of whose members is fully impressed with the knowledge of these blessings, could meet for any purpose inimical to that rule to which we owe so much? [Cheers.]

The thing is absurd. Let us speak out like men and proclaim that we are loyal to the backbone [cheers]; that we understand the benefits English rule has conferred upon us; that we thoroughly appreciate the education that has been given to us, the new light which has been poured upon us, turning us from darkness into light and teaching us the new lesson that kings are made for the people, not people for their kings; and this new lesson we have learned amidst the darkness of Asiatic despotism only by the light of free English civilization. [Loud cheers.]

The Moral Impoverishments of India

The frustration felt by the swelling ranks of educated Indians who were excluded from government positions is well expressed in Dādābhāi's memorandum of 1880. Note the veiled threat with which this selection concludes.

[From *Essays, Speeches, Addresses, and Writings of the Hon'ble Dādābhāi Naoroji,* pp. 465-67]

In this Memorandum I desire to submit for the kind and generous consideration of His Lordship the Secretary of State for India, that from the same cause of the deplorable drain, besides the material exhaustion of India, the moral loss to her is no less sad and lamentable.

With the material wealth go also the wisdom and experience of the country. Europeans occupy almost all the higher places in every department of government, directly or indirectly under its control. While in India they acquire India's money, experience, and wisdom, and when they go, they carry both away with them, leaving India so much poorer in material and moral wealth. Thus India is left without, and cannot have, those elders in wisdom and experience, who in every country are the natural guides of the rising generations in their national and social conduct, and of the destinies of their country—and a sad, sad loss this is!

Every European is isolated from the people around him. He is not their mental, moral or social leader, or companion. For any mental or moral influence or guidance or sympathy with the people, he might just as well be living in the moon. The people know not him, and he knows not, nor cares for the people. Some honourable exceptions do, now and then, make an effort to do some good they can, but in the very nature of things, these efforts are always feeble, exotic, and of little permanent effect. These men are not always in the place, and their works die away when they go.

The Europeans are not the natural leaders of the people. They do not belong to the people. They cannot enter into their thoughts and feelings; they cannot join or sympathize with their joys or griefs. On the contrary, every day the estrangement is increasing. Europeans deliberately and openly widen it more and more. There may be very few social institutions started by Europeans in which natives, however fit and desirous to join, are not deliberately and insultingly excluded. The Europeans are and make themselves strangers in every way. All they effectually do is to eat the substance of India, material and moral, while living there, and when they go, they carry away all they have acquired, and their pensions and future usefulness besides.

This most deplorable moral loss to India needs most serious consideration, as much in its political as in its national aspect. Nationally disastrous as it is, it carries politically with it its own nemesis. Without the guidance of elderly wisdom and experience of their own natural leaders, the education which the rising generations are now receiving is naturally leading them (or call it misleading them, if you will) into directions which bode no good to the rulers, and which, instead of being the strength of the rulers as it ought to and can be, will turn out to be their great weakness. The fault will be of the rulers themselves for such a result. The power that is now being raised by the spread of education, though yet slow and small, is one that in time must, for weal or woe, exercise great influence. In fact it has already begun to do so. However strangely the English rulers, forgetting their English manliness and moral courage, may, like the ostrich, shut their eyes by gagging acts or otherwise, to the good or bad influences they are raising around them, this good or evil is rising nevertheless. The thousands that are being sent out by the universities every year find themselves in a most anomalous position. There is no place for them in their motherland. They may beg in the streets or break stones on the roads, for aught the rulers seem to care for their natural rights, position, and duties in their own country. They may perish or do what they like or can, but scores of Europeans must go from this country to take up what belongs to them, and that, in spite of every profession for years and years past and up to the present day, of English statesmen, that they must govern India for India's good, by solemn acts and declarations of Parliament, and above all, by the words of the August Sovereign Herself. For all practical purposes all these high promises have been hitherto, almost wholly, the purest romance, the reality being quite different.

The educated find themselves simply so many dummies, ornamented with the tinsel of school education, and then their whole end and aim of life is ended. What must be the inevitable consequence? A wild, spirited horse, without curb or reins, will run away wild, and kill and trample upon every one that came in his way. A misdirected force will hit anywhere and destroy anything. The power that the rulers are, so far to their credit, raising, will, as a nemesis recoil against themselves, if with this blessing of education they do not do their whole duty to the country which trusts to their righteousness, and thus turn this good power to their own side. The nemesis is as clear from the present violence to nature as disease and death arise from uncleanliness and rottenness. The voice of the power of the rising education is, no doubt, feeble at present. Like the infant, the present dissatisfaction is only crying at the pains it is suffering. Its notions have not taken any form or shape or course yet, but it is growing. Heaven only knows what it will grow to! He who runs may see that if the present material and moral destruction of India continued, a great convulsion must inevitably arise, by which either India will be more and more crushed under the iron heel of despotism and destruction, or may succeed in shattering the destroying hand and power. Far, far is it from my earnest prayer and hope that such should be the result of the British rule.

"Surrender-Not" Banerjea: Bengali Moderate

The Hindu renaissceance in nineteenth-century Bengal was accompanied by a gradual political awakening in that province. Politics, however, unlike religion, came as a comparatively new category of thought to Bengali Hindus after centuries of domination by Muslim rulers. The example set by Rāmmohun Roy thus lay neglected until the new English-educated middle-class gave birth several generations later to a group of men infused with new ideals of patriotism and self-government.

To this group Allan Octavian Hume, the retired civil servant who fathered the organization of the Indian National Congress, appealed with his letter of 1883, addressing the graduates of Calcutta University. "You are the salt of the land," he wrote. "And if amongst even you, the elite, fifty men cannot be found with sufficient power of self-sacrifice, sufficient love for and pride in their country, sufficient genuine and unselfish heart-felt patriotism to take the initiative, and if needs be, devote the rest of their lives to the Cause—then there is no hope for India".[5]

To one Calcutta University graduate Hume's appeal was entirely superfluous, for Surendranāth Banerjea (1848–1926) had already cast himself into the stormy sea of national service. A brāhman and the son of a doctor, Surendranāth had been one of the first Indians to be admitted to the select Indian Civil Service, the so-called "steel frame" of British administration; but his failure to correct a false report prepared in his name by a subordinate had caused him to be dismissed—a punishment far more severe than English members of the I.C.S. received for similar oversights. Undismayed, Surendranāth journeyed to London to appeal his case. When the appeal was denied, he appeared for bar examinations, only to be refused again. With the two swiftest roads to success—the civil service and the law—closed to him, Surendranāth returned to Calcutta, convinced that "the personal wrong done to me was an illustration of the impotency of our people," and determined to spend his life "redressing our wrongs and protecting our rights, personal and collective."[6]

The rest of his long life was only the acting out of this resolve. Starting as a teacher, he soon founded a patriotic association, then a newspaper, then a college. As Keshub Chunder Sen had captivated audiences in many parts of the land with his revivalist sermons, so Surendranāth used his oratorical gifts to rouse Indians from Bengal to the Punjab to a greater sense of loyalty to their country. When he was jailed for criticizing a British judge, he started the tradition (still popular in India) of welcoming imprisonment in order to demonstrate the injustice of a governmental law or policy.

Surendranāth's career dramatizes the change of heart in countless educated Indians from blind loyalty to British rule to stubborn resistance against its evils. Despite his sufferings at the hands of the authorities, Surendranāth insisted that only constitutional means be used in the struggle for self-government. When the Extremists cried for more drastic measures against the foreigner, he opposed them as firmly as he opposed the British. Twice president of the Congress, he left it in 1918 to head the All-India Liberal Federation when the younger Congress leaders threatened to obstruct the introduction of the important Montagu-Chelmsford Reforms. His persistence in his chosen course earned him the respect of Indians and British alike and won him the aptly coined nickname of "Surrender-not" Banerjea.

Surendranāth Benerjea

The Need for Indian Unity

Understanding between Hindus and Muslims formed a major plank in the Moderates' platform. In one of Surendranath's earliest speeches (in 1878) he exhorted the young men of the country to strive for unity as a patriotic duty.

[From *Speeches and Writings of Hon. Surenderanāth Banerjea*, pp. 227–31]

Young men, whom I see around me in such large numbers, you are the hopes of your families. May I not also say, you are the hopes of your country? Your country expects great things from you. Now I ask, how many of you are prepared, when you have finished your studies at the college, to devote your lives, to consecrate your energies to the good of your country? I repeat the question and I pause for a reply. [Here the speaker paused for a few seconds. Cries of "all, all" from all sides of the gallery]. The response is in every way worthy of yourselves and of the education which you are receiving. May you prove true to your resolve, and carry out in life the high purposes which animate your bosoms.

Gentlemen, I have a strong conviction and an assured belief that there comes a time in the history of a nation's progress, when every man may verily be said to have a mission of his own to accomplish. Such a time has now arrived for India. The fiat has gone forth. The celestial mandate has been issued that every Indian must now do his, duty, or stand condemned before God and man. There was such a time of stirring activity in the glorious annals of England, when Hampden offered up his life for the deliverance of his own country, when Algernon Sydney laid down his head on the block to rid his country of a hated tyrant, when English bishops did not hesitate in the discharge of their duty to their Fatherland to descend from the performance of their ecclesiastical functions and appear as traitors before the bar of a Criminal Court. These are glorious reminiscences in England's immortal history, which Englishmen to this day look back upon with pride and satisfaction. It is not indeed necessary for us to have recourse to violence in order to obtain the redress of our grievances. Constitutional agitation will secure for us those rights, the privileges which in less favoured countries are obtained by sterner means. But peaceful as are the means to be enforced, there is a stern duty to be performed by every Indian. And he who fails in that duty is a traitor before God and man.

In holding up for your acceptance the great principle of Indian unity, I do not lay claims to originality. Three hundred years ago, in the Punjab, the immortal founder of Sikhism, the meek, the gentle, the blessed Nānak preached the great doctrine of Indian unity and endeavoured to knit together Hindus and Musulmans under the banner of a common faith. That attempt was eminently successful. Nānak became the spiritual founder of the Sikh empire. He preached the great doctrine of peace and goodwill between Hindus and Musulmans. And standing in the presence of his great example, we too must preach the great doctrine of peace and goodwill between Hindus and Musulmans, Christians and Parsees, aye between all sections of the great Indian community. Let us raise aloft the banner of our country's progress. Let the word "Unity" be inscribed there in characters of glittering gold. We have had enough of past jealousies, past dissensions, past animosities. The spirits of the dead at Paniput[7] will testify to our bloody strifes. The spirits of the dead in other battlefields will testify to the same fact. There may be religious differences between us. There may be social differences between us. But there is a common platform where we may all meet, the platform of our country's welfare. There is a common cause which may bind us together, the cause of Indian progress. There is a common Divinity, to whom we may uplift our voices in adoration, the Divinity who presides over the destinies of our country. In the name then of a common country, let us all, Hindus, Musulmans, Christians, Parsees, members of the great Indian community, throw the pall of oblivion over jealousies and dissensions of bygone times and embracing one another in fraternal love and affection, live and work for the benefit of a beloved Fatherland. Under English auspices there is indeed a great future for India. I am confident of the great destinies that are in store for us. You and I may not live to see that day. These eyes of ours may not witness that spectacle of ineffable beauty. It may not be permitted to us to exclaim Simeonlike, "Now Lord, lettest thou thy servant depart in peace." It may not be permitted to us to exclaim like the Welsh Bard on the heights of Snowdon, "Visions of glory, spare my aching sight." But is it nothing to know when you are dying, when you are about to take leave of this world, of its joys and sorrows, when the past of your life is unfurled before you, when eternity opens wide its portals, is it nothing to know at that last awful, supreme moment of your lives, that you have not lived in vain, that you have lived for the benefit of others, that you have lived to help in the cause of your country's regeneration? Let us all lead worthy, honourable and patriotic lives, that we may all live and die happily and that India may be great. This is my earnest and prayerful request. May it find a response in your sympathetic hearts.

Faith in England

The backbone of the Moderates' creed was faith that the British would grant self-government to India when she was prepared for it. Surendranāth enunciated this creed in the peroration of his presidential address to the Congress in 1895.

[From *Speeches and Writings of the Hon. Surendranāth Banerjea,* pp. 93-96]

We feel that in this great struggle in which we are engaged, the moral sympathies of civilized humanity are with us. The prayers of the good and the true in all parts of the world follow us. They will welcome as glad tidings of great joy the birth of an emancipated people on the banks of the Ganges. For, have they not all read about our ancient civilization; how, in the morning of the world, before the Eternal City had been built upon the Seven Hills, before Alexander had marched his army to the banks of the Tigris, before Babylonian astronomers had learnt to gaze upon the starry world, our ancestors had developed a great civilization, and how that civilization has profoundly influenced the course of modern thought in the highest concerns of man? Above all, we rely with unbounded confidence on the justice and generosity of the British people and of their representatives in Parliament.

It is not that we mistrust the authorities here. But the higher we mount the purer is the atmosphere. The impurities generated by local causes cannot touch those who, removed from local influences, represent in a loftier sphere of responsibility the majesty and the greatness of the English nation. Let us freely acknowledge the tribute we owe to the British government in India. What government could have accorded a speedier recognition to Congress claims than the government of India has done? Within the lifetime of a generation we have achieved changes—beneficent changes of far-reaching moment—which it would have taken many generations to accomplish elsewhere, which in less fortunately situated countries could not have been accomplished except, perhaps, after bloodshed and tumult. All this we freely acknowledge. For all this we are truly grateful. All this fills [us] with hope for the future.

Nevertheless we feel that much yet remains to be done, and the impetus must come from England. To England we look for inspiration and guidance. To England we look for sympathy in the struggle. From England must come the crowning mandate which will enfranchise our people. England is our political guide and our moral preceptor in the exalted sphere of political duty. English history has taught us those principles of freedom which we cherish with our lifeblood. We have been fed upon the strong food of English constitutional freedom. We have been taught to admire the eloquence and genius of the great masters of English political philosophy. We have been brought face to face with the struggles and the triumphs of the English people in their stately march towards constitutional freedom. Where will you find better models of courage, devotion, and sacrifice; not in Rome, not in Greece, not even in France in the stormy days of the Revolution—courage tempered by caution, enthusiasm leavened by sobriety, partisanship softened by a large-hearted charity—all subordinated to the one predominating sense of love of country and love of God.

We should be unworthy of ourselves and of our preceptors—we should, indeed, be something less than human—if, with our souls stirred to their inmost depths, our warm Oriental sensibilities roused to an unwanted pitch of enthusiasm by the contemplation of these great ideals of public duty, we did not seek to transplant into our own country the spirit of those free institutions which has made England what she is. In the words of Lord Lansdowne, a wave of unrest is passing through this country. But it is not the unrest of discontent or disloyalty to the British government—it is the unrest which is the first visible sign of the awakening of a new national life. It is the work of Englishmen—it is the noblest monument of their rule–it is the visible embodiment of the vast moral influence which they are exercising over the minds of the people of India. Never in the history of the world have the inheritors of an ancient civilization been so profoundly influenced by the influx of modern ideas. In this Congress from year to year we ask England to accomplish her glorious work. The course of civilization following the path of the sun has travelled from East to West. The West owes a heavy debt to the East. We look forward to the day when that debt will be repaid, not only by the moral regeneration, but by the political enfranchisement of our people.

Faith in Social Progress

In concluding his memoirs in his old age, Surendranāth looked back at the changes that had taken place in Hindu society during his lifetime, and summed up that faith in gradual reform which is one of the hallmarks of a Moderate.

[From *A Nation in Making,* pp. 397–98]

I feel that if we have to advance in social matters, we must, so far as practicable, take the community with us by a process of steady and gradual uplift, so that there may be no sudden disturbance or dislocation, the new being adapted to the old, and the old assimilated to the new. That has been the normal path of progress in Hindu society through the long centuries. It would be idle to contend that Hindu society is today where it was two hundred years ago. It moves slowly, perhaps more slowly than many would wish, but in the words of Galileo "it does move," more or less according to the lines of adaptation that I have indicated. The question of sea-voyage, or child-marriage, or even enforced widowhood, is not today where it was in the latter part of the last century. Fifty years ago I was an outcaste (being an England-returned Brahmin) in the village where I live. Today I am an honoured member of the community. My public services have, perhaps, partly contributed to the result. But they would have been impotent, as in the case Ram Mohun Roy for many long years after his death, if they were not backed by the slow, the silent, the majestic forces of progress, working noiselessly but irresistibly in the bosom of society, helping on the fruition of those ideas which have been sown in the public mind. Remarkable indeed have been, in many respects, the relaxations and the removal of restrictions of caste. Dining with non-Hindus, which was an abomination not many years ago, is now connived at, if not openly countenanced. A still more forward step towards loosening the bonds of caste has been taken within the last few years. The barriers of marriage between some sub-castes have been relaxed, and marriages between hitherto prohibited sub-castes of Brahmins and Kayasthas [scribes] are not infrequent, and I have had some personal share in this reform. Beneficent are the activities of the Brāhmo Samāj, but behind them is the slower but larger movement of the general community, all making towards progress.

M.G. Rānade: Pioneer Mahārāshtrian Reformer

Western cultural influence, like British rule itself, came to different parts of India at different times. The coastal ports founded in the sixteenth and seventeenth centuries—Madras, Bombay, Calcutta—became and remain today the centres of the new order of life and thought. The spread of this order into the hinterland, however, was a slow and irregular process. Bengal, the home of a number of thinkers considered thus far, was the first province to fall entirely under British sway and therefore the first to react to the impact of Western ways and ideas.

On the opposite side of the Indian subcontinent, protected by their mountain fortresses in the Western Ghats, the proud kingdoms of Mahārāshtra were among the last to surrender to foreign rule. The leadership which made this prolonged resistance possible came notably from two caste groups. The fighting Marāthā-Kunbi castes under Shivaji (1630-1680) and his descendants, provided most of the military force, while the small but influential Chitpavan brāhman caste provided the peshwas (prime ministers) and intellectual leaders of later times. Even after the final defeat of the Peshwa's government is 1818 the city of Poona remained the centre of Mahārāshtrian intellectual life. In the closing decades of the nineteenth century the Chitpavan brāhman caste produced three leaders whose names were to be inscribed in Indian nationalism's hall of fame—Rānade, Gokhale, and Tilak.

Mahādev Govind Rānade, the eldest of three children, was born in 1842 in a strictly orthodox household. An extremely serious student, he begged his father to send him to school in Bombay to complete his English education. At fourteen he entered the Elphinstone Institution, and at seventeen took his place in the first class to enroll in the new Bombay University. He distinguished himself by his diligence and originality of thought, and became a teacher of economics and later of history and literature at his first alma mater, now called the Elphinstone College. But he chose to make his career in the law, and before he was thirty received his first appointment as a subordinate judge in the government courts at Poona.

During his thirty years as a judge, Rānade gently but firmly worked for the reform of such social evils as child marriage, the non-remarriage of widows, and the seclusion of women. In many ways his efforts resembled those of Rāmmohun Roy, whom he admired as a patriot and as a godly man. Rānade was one of the early members of the Prārthanā Samaj (Prayer Society, modeled after the Brāhmo Samāj), whose founding in 1867 was sparked by Keshub Chandra Sen's earlier visits to Bombay. Under Rānade's judicious guidance, the Prārthanā Samāj did not cut itself off from the rest of Hindu society, but strove gradually to bring the orthodox around to its position. Despite the vociferous and sometimes violent opposition of Tilak and his school, Rānade's policy of moderation in social reform met with increasing success.

Disqualified from entering active politics by his judgeship. Rānade's contribution to the nationalist movement was largely in the realm of social and economic reform. In 1887, he founded the Indian National Social Conference as a separate organization which met concurrently with the annual Congress sessions, and in 1890 inaugurated the Industrial Association of Western India. Rānade's views on economics grew out of his long and patient study of Indian problems. He concluded that their constructive solution lay in a vigorous policy of industrial and commercial development under British government auspices.

Rānade's infinite capacity for taking pains, his saintly disposition, and his devotion to the welfare of India inspired to greater patriotic endeavour the hundreds of younger men with whom he maintained contact in person or through correspondence. He was a Moderate in the best sense of the term—scholarly, patient, practical, constructive, never wasting his time in denouncing those who held other views. After his death in 1901 his memory continued to inspire the leaders of Western India—Gokhale, and after him Gāndhi, carrying on the tradition he initiated of social and economic reform as an integral part of selfless public service.

Mahādev Govind Rānade

Revivalism versus Reform

The ludicrous impracticability of reviving ancient traditions merely because they were ancient was tellingly demonstrated by Rānade in one of his Social Conference addresses. Having explained why he rejected the suggestion of the Brāhmo and Ārya Samājists that all social reformers should convert to those faiths, he went on to analyze the four basic causes of the degeneration of Indian society.

[From Chintamini, *Indian Social Reform,* Part II, pp. 89-95]

While the new religious sects condemn us for being too orthodox, the extreme orthodox section denounce us for being too revolutionary in our methods. According to these last, our efforts should be directed to revive, and not to reform. I have many friends in this camp of extreme orthodoxy, and their watchword is that revival, and not reform, should be our motto. They advocate a return to the old ways, and appeal to the old authorities and the old sanction.

Here also, as in the instance quoted above, people speak without realizing the full significance of their own words. When we are asked to revive our institutions and customs, people seem to be very much at sea as to what it is they seem to revive. What particular period of our history is to be taken as the old? Whether the period of the Vedas, of the Smritis, of the Puranas or of the Mohammedan or modern Hindu times? Our usages have been changed from time to time by a slow process of growth, and in some cases of decay and corruption, and we cannot stop at a particular period without breaking the continuity of the whole. When my revivalist friend presses his argument upon me, he has to seek recourse in some subterfuge which really furnishes no reply to the question—what shall we revive? Shall we revive the old habits of our people when the most sacred of our caste indulged in all the abominations as we now understand them of animal food and drink which exhausted every section of our country's zoology and botany? The men and the gods of those old days ate and drank forbidden things to excess in a way no revivalist will now venture to recommend. Shall we revive the twelve forms of sons, or eight forms of marriage, which included capture, and recognized mixed and illegitimate intercourse? Shall we revive the Niyoga system of procreating sons on our brother's wives when widowed? Shall we revive the old liberties taken by the Rishis and by the wives of the Rishis with the marital tie? Shall we revive the hecatombs of animals sacrificed from year's end to year's end, and in which human beings were not spared as propitiatory offerings? Shall we revive the Shakti worship of the left hand with its indecencies and practical debaucheries? Shall we revive the sati and infanticide customs, or the flinging of living men into rivers, or over rocks, or hookswinging, or the crushing beneath Jagannath car?[8] Shall we revive the internecine wars of the Brahmins and Kshatriyas, or the cruel persecution and degradation of the aboriginal population? Shall we revive the custom of many husbands to one wife or of many wives to one husband? Shall we require our Brahmins to cease to be landlords and gentlemen, and turn into beggars and dependants upon the king as in olden times? These instances will suffice to show that the plan of reviving the ancient usages and customs will not work our salvation, and is not practicable. If these usages were good and beneficial, why were they altered by our wise ancestors? If they were bad and injurious, how can any claim be put forward for their restoration after so many ages? Besides, it seems to be forgotten that in a living organism, as society is, no revival is possible. The dead and the buried or burnt are dead, buried, and burnt once for all, and the dead past cannot therefore be revived except by a reformation of the old materials into new organized beings. If revival is impossible, reformation is the only alternative open to sensible people, and now it may be asked what is the principle on which this reformation must be based? People have very hazy ideas on this subject. It seems to many that it is the outward form which has to be changed, and if this change can be made, they think that all the difficulties in our way will vanish. If we change our outward manners and customs, sit in a particular way, or walk in a particular fashion, our work according to them is accomplished. I cannot but think that much of the prejudice against the reformers is due to this misunderstanding. It is not the outward form, but the inward form, the thought and the idea which determines the outward form, that has to be changed if real reformation is desired.

Now what have been the inward forms or ideas which have been hastening our decline during the past three thousand years? These ideas may be briefly set forth as isolation, submission to outward force or power more than to the voice of the inward conscience, perception of fictitious differences between men and men due to heredity and birth, passive acquiescence in evil or wrong doing, and a general indifference to secular well-being, almost bordering upon fatalism. These have been the root ideas of our ancient social system. They have as their natural result led to the existing family arrangements where the woman is entirely subordinated to the man and the lower castes to the higher castes, to the length of depriving men of their natural respect for humanity. All the evils we seek to combat result from the prevalence of these ideas. They are mere corollaries to these axiomatic assumptions. They prevent some of our people from realizing what they really are in all conscience, neither better nor worse than their fellows, and that whatever garb men may put on, they are the worse for assuming dignities and powers which do not in fact belong to them. As long as these ideas remain operative on our minds, we may change our outward forms and institutions, and be none the better for the change. These ideas have produced in the long course of ages their results on our character, and we must judge their good or bad quality, as Saint Paul, by the fruits they have borne. Now that these results have been disastrous, nobody disputes or doubts, and the lesson to be drawn for our guidance in the future from this fact is that the current of these ideas must be changed, and in the place of the old worship we paid to them, we must accustom ourselves and others to worship and reverence new ideals. In place of isolation, we must cultivate the spirit of fraternity or elastic expansiveness. At present it is everybody's ambition to pride himself upon being a member of the smallest community that can be conceived, and the smaller the number of those with whom you can dine, or marry, or associate, the higher is your perfection and purity, the purest person is he who cooks his own food, and does not allow the shadow of even his nearest friend to fall upon his cooked food. Every caste and every sect has thus a tendency to split itself into smaller castes and smaller sects in practical life. Even in philosophy and religion, it is a received maxim that knowledge is for the few, and that salvation is only possible for the esoteric elect with whom only are the virtues of sanctity and wisdom, and that for the rest of mankind, they must be left to wander in the wilderness, and grovel in superstition and even vice, with only a colouring of so-called religion to make them respectable. Now all this must be changed. The new mould of thought on this head must be, as stated above, cast on the lines of fraternity, a capacity to expand outwards, and to make more cohesive inwards the bonds of fellowship. Increase the circle of your friends and associates, slowly and cautiously if you will, but the tendency must be towards a general recognition of the essential equality between man and man. It will beget sympathy and power. It will strengthen your own hands, by the sense that you have numbers with you, and not against you, or as you foolishly imagine, below you.

The next idea which lies at the root of our helplessness is the sense that we are always intended to remain children, to be subject to outside control and never to rise to the dignity of self-control by making our conscience and our reason the supreme, if not the sole, guide to our conduct. All past history has been a terrible witness to the havoc committed by this misconception. We are children, no doubt, but the children of God, and not of man, and the voice of God is the only voice [to] which we are bound to listen. Of course, all of us cannot listen to this voice when we desire it, because from long neglect and dependence upon outside help, we have benumbed this faculty of conscience in us. With too many of us, a thing is true or false, righteous or sinful, simply because somebody in the past has said that it is so. Duties and obligations are duties and obligations, not because we feel them to be so, but because somebody reputed to be wise has laid it down that they are so. In small matters of manners and courtesies, this outside dictation is not without its use. But when we abandon ourselves entirely to this helpless dependence on other wills, it is no wonder that we become helpless as children in all departments of life. Now the new idea which should take up the place of this helplessness and dependence is not the idea of a rebellious overthrow of all authority, but that of freedom responsible to the voice of God in us. Great and wise men in the past, as in the present, have a claim upon our regards, but they must not come between us and our God—the Divine principle enthroned in the heart of every one of us high or low. It is this sense of self-respect, or rather respect for the God in us, which has to be cultivated. It is a very tender plant which takes years and years to make it grow. But there is the capacity and the power, and we owe it as a duty to ourselves to undertake the task. Revere all human authority, pay your respects to all prophets and all revelations, but never let this reverence and respect come in the way of the dictates of conscience, the Divine command in us.

Similarly there is no doubt that men differ from men in natural capacities, and aptitudes, and that heredity and birth are factors of considerable importance in our development. But it is at the same time true they are not the only factors that determine the whole course of our life for good or for evil, under a law of necessity. Heredity and birth explain many things, but this Law of Karma does not explain all things! What is worse, it does not explain the mystery that makes man and woman what they really are, the reflection and the image of God. Our passions and our feelings, our pride and our ambition lend strength to these agencies, and with their help the Law of Karma completes our conquest, and in too many cases enforces our surrender. The new idea that should come in here is that this Law of Karma can be controlled and set back by a properly trained will, when it is made subservient to a higher will than ours. This we see in our everyday life, and Necessity, or the Fates are, our own texts tell us, faint obstacles in the way of our advancement if we devote ourselves to the law of Duty. I admit that this misconception is very hard to remove, perhaps the hardest of the old ideas. But removed it must be, if not in this life or generation, in many lives and generations, if we are ever to rise to our full stature.

The fourth old form or idea to which I will allude here is our acquiescences in wrong or evil doing as an inevitable condition of human life, about which we need not be very particular. All human life is a vanity and a dream, and we are not much concerned with it. This view of life is in fact atheism in its worst form. No man or woman really ceases to be animal who does not perceive or realize that wrong or evil-doing, impurity and vice, crime and misery, and sin of all kinds, is really our animal existence prolonged. It is the beast in us which blinds us to impurity and vice, and makes them even attractive. There must nautches[9] in our temples, say our priests, because even the Gods cannot do without these impure fairies. This is only a typical instance of our acquiescence in impurity. There must be drunkenness in the world, there must be poverty and wretchedness and tyranny, there must be fraud and farce, there must be thieves and the law to punish them. No doubt these are facts, and there is no use denying their existence, but in the name of all that is sacred and true, do not acquiesce in them, do not hug these evils to your bosom, and cherish them. Their contact is poisonous, not the less deadly because it does not kill, but it corrupts men. A healthy sense of the true dignity of our nature, and of man's high destiny, is the best corrective and antidote to this poison. I think I have said more than enough to suggest to your reflecting minds what it is that we have to reform. All admit that we have been deformed. We have lost our stature, we are bent in a hundred places, our eyes lust after forbidden things, our ears desire to hear scandals about our neighbours, our tongues lust to taste forbidden fruit, our hands itch for another man's property, our bowels are deranged with indigestible food. We cannot walk on our feet, but require stilts or crutches. This is our present social polity, and now we want this deformity to be removed; and the only way to remove it is to place ourselves under the discipline of better ideas and forms such as those I have briefly touched above. Now this is the work of the Reformer. Reforms in the matter of infant marriage and enforced widowhood, in the matter of temperance and purity, intermarriage between castes, the elevation of the low castes, and the readmission of converts, and the regulation of our endowments and charities, are reforms only so far and no further as they check the influence of the old ideas and promote the growth of the new tendencies. The Reformer has to infuse in himself the light and warmth of nature, and he can only do it by purifying and improving himself and his surroundings. He must have his family, village, tribe, and nation recast in other and new moulds, and that is the reason why Social Reform becomes our obligatory duty, and not a mere pastime which might be given up at pleasure. Revival is, as I have said, impossible; as impossible as mass-conversion into other faiths. But even if it were possible, its only use to us would be if the reforms elevated us and our surroundings, if they made us stronger, braver, truer men with all our faculties of endurance and work developed, with all our sympathies fully awakened and refined, and if with our heads and hearts acting in union with a purified and holy will, they made us feel the dignity of our being and the high destiny of our existence, taught us to love all, work with all, and feel for all.

Hindu-Muslim Cooperation

In his speech to the Indian Social Conference of 1890, Rānade stressed the importance of religious toleration, suggesting that the members of each community avoid mutual recriminations, and cooperate instead in the work of social reform.

[From Chintamini, *Indian Social Reform,* Part II, pp. 122-25]

If the lessons of the past have any value, one thing is quite clear, namely, that in this vast country no progress is possible unless both Hindus and Mahomendans join hands together, and are determined to follow the lead of the men who flourished in Akbar's time and were his chief advisers and councillors, and sedulously avoid the mistakes which were committed by his greatgrandson Aurangzib. Joint action from a sense of common interest, and a common desire to bring about the fusion of the thoughts and feelings of men so as to tolerate small differences and bring about concord—these were the chief aims kept in view by Akbar and formed the principle of the new divine faith formulated in the Din-i-ilahi.[10] Every effort on the part of either Hindus or Mahomedans to regard their interests as separated and distinct, and every attempt made by the two communities to create separate schools and interests among themselves, and not to heal up to wounds inflicted by mutual hatred of caste and creed, must be deprecated on all hands? It is to be feared that this lesson has not been sufficiently kept in mind by the leaders of both communities in their struggle for existence and in the acquisition of power and predominance during recent years. There is at times a great danger of the work of Akabr being undone by losing sight of this great lesson which the history of his reign and that of his two successors is so well calculated to teach. The Conference which brings us together is especially intended for the propagation of this "din"[11] or "dharma," and it is in connection with that message chiefly that I have ventured to speak to you today on this important subject. The ills that we are suffering from are most of them self-inflicted evils, the cure of which is to a large extent in our own hands. Looking at the series of measures which Akbar adopted in his time to cure these evils, one feels how correct was his vision when he and his advisers put their hand on those very defects in our national character which need to be remedied first before we venture on higher enterprises. Pursuit of high ideas, mutual sympathy and cooperation, perfect tolerance, a correct understanding of the diseases from which the body politic is suffering, and an earnest desire to apply suitable remedies—this is the work cut out for the present generation. The awakening has commenced, as is witnessed by the fact that we have met in this place from such distances for joint consultation and action. All that is needed is that we must put our hands to the plow, and face the strife and the struggle. The success already achieved warrants the expectation that if we perservere on right lines, the goal we have in view may be attained. That goal is not any particular advantage to be gained in power and wealth. It is represented by the efforts to attain it, the expansion and the evolution of the heart and the mind, which will make us stronger and braver, purer and truer men. This is at least the lesson I draw from our more recent history of the past thousand years, and if those centuries have rolled away to no purpose over our heads, our cause is no doubt hopeless beyond cure. That is however not the faith in me; and I feel sure it is not the faith that moves you in this great struggle against our own weak selves, than which nothing is more fatal to our individual and collective growth. Both Hindus and Mahomendans have their work cut out in this struggle. In the backwardness of female education, in the disposition to overleap the bounds of their own religion, in matters of temperance, in their internal dissensions between castes and creeds, in the indulgence of impure speech, thought, and action on occasions when they are diposed to enjoy themselves, in the abuses of many customs in regard to unequal and polygamous marriages, in the desire to be extravagant in their expenditure on such occasions, in the neglect of regulated charity, in the decay of public spirit in insisting on the proper management of endowments—in these and other matters both communities are equal sinners, and there is thus much ground for improvement on common lines. Of course the Hindus, being by far the majority of the population, have other difficulties of their own to combat with; and they are trying in their gatherings of separate castes and communities to remedy them each in their own way. But without coperation and conjoint action of all communities, success is not possible, and it is on that account that the general Conference is held in different places each year to rouse local interest, and help people in their separate efforts by a knowledge of what their friends similarly situated are doing in other parts. This is the reason of our meeting here, and I trust that this message I have attempted to deliver to you on this occasion will satisfy you that we cannot conceive a nobler work than the one for which we have met here today.

India's Need: State Guidance of Economic Development

Rānade's essay of 1892 on "Indian Political Economy" may be regarded as the cornerstone of the economic theory which underlies the present Five Year Plans. He first showed that English *laissez faire* doctrines were being challenged by more recent theories of the science of economics and were not necessarily relevant to India's problems; then continued with diagnosis of the Indian economy.

[From *Rānade, Essay on Indian Economics*, pp. 22-25, 33-36]

This resumé of the past and contemporary history of the growth of economic Sciences in England, France, Germany, Italy, and America will satisfy the student that modern European thought does not at all countenance the view of the English writers of the Ricardian

School, that the principles of the science, as they have enuniated them in their textbooks, are universally and necessarily true for all times and places, and for all stages of advancement. Modern thought is veering to the conclusion that the individual and his interests are not the centre round which the theory should revolve, that the true centre is the body politic of which that individual is a member, and that collective defense and well-being, social education and discipline, and the duties, and not merely the interests, of men, must be taken into account, if the theory is not to be merely utopian. The method to be followed is not the deductive but the historical method, which takes account of the past in its forecast of the future; and relativity, and not absoluteness, characterizes the conclusions of economical science. There are those who seek to get over this difficulty by differentiating the science from what they are disposed to call the art of economy. This divorce of theory and practice is, however, a mischievous error, which relegates the science to the sterility of an ideal dream or a puzzle, and condemns the art to the position of a rule of the thumb. Theory is only enlarged practice, practice is theory studied in its relation to proximate causes. The practice is predetermined by the theory which tests its truth, and adapts it to different conditions by reason of its grasp of the deep-seated, permanent, and varied basal truths. I hope thus to have shown that the nature of the subject itself as a branch of social science, which is best studied historically and not deductively, the actual practice of the most civilized nations and the history of the growth of its theory given above alike establish the doctrine of relativity, and the predominant claim of collective welfare over individual interests, as the principal features in which the highest minds of the present day chiefly differ from the economical writers of the old school, with their *a priori* conclusions based on individual self-interest and unrestricted competition.

We have next to consider the bearings of this enlarged view of the science in its Indian aspects. The characteristics of our social life are the prevalence of status over contract, of combination over competition. Our habits of mind are conservative to a fault. The aptitudes of climate and soil facilitate the production of raw materials. Labour is cheap and plentiful, but unsteady, unthrifty, and unskilled. Capital is scarce, immobile, and unenterprising. Cooperation on a large scale of either capital or labour is unknown. Agriculture is the chief support of nearly the whole population, and this agriculture is carried on under conditions of uncertain rainfall. Commerce and manufactures on a large scale are but recent importations, and all industry is carried on, on the system of petty farming, retail dealing, and job working by poor people on borrowed capital. There is an almost complete absence of a landed gentry or wealthy middle class. The land is a monopoly of the State. The desire for accumulation is very weak, peace and security having been almost unknown over large areas for any length of time till within the last century. Our laws and institutions favour a low standard of life, and encourage subdivision and not concentration of wealth. The religious ideals of life condemn the ardent pursuit of wealth as a mistake to be avoided as far as possible. These are old legacies and inherited weaknesses. Stagnation and dependence, depression and poverty––these are written in broad characters on the face of the land and its people. To these must be added the economical drain of wealth and talents, which foreign subjection has entailed on the country. As a compensation against all these depressing influences, we have to set off the advantage of a free contact with a race which has opened the country to the commerce of the world, and by its superior skill and resources has developed communications in a way previously unknown. If we wish to realize our situation fully, we may not overlook this factor, because, it represents the beam of light which alone illumines the prevailing darkness. It cannot well be a mere accident that the destinies of this country have been entrusted to the guidance of a nation whose characteristic strength is opposed to all our weaknesses, whose enterprise, chiefly in commerce and manufactures, knows no bounds, whose capital overflows the world, among whom contract has largely superseded status, and competition and cooperation play a predominant part, whose view of life is full of hope, and whose powers of organization have never been surpassed.

Rānade next advanced several reasons why industrial enterprise should be encouraged, and urged government action to populate untilled lands, protect peasants against excessive taxation, and prevent exploitation by landlords or money-lenders. In his conclusion he argued that the state should play a more active role in the economic development of the country.

Lastly comes the great department of governmental interference. The meddlesomeness of the mercantile system provoked a reaction against state control and guidance towards the end of the last century in favour of natural liberty. The doctrines of this negative school have now in their turn been abused by a too logical extension of its principles. There is a decided reaction in Europe against the *laissez faire* system. Even in England, the recent factory legislation, the qualified recognition by law of Trades-Unionism, the poor law system, and the Irish Land Settlement, are all instances which indicate the same change of view. Speaking roughly, the province of state interference and control is practically being extended so as to restore the good points of the mercantile system without its absurdities. The State is now more and more recognized as the national organ for taking care of national needs in all matters in which individual and co-operative efforts are not likely to be so effective and economic as national effort. This is the correct view to take of the true functions of a state. To relegate them to the simple duty of maintaining peace and order is really to deprive the community of many of the advantages of the social union. Education, both liberal and technical, posts and telegraphs, railway and canal communications, the pioneering of new enterprise, the insurance of risky undertakings—all these functions are usefully discharged by the State. The question is one of time, fitness, and expediency, not one of liberty and rights. In our own country the State has similarly enlarged its functions with advantage. The very fact that the rulers belong to a race with superior advantage imposes this duty on them of attempting things which no native rulers, past or present, could as well achieve, or possibly even think of. This obligation is made more peremptory by the fact that the State claims to be the sole landlord, and is certainly the largest capitalist in the country. While the State in India has done much in this way in the working of iron and coal fields, and in the experiments made about cotton and tobacco, and in tea and coffee and cinchona Plantations, it must be admitted that, as compared with its resources and the needs of the country, these attempts are as nothing by the side of what has been attempted with success in France, Germany, and other countries, but which, unhappily, has not been attempted in this country. Even if political considerations forbid independent action in the matter of differential duties, the pioneering of new enterprises is a duty which the government might more systematically undertake with advantage. In truth, there is no difference of principle between lending such support and guidance, by the free use of its credit and superior organization, in pioneering industrial undertaking or subsidizing private cooperative effort, and its guaranteeing minimum interest to railway companies. The building up of national, not merely state, credit on broad foundations by helping people to acquire confidence in a free and largely ramified banking system, so advantageously worked in Europe under different forms, has also not been attempted here. There is, lastly, the duty cast on it of utilizing indigenous resources, and organizing them in a way to produce in India in state factories all products of skill which the state departments require in the way of stores. These are only a few of the many directions in which, far more than exchange and frontier difficulties, the highest statesmanship will have a field all its own for consideration and action. They will, no doubt, receive such consideration if only the minds of the rulers were once thoroughly freed from the fear of offending the so-called maxims of rigid economical science. It is time that a new departure should take place in this connection, and it is with a view to drawing public attention to this necessity that I have ventured to place before you the results of modern economic thought. In this, as in other matters, the conditions of Indian life are more faithfully reproduced in some of the continental countries and in America than in happy England, proud of its position, strong in its insularity, and the home of the richest and busiest community in the modern industrial world. If the attempt I have made leads to a healthy and full discussion of the change of policy I advocate, I shall regard myself amply repaid for my trouble.

G.K. Gokhale : Servant of India

The work of reform begun by Rānade was ably shouldered by his younger friend and colleague G.K. Gokhale. So close was the personal relationship between the two men during Rānade's lifetime—for years they met weekly to discuss their ideas and projects—that Gokhale's excursions into active politics can be regarded as the logical extension of his teacher's endeavours. Sprung from the same proud Mahārāshtrian stock, both leaders nevertheless clung to the policy of cooperation with the government and of moderate opposition to its evils. Gokhale, however, had to endure the merciless attacks of the Extremists during the stormiest decade in Indian politics up to that time.

Gopāl Krishna Gokhale (1866 – 1915) dedicated his life to public service at the age of nineteen, on his graduation from Elphinstone College, by joining the Deccan Education Society in Poona. Members of the Society took a vow of poverty for twenty years in order to devote their time exclusively to educating their fellow-countrymen. For his part, Gokhale became a teacher of English and Mathematics in the Fergusson College which the Society founded in 1885. He soon met Justice Rānade and began his long and fruitful apprenticeship under him—examining documents, weighing evidence, analyzing fiscal data, and preparing comprehensive memoranda on public questions.

Gokhale attracted public attention with the sagacity of his carefully prepared speeches, and in 1899 was elected a member of the recently formed Legislative Council for the state of Bombay. When only thrity-six, he became the Indian representative of this state on the Imperial Legislative Council, despite its limited powers the highest law-making body in India. For the last thirteen years of his life he wore himself out with his efforts to secure government cooperation in granting much needed financial and administrative reforms for India. "No taxation without representation," was the essence of his demand, and his annual speeches on the imperial budget effected many concessions from harassed ministers of finance.

In 1905 Gokhale founded the Servants of India Society in Poona, modeling it after the lay and monastic orders of the Catholic Church. Famine relief, education, Hindu-Muslim unity, and the elevation of the lowest castes were among the fields in which it carried on the work begun by its founder. Gokhale also took great interest in the problems of Indian emigrants to South Africa, giving freely of his advice and encouragement to their leader, M.K. Gāndhi. Although bitterly reviled by Tilak and other advocates of violent action to end foreign rule, Gokhale's readiness to cooperate with the British in introducing gradual reforms helped to pave the way for the eventual peaceful transfer of power to an independent India.

Gopāl Krishna Gokkhale

Taxation Without Representation

Soon after taking his place in the Imperial Legislative Council, Gokhale made the first of his annual budget speeches. His attacks on the government's taxation policy are representative of the Moderates' preoccupation with the economic shortcomings of British rule.

[From *Speeches of the Honourable Mr. G.K. Gokhale*, pp. 1–2, 8–11]

Your Excellency, I fear I cannot conscientiously join in the congratulations which have been offered to the Hon'ble Finance Member on the huge surplus which the revised estimates show for the last year. A surplus of seven crores[12] of rupees is perfectly unprecedented in the history of Indian finance, and coming as it does on the top of a series of similar surpluses realized when the country has been admittedly passing through very trying times, it illustrates to my mind in a painfully clear manner the utter absence of a due correspondence between the condition of the people and the condition of the finances of the country. Indeed, my Lord, the more I think about this matter the more I feel–and I trust Your Lordship will pardon me for speaking somewhat bluntly–that these surpluses constitute a double wrong to the community. They are a wrong in the first instance in that they exist at all'–that government should take so much more from the people than is needed in times of serious depression and suffering; and they are also wrong, because they lend themselves to easy misinterpretation and, among other things, render possible the phenomenal optimism of the Secretary of State for India, who seems to imagine that all is for the best in this best of lands. A slight examination of these surpluses suffices to show that they are mainly, almost entirely, currency surpluses, resulting from the fact that government still maintain the same high level of taxation which they considered to be necessary to secure financial equilibrium when the rupee stood at its lowest. ...

A taxation so forced as not only to maintain a budgetary equilibrium but to yield as well "large, continuous, progressive surpluses"–even in years of trial and suffering–is, I submit, against all accepted canons of finance. In European countries, extraordinary charges are usually met out of borrowings, the object being to avoid, even in times of pressure, impeding the even, normal development of trade and industry by any sudden or large additions to the weight of public burdens. In India, where the economic side of such questions finds such scant recognition, and the principle of meeting the charges of the year with the resources of the year is carried to a logical extreme, the anxiety of the Financial Administration is not only to make both ends meet in good and bad years alike, but to present large surpluses year after year. The Hon'ble Finance Member remarks in his Budget Statement under "Army Services": "It must be remembered that India is defraying from revenues the cost of undertaking both rearmament and the reform of military reorganization in important departments. I believe that this is an undertaking which has not been attempted by other countries without the assistance of loans in some form or other. Even in England, extraordinary military requirements for fortifications and barracks have been met by loans for short terms of years repayable by installments out of revenues. If profiting by a period of political tranquility we can accomplish this task without the raising of a loan and the imposition of a permanent burden on future generations, I think that we shall be able to congratulate ourselves on having done that which even the richest nations of Europe have not considered it advisable to attempt."

Every word of this citation invites comment. How comes it that India is doing in regard to these extraordinary charges that which even the richest nations of Europe have not considered it advisable to attempt? The obvious answer is that in those countries it is the popular assemblies that control taxation and expenditure; in India the tax-payer has no constitutional voice in the shaping of these things. If we had any votes to give, and the government of the country had been carried on by an alternation of power between two parties, both alike anxious to conciliate us and bid for our support, the Hon'ble Member would assuredly have told a different tale. But I venture to submit, my Lord, that the consideration which the people of Western countries receive in consequence of their voting power should be available to us, in matters of finance at any rate, through an "intelligent anticipation"–to use a phrase of Your Lordship's – of our reasonable wishes on the part of government.

But even thus–after doing what the richest nations of Europe shrink from attempting–meeting all sorts of extraordinary charges, amounting to about 70 crores in sixteen years, out of current revenues– we have "large, continuous, progressive surpluses," and this only shows, as Colonel Chesney points out in the March number of the *Nineteenth Century and After,* that more money is being taken from the people than is right, necessary, or advisable, or, in other words, the weight of public taxation has been fixed and maintained at an unjustifiably high level. Taxation for financial equilibrium is what we all can understand, but taxation kept up in the face of the difficulties and misfortunes of a period of excessive depression and for "large, continuous and progressive surpluses" is evidently a matter which requires justification. At all events, those who have followed the course of the financial history of the period will admit that the fact viewed *per se* that "such large, continuous, and progressive surpluses" have occurred during the period–as a result not of a normal expansion of fiscal resources but of a forced up and heavy taxation–does not connote, as Lord George Hamilton contends, an advancing material prosperity of the country or argue any marvellous recuperative power on the part of the masses–as the Hon'ble Sir Edward Law urged last year. To them, at any rate, the apparent paradox of a suffering country and an overflowing treasury stands easily explained and is a clear proof of the fact that the level of national taxation is kept unjustifiably high, even when government are in a position to lower that level.

Improving the Lot of Low–Caste Hindus

One of Gokhale's chief concerns in the realm of social reform was the lot of the so-called "untouchables." The appeal launched in this speech to a social conference in 1903 was answered after his death by Gāndhi's devotion to their cause.

[From *Speeches of the Honourable Mr. G.K. Gokhale,* pp. 740–47]

Mr. President and Gentlemen : The proposition which has been entrusted to me runs thus– "That this Conference holds that the present degraded condition of the low castes is, in itself and from the national point of view, unsatisfactory, and is of opinion that every well-wisher of the country should consider it his duty to do all he can to raise their moral and social condition by trying to rouse self-respect in these classes and placing facilities for education and employment within their reach."

Gentlemen, I hope I am not given to the use of unnecessarily strong language and yet I must say that this resolution is not as strongly worded as it should have been. The condition of the low castes–it is painful to call them low castes–is not only unsatisfactory as this resolution says, it is so deeply deplorable that it constitutes a grave blot on our social arrangements; and, further, the attitude of our educated men towards this class is profoundly painful and humiliating. I do not propose to deal with this subject as an antiquarian; I only want to make a few general observations from the standpoint of justice, humanity, and national self interest. I think all fair-minded persons will have to admit that it is absolutely monstrous that a class of human beings, with bodies similar to our own, with brains that can think and with hearts that can feel, should be perpetually condemned to a low life of utter wretchedness, servitude, and mental and moral degradation, and that permanent barriers should be placed in their way so that it should be impossible for them ever to overcome them and improve their lot. This is deeply revolting to our sense of justice. I believe one has only to put oneself mentally into their place to realize how grievous this injustice is. We may touch a cat, we may touch a dog, we may touch any other animal, but the touch of these human beings is pollution! And so complete is now the mental degradation of these people that they themselves see nothing in such treatment to resent, that they acquiesce in it as though nothing better than that was their due.

I remember a speech delivered seven or eight years ago by the late Mr. Rānade in Bombay, under the auspices of the Hindu Union Club. That was a time when public feeling ran high in India on the subject of the treatment which our people were receiving in South Africa. Our friend, Mr. Gāndhi, had come here on a brief visit from South Africa and he was telling us how our people were treated in Natal and Cape Colony and the Transvaal–how they were not allowed to walk on footpaths or travel in first-class carriages on the railway, how they were not admitted into hotels, and so forth. Public feeling, in consequence, was deeply stirred, and we all felt that it was a mockery that we should be called British subjects, when we were treated like this in Great Britain's colonies. Mr. Rānade felt this just as keenly as any one else. He had been a never-failing adviser of Mr. Gāndhi, and had carried on a regular correspondence with him. But it was Mr. Rānade's peculiar greatness that he always utilized occasions of excitement to give a proper turn to the national mind and cultivate its sense of proportion. And so, when every one was expressing himself in indignant terms about the treatment which our countrymen were receiving in South Africa, Mr. Rānade came forward to ask if we had no sins of our own to answer for in that direction. I do not exactly remember the title of his address. I think it was "Turn the searchlight inwards," or some such thing. But I remember that it was a great speech–one of the greatest that I have ever been privileged to hear. He began in characteristic fashion, expressing deep sympathy with the Indians in South Africa in the struggle they were manfully carrying on. He rejoiced that the people of India had awakened to a sense of the position of their countrymen abroad, and he felt convinced that this awakening was a sign of the fact that dead bones in the valley were once again becoming instinct with life. But he proceeded to ask: "Was this sympathy with the oppressed and downtrodden Indians to be confined to those of our countrymen only who had gone out of India? Or was it to be general and to be extended to all cases where there was oppression and injustice?" It was easy, he said, to denounce foreigners, but those who did so were bound in common fairness to look into themselves and see if they were absolutely blameless in the matter. He then described the manner in which members of low caste were treated by our own community in different parts of India. It was a description which filled the audience with feelings of deep shame and pain and indignation. And Mr. Rānade very justly asked whether it was for those who tolerated such disgraceful oppression and injustice in their own country to indulge in all that denunciation of the people of South Africa. This question, therefore, is, in the first place, question of sheer justice.

Next, as I have already said, it is a question of humanity. It is sometimes urged that if we have our castes, the people in the West have their classes, and after all, there is not much difference between the two. A little reflection will, however, show that the analogy is quite fallacious. The classes of the West are a perfectly elastic institution, and not rigid or cast-iron like our castes. Mr. Chamberlain, who is the most masterful personage in the British empire today, was at one time a shoemaker and then a screwmaker. Of course, he did not make shoes himself, but that was the trade by which he made money. Mr. Chamberlain today dines with royalty, and mixes with the highest in the land on terms of absolute equality. Will a shoemaker ever be able to rise in India in the social scale in a similar fashion, no matter how gifted by nature he might be? A great writer has said that castes are eminently useful for the preservation of society, but that they are utterly unsuited for purposes of progress. And this I think is perfectly true. If you want to stand where you were a thousand years ago, the system of castes need not be modified in any material degree. If, however, you want to emerge out of the slough in which you have long remained sunk, it will not do for you to insist on a rigid adherence to caste. Modern civilization has accepted greater equality for all as its watchword, as against privilege and exclusiveness, which were to root-ideas of the old world. And the larger humanity of these days requires that we should acknowledge its claims by seeking the amelioration of the helpless condition of our downtrodden countrymen.

Finally, gentlemen, this is a question of national self-interest. How can we possibly realize our national aspirations, how can our country ever hope to take her place among the nations of the world, if we allow large numbers of our countrymen to remain sunk in ignorance, barbarism, and degradation? Unless these men are gradually raised to a higher level, morally and intellectually, how can they possibly understand our thoughts or share our hopes or cooperate with us in our efforts? Can you not realize that so far as the work of national elevation is concerned, the energy, which these classes might be expected to represent, is simply unavailable to us? I understand that the great thinker and observer–Swāmī Vivekānanda–held this view very strongly. I think that there is not much hope for us as a nation unless the help of all classes, including those that are known as low castes, is forthcoming for the work that lies before us. Moreover, is it, I may ask, consistent with our own self-respect that these men should be kept out of our houses and shut out from all social intercourse as long as they remain within the pale of Hinduism, whereas the moment they put on a coat and a hat and a pair of trousers and call themselves Christians, we are prepared to shake hands with them and look upon them as quite respectable. No sensible man will say that this is a satisfactory state of things. Of course, no one expects that these classes will be lifted up at once morally and intellectually to a position of equality with their more-favoured countrymen.

This work is bound to be slow and can only be achieved by strenuous exertions for giving them education and finding for them honourable employment in life. And, gentlemen, it seems to me that, in the present state of India, no work can be higher or holier than this. I think if there is one question of social reform more than another that should stir the enthusiasm of our educated young men and inspire them with an unselfish purpose, it is this question of the degraded condition of our low castes. Cannot a few men–five percent, four percent, three, two, even one percent–of the hundreds and hundreds of graduates that the university turns out every year, take it upon themselves to dedicate their lives to this sacred work of the elevation of low castes? My appeal is not to the old or the middle-aged–the grooves of their lives are fixed–but I think I may well address such an appeal to the young members of our community–to those who have not yet decided upon their future course and who entertain the noble aspiration of devoting to a worthy cause the education which they have received. What the country needs most at the present moment is a spirit of self-sacrifice on the part of our educated young men, and they may take it from me that they cannot spend their lives in a better cause than raising the moral and intellectual level of these unhappy low castes and promoting their general well-being.

The Servants of India Society

The charter of the Servants of India Society embodies Gokhale's most cherished aims for the uplift of his country.

[From *Speeches of the Honourable Mr. G.K. Gokhale,* Appendix, pp. 182–83, 184]

For some time past, the conviction has been forcing itself on many earnest and thoughtful minds that a stage has been reached in the political education and national advancement of the Indian people, when, for further progress, the devoted labours of a specially trained agency, applying itself to the task in a true missionary spirit, are required. The work that has so far been done has indeed been of the highest value. The growth, during the last fifty years, of a feeling of common nationality, based upon common tradition, common disabilities, and common hopes and aspirations, has been most striking. The fact that we are Indians first, and Hindus, Mohamedans, Parsees, or Christians afterwards, is being realized in a steadily increasing measure, and the idea of a united and renovated India, marching onwards to a place among the nations of the world worthy of her great past, is no longer a mere idle dream of a few imaginative minds, but is the definitely accepted creed of those who form the brain of the community–the educated classes of the country. A creditable beginning has already been made in matters of education and of local self-government; and all classes of the people are slowly but steadily coming under the influence of liberal ideas. The claims of public life are every day receiving wider recognition, and attachment to the land of our birth is growing into a strong and deeply cherished passion of the heart. The annual meetings of the National Congress and of provincial and other conferences, the work of political associations, the writings in the columns of the Indian press–all bear witness to the new life that is coursing in the veins of the people. The results achieved so far are undoubtedly most gratifying, but they only mean that the jungle has been cleared and the foundations laid. The great work of rearing the superstructure has yet to be taken in hand, and the situation demands, on the part of workers, devotion and sacrifices proportionate to the magnitude of the task.

The Servants of India Society has been established to meet in some measure these requirements of the situation. Its members frankly accept the British connection, as ordained, in the inscrutable dispensation of Providence, for India's good. Self-government on the lines of English colonies is their goal. This goal, they recognize, cannot be attained without years of earnest and patient work and sacrifices worthy of the cause. Moreover, the path is beset with great difficulties–there are constant temptations to turn back–bitter disappointments will repeatedly try the faith of those who have put their hand to the work. But the weary toil can have but one end, if only the workers grow not fainthearted on the way. One essential condition of success is that a sufficient number of our countrymen must now come forward to devote themselves to the cause in the spirit in which religious work is undertaken. Public life must be spiritualized. Love of country must so fill the heart that all else shall appear as of little moment by its side. A fervent patriotism which rejoices at every opportunity of sacrifice for the motherland, a dauntless heart which refuses to be turned back from its object by difficulty or danger, a deep faith in the purpose of Providence that nothing can shake–equipped with these, the worker must start on his mission and reverently seek the joy which comes of spending oneself in the service of one's country.

The Servants of India Society will train men, prepared to devote their lives to the cause of the country in a religious spirit, and will seek to promote, by all constitutional means, the national interests of the Indian people. Its members will direct their efforts principally towards: (1) creating among the people, by example and by precept, a deep and passionate love of the motherland, seeking its highest fulfillment in service and sacrifice; (2) organizing the work of political education and agitation and strengthening the public life of the country; (3) promoting relations of cordial goodwill and cooperation among the different communities; (4) assisting educational movements, especially those for the education of women, the education of backward classes and industrial and scientific education; and (5) the elevation of the depressed classes. The headquarters of the Society will be at Poona, where it will maintain a Home for its members, and attached to it, a library for the study of political questions. The following constitution has been adopted for the Society.

1. The Society shall be called "The Servants of India Society".
2. The objects of the Society are to train men to devote themselves to the service of India as national missionaries and to promote by all constitutional means the national interests of the Indian people...

   [Items 3 to 8 and 10 onward deal with organizational questions.]

9. Every member, at the time of admission, shall take the following seven vows:
   (a) That the country will always be the first in his thoughts and the will give to her service the best that is in him.
   (b) That in serving the country he will seek no personal advantage for himself.
   (c) That he will regard all Indians as Brothers, and will work for the advancement of all, without distinction of caste or creed.

(d) That he will be content with such provision for himself and his family, if he has any, as the Society may be able to make. He will devote no part of his energies to earning money for himself.

(e) That he will lead a pure personal life.

(f) That he will engage in no personal quarrel with any one.

(g) That he will always keep in view the aims of the Society and watch over its interests with the utmost zeal, doing all he can to advance its work. He will never do anything which is inconsistent with the objects of the Society.

References

1. R.P. Masani, *Dādābhāi Naoroji: The Grand Old Man of India,* p.25.
2. Armed thieves, highway murders, robber bands.
3. Dādābhāi refers to the export from Inida of the savings and pensions of British officials, and to other costs of British rule such as supplies and military expenditures.
4. Vikramāditya, a great and good king in Indian legend.
5. William Wedderburn, *Allan Octavian Hume, C.B.*, pp. 51–52.
6. Surendranāth Banerjea, *A Nation in Making, Being the Reminis-cences of Fifty Years in Public Life,* p. 33.
7. Pānipāt, the site of numerous pitched battles in Indian history. It lies about fifty miles north of Delhi.
8. A huge wagon used to carry the idol of Jagannāth, "the Lord of the Universe," in the city of Puri. In fits of frenzy devotees would hurl themselves in front of its wheels. The word "juggernaut" derives from this source.
9. Women attached to temples as dancers (and sometimes as prostitutes).
10. "Divine Faith," the synthesis of Hindu and Muslim religious ideas proclaimed by the Mughal Emperor Akbar.
11. Arabic term for which the English word "religion" is only an approximate translation.
12. One crore equals ten millions.

4

The Indian Struggle for Independence 1885 to 1909

The absence or revolutionary warfare, in comparison with other Asian experiences, charcterizes the Indian struggle for independence. This was true even before Gandhi devised his non-violent approach to Indian freedom. In the analysis of the pre-Gandhian Indian movement for independence, the question is *why a military confrontation or violent opposition against the British did not characterize the Indian freedom movement from 1885, the year of founding of the Indian National Congress to 1909, the year which marks the end of the first phase of Indian Government-Congress relations.*[1]

The above question is even more pertinent when one remembers that the leaders of the national movement were western educated and very much aware of developments both in the West and Asia. *The West surely supplied a surfeit of examples of successful violent revolution, and the Japanese demonstrated the applicability of this violence against the West in Russo-Japanese war of 1904-1905. Violent militant confrontation with the British would certainly be one option open to the leaders in their struggle for Independence.*

My hypothesis is that the *scope of issue perception on the part of both the Indians and the British provides the key to the nature of the struggle for Independence during those years.* The value of focussing on the issues of perception debated by both the British and the Indians lies in the conceptualization of the nature of the Indian struggle for

Independence. The historian's treatment of this movement has resulted in little understanding of the dynamics of conflict between the British and the Indians. When this has been best accomplished, attention has been directed towards Gandhi and his satyagrahas; Joan Bondurant's *Conquest of Violence* is a good example.[2] The pre-Gandhi movement has not received such treatment. A typical example of the interpretation of the independence movement is Daniel Argov's description:

> The national movement in India is distinguished from other searches for independence and national identity by the quality of intellectual debate among the political leaders.[3]

Although Argov, who is analyzing the Indian nationalist movement from within and focusing on the process of Indian demands, succeeds in providing and enumerating the positions taken by both the British and the Indians. His treatment does not provide any answers to such questions as to *why the Indians were content to agitate peacefully, even when it became clear that their demands and British interests were incompatible.* I wish to go one step further and suggest that the content of the issues in that "debate" are of great importance in ascertaining the nature of the early struggle for independence. Recent conflict studies suggest that whether the issues perceived are symbolic and reified or concrete and specific indicate whether the confrontation may assume violent configurations or not.

Recent studies in conflict analysis provide insight into the dynamics of relationship between protagonist and antagonist.[4]

Two important concepts in this paper are conflict and the "scope" of the conflict. For a definition of conflict, Kenneth Boulding provides a satisfactory beginning.

> A situation of competition in which the parties are aware of the incompatibility of potential future positions and in which each party wishes to occupy a position that is incompatible with the wishes of others.[5]

At the core of the conflict are certain issues that the individuals perceive to represent the conflict. The scope of the conflict then is how the participants view it; whether it is concentrated upon specific issues or questions or whether it is concentrated upon nebulous or symbolic issues would make the scope narrow or wide by our definition. Evidence suggests that resolution of a conflict depends on what kind of issues the decision makers are viewing at the time.[6]

Also, the findings in conflict studies provide a means of suggesting one factor, issues, pertinent to the shape and direction the Indian struggle for independence followed, i.e., further, one can also suggest reasons for variations within the method of opposition to the British. By this I am referring to the Extremist, Moderate split that finalized in 1907. The issue perception and pronouncements by both the British and the leaders of Congress have great impact on the timing of Indian terrorism, or even its appearance.

A psychological premise exists that relates issue perception to the probability of overt violence. Daniel Katz, in his article, "The Psychological Barriers to Communication,"[7] maintains that one problem in communication is the difficulty of differentiation between words which refer to actual reality and those which refer to concepts. People tend to reify concepts, and if the communication takes place in a stress situation, people undergo a reaction which may narrow the stressed individual's focus. Thus, if there is a failure to differentiate between reality and concepts in a stress situation, issue perception may become focussed narrowly on a reified concept. This holds great great importance in a conflict situation where the decision makers cast their choices in accordance with their issue perception.

A corollary to the importance of issue perception that has pertinence to the Indian movement is the observation that hostility rises when incompatible interests are present. And, "once set in motion, hostility can sustain conflict unaided by disagreement about particular issues. The original issues may be settled, yet the controversy continues unabated. The antagonistic relationship has now become direct; it no longer draws sustenance from an outside element—an issue."[8] This holds importance for subsequent behaviour of the "extremists" of the Indian independence movement.

James Coleman has developed a model of conflict that provides a means of measuring the development of the dynamics between the British and the Indians.[9] In the focus on issues, Coleman maintains that if the conflict eventuates in violence, fundamental transformations take place in the course of a conflict—the issues move from the specific to the general; new and different issues arise; and what began as disagreement ends up in antagonism between the parties. The lack of these developments strongly indicates an adumbration of violent conflict occurring.[10] When decision-makers have to decide whether a conflict is essential, and the perceived issues are general and symbolic, compromise is much less likely and violence much more probable. Conversely, if the focus on issues remains relatively stable, or they only change over long periods of time and are specific, the possibilities of resolution short of violence is likely.

This paper explores the probability that one factor in the lack of violent confrontation between the British and Indians from 1885 to 1919 was the *ability of both the British and Indians to remain focussed upon specific issues. A consequence of this thesis is that the relatively violent period of British-Indian relations from 1905-1916 coincides with the allusion to more symbolic referents by both the British and Indians.* To test this hypothesis, the issues and goals of both the National Congress and the Government of India have been analysed to ascertain the nature of the scope of perception.

The period from 1885 to 1905 certainly was not one of immoderation on the part of Congress. Indeed, within the definition of this paper, it is not likely that a "conflict' existed between the Congress leaders and the Government of India. But the continuity of demands raised by Congress beginning in 1885 until 1905 form a commentary on the nature of the early Congress. It is significant to record the earliest resolution, if only to illustrate the specificity of the demands and the lack of symbolic issues.

The Congress in 1885 asked for the abolition of the Council of Secretary of State, to be replaced by a standing committee in Parliament. This was an early recognition of the need for a legislative check on government machinery that made the Government and the policies of the Secretary of State for India virtually autonomous. The resolution continued that since this object was not likely to be acceded to, a reform of the Council should take place. The character of the Council would be advisory, not administrative, and members of the Council would be partly elected and partly nominated.[11] In reference to constitutional changes, the first and second sessions called for the local legislative councils to be expanded with elected Indian members. In the second session, the percentage of elected Indians was to be fifty percent and provided for appeals against executive action by the Government of India.[12]

An explanation for the moderation of the first congresses, beyond that of a young organization seeking recognition by the Indians as a spokesman and by the Government of India as a surveyor of Indian grievances is found in the social–economic–educational background of the leaders. The importance of this western educated middle class Indian background is found in the early Congress speech of Gokhale.

> Liberalism and moderation will be the watch-words of our association. The spirit of liberalism implies a freedom from race and creed prejudices and a steady devotion to all that seeks to do justice between man and man, giving to the rulers the loyalty due to the law that they are bound to administer, but securing at the same time to the people the equality which is their right under the law. Moderation implies the conditions of never vainly aspiring after the impossible or after too remote ideals, but striving each day to take the next step in the order of natural growth that lies nearest to our hands in a spirit of compromise and fairness.[13]

This spirit set the context of National Congress resolutions for the next ten years. When the Ilbert Bill served to solidify both the British position and the Indian attitude, insight into the leaders' thinking is provided by the candid explanation of Banerjea as he returned to Calcutta with the failure of passage of the bill:

> "We have everything to lose, nothing to gain by the severance of our connection with England. We owe whatever position or prestige we have acquired to our English education and culture. If you were to leave the country, our English education and culture would be at a discount. We are not particularly anxious to commit political suicide."[14]

The early Congress leaders, then, pinned their hopes on the Liberal party in England and justified their requests for Indian representation in the British Government of India on the basis of England's pledges to India by Munro, Lawrence and Queen Victoria. However, the Viceroys and Secretaries of State for India repudiated the feasibility of introducing those institutions until 1917. The effect of the latter's actions may perhaps be summed in the statement:

> A time may conceivably come...to leave India to herself but for the present it is necessary to govern her as if we were to govern her forever.[15]

Although this reluctance would come to define a conflict situation between the British and the Indians, this was not immediately so. On the contrary, the British demonstrated the trait so responsible for moderation on both sides. Lord Dufferin, by 1982, saw fit to acknowledge demands Congress had been making. This was the Indian Councils Act of 1892. With the aid of a Council of India committee, Dufferin drew up "a plan for the enlargement of our Provincial Councils, for the enhancement of their status, the multiplication of their functions, the partial introduction...of the elective principle, and the liberalisation of their general character as political institutions."[16] The bill finally provided for enlarged membership in the Provincial Councils, such membership at the discretion of nomination by the Governor-General. This was to allow a means of incorporating elected members into the Councils. The Act also allowed the Councils to *discuss,* not vote, the budget and indulge in criticism of the financial policy of the Government. Finally, the members of Councils were granted the right of questioning on matters of public interest, this being subject to conditions prescribed by the Governor-General or the Provincial Governor.[17] Thus reinforced in the manner and mode of their demands, Congress continued making essentially the same overtures to the Government of India until the nineteen hundreds.

With precedent set for Indian involvement in the local and Provincial councils, the National Congress took up the matter of the rule of the Government of India. Demands were made for representation in the House of Commons, for expansion of the Councils in the country, and appointment of Indians to the Council of Secretary of State and Executive Council.[18] These 1904 resolutions were reiterated by Gokhale in his 1905 address to the National Congress. He stated there that Congress sought those reforms "which aim at securing for our people a larger and larger share in the administration and control of our affairs; these include a reform of our legislative councils, the appointment of Indians to the Secretary of States Council (In London) and the Executive Council in India, and a steady substitution of the Indian for the European agency in the public service of the country."[19] However, beneath the surface of these specific suggestions, a changed attitude and approach soon appeared.

During the five-year period from 1900 to 1905, the questions of the partition of Bengal and employment of Indians in the higher Civil Service dominated. The method of approach and handling these two issues by Lord Curzon had no small effect on the National Congress. Congress had been reaching out from the specific proposals of Gokhale in 'the 1880's to the widening of the perception of issues as noted in 1903 when Sir Henry Cotton, President of the National Congress, addressed his fellow members. "The ideal of an Indian patriot of the establishment of a federation of free and separate states, the United States of India, placed on a fraternal footing with the self-governing colonies, each with its own local autonomy, cemented together under the aegis of Great Britain."[20] The specific proposals of Congress were directed toward this end.

When in 1904, Congress emphasized employment of Indians in the Civil Service, Curzon's response constituted a focus on a symbolic issue that hardened feelings on both sides. Curzon intimated that British rule would be for a long time to come and repudiated hopes that Indians share in the administration of government.

> The highest ranks of civil employment in India must as a general rule be held by Englishmen for the reason that they possess partly by heredity, partly by upbringing, and partly by education, the habits of mind and the vigour of character which are essential for the task; and that the rule of India being a British rule and every other rule being in the circumstances of the case impossible, the tone and standard should be set by those who have created and are responsible for it."[21]

This coupled with the deep suspicion that Curzon's proposed partition of Bengal was to effect a demise of Bengali interests and articulation, made partition a symbol of Indian grievances and provoked a change in the tone and substance of subsequent Congress resolutions.

The introductory speech of the 1905 Congress set the tone. India was declared to be "distracted, discontented, despondent, the victim of many misfortunes, political and others'; the "*cup of national indignation had been filled to over-flowing by the Partition designed to break down the political power and influence of the educated opinion of Bengal.*"[22] The combination of Curzon's racism and the evolution of Congress demands sustained a more symbolic resolution in 1906. Gokhale, in London, told Morley that the aim of Congress was self-government within the Empire.[23] In the 1906 Congress, Swaraj was mentioned for the first time in a presidential address and this loosely defined goal was posited as the object of Congress activities.[24] However, the question of whether agitation of self-government was to be outside or within the Government of India marked the divergence between the moderate and extremist factions of Congress.

The possible development of Indian Nationalism along uncompromising symbolic lines is indicated by statements in the Bengali newspapers. The *New India wrote: "Absolute national autonomy is the goal. The nation must succeed in gaining it or must perish in the attempt. Revolution is inevitable."*[25] The *Yugantar* commented that war of revolution was far better than death in peace and it urged the Indians to draw inspiration from Japan's victory over Russia.

The transformation for many Congress leaders can be seen in the words of Bipin C. Pal.

> We loved the abstraction we called India but hated the thing it actually was. Our patriotism was not composed of our love for our own history, literature, arts, industries, culture and institutions, but as a prototype of England which we wished her to be. The new spirit cured us of an imaginary and abstract patriotism. Love of India means a love for its rivers and mountains, for its paddy fields and its sandy lands, its towns and villages and poor people, for its languages, literature, philosophy, religion, culture and civilization.[26]

When one juxtaposes the nationalist attachment to "mother India" with Gokhale's statement of commitment to western liberalism, the degree of separation and transformation of issue perception from 1885 to 1905 is apparent. Although the years from 1905 to 1916 mark the most radical and violent opposition to British rule, neither the Anarchist movement nor the Extremist New Party faction fomented an Indian revolution. One key to this development is the British reaction to Congress's proclamation of home-rule and swadeshi.

On June 6, 1906, Morely wrote to Lord Minto to the effect that informed Indian watchers were of the opinion that it was not possible "to go on governing in the same spirit; you have got to deal with the

Congress Party and Congress principles."[27] As a fist step, Minto in August of 1906 stated his objective of possible reform: "(a) a Council of princes, and should this be impossible, whether they might be represented in the Viceroy's Legislative Council; (b) an Indian member of the Viceroy's Executive Council; (c) increased representation on the Legislative Council of the Viceroy and of Local Governments; and (d) prolongation of the budget debate and increased power of moving amendments."[28] Instead of an emotional outburst which would match the emotional quality of Indian pronouncements, the British remained focussed on specific issues, and acknowledged Congress demands. That this did not have to be the course of British reaction is illustrated by the *Civil and Military Gazette,* a spokesman for the English in India.

> We must hold the country with the power of the sword and in the interests of our women and children and the Empire. We must see that the edge of the sword is not dulled... The only thing an oriental respects is power.[29]

However, the Morley-Minto Reforms remained tied to specific issues, although they did raise the new issues of weightage with regard to Muslim representation.

Again the notable aspect of the Indian Councils Act of 1909 is the specificity of its provisions. The size of the Legislative Councils was enlarged, and additional members of the Governor General's Council provided. It was also provided that the Imperial Legislative Council would consist of 37 official and 32 non-official members.

This retained a substantial official majority for the Indian government. The Act did not provide for official majority in the Provincial Legislative Councils, and it was in the Legislative Councils that the Indian realized the greatest gains. The majority of the members were to be non-officials. Although this did not mean elected majorities in the Provincial Council, the possibility of this development in the future was ensured. In the Legislative Councils, the functions of the Councils were increased. This included discussion of the budget and other financial matters. Members were allowed to ask any pertinent questions thought necessary, and to move resolutions. These would be in form of a definite recommendation to the Government. In terms of local power, municipalities and other local government institutions were to elect members.[30]

The development of the Congress mentality from loyal British subjects to the nationalism (albeit moderate) visible in Pal's statement wrested the initiative from the Government of India. With the proclamation of swaraj, and the inauguration of boycott and swadeshi, the British were faced with demands perhaps incompatible with their objectives. Hence, what were British objectives in India became the most crucial question for the Government of India. Congress wanted autonomy at least, absolute independence at most, and was being fast convinced that England was not really committed to either possibility. The moderates pinned their hopes on the Liberal victory in Parliament in England and the New Governor General and Secretary of State for India, Lord Minto and John Morley respectively. Just what were the goals and shades of political thinking of these two gentlemen has been the subject of considerable debate.[31] The resolution of that interpretation, however, is not a purpose of this paper.

One clue to British reaction to a more militant Congress is the position of the aforementioned question and its answer by John Morley in 1908. "What are we in India for?" he challenged Minto."Surely in order to implant—slowly, prudently, judiciously,—those ideas of justice, law, humanity, which are the foundation of our own civilization."[32] Whether the motivation for this statement, and for the 1909 reforms was to lay the framework for final self-rule is immaterial. What is important is that the symbolic referent was not the glory of Empire, or the permanency of British rule, rather it was an outline that demanded specific issues be spelled out to accomplish such an aim. The compatibility of such an outline is demonstrated in the speech of the same year by Gokhale. He stated that Indians might gain provincial self-government in ten years and explained: "It is no use trying to overthrow the present administration before we have something to put in its place."[33]

The result of the 1909 reforms had significance for the possibility of violent confrontation with the Congress party. Until 1909, Congress fulfilled the task of criticizing Government of India from without, and the Government regarded Congress as a body which articulated educated Indians' thoughts and demands. With the expansion of the Councils and Legislative Councils and the incorporation of many Congress members into these bodies, Congress no longer served the same function. Criticism now came from within the various organs of Government. This not only increased the specificity of the debates between the two, in terms of conflict resolution, this development greatly ameliorated the amount of hostility between Congress and the Government of India.

It was not that the Reforms did not arouse any reaction from Congress. As with partition, the Reforms created a new issue, "weightage." And Congress, while thanking the British Government for many of the provisions in the Reforms expressed its unhappiness with the general tone of the reform (prejudicial to educated Indians) and with the weighted representation the Muslims received. But Congress ended the 1909 reform with a call for a reform of the reforms, quite a specific resolution.

—Lynn Triplett

References

1. Indian nationalism always presents a problem for the scholar who wishes to take an integral approach. The phrase "Indian struggle" immediately leads one to ask which Indians—*Hindu, Muslim, Bengali, Punjabi or Maharashtrian*? Our first problem is to define who are talking about when we say *issue perception on the part of the Indians.* Despite the multiple nature of Indian participation, few will argue that *the main thrust of Indian nationalism developed within the context of the Indian National Congress.* Therefore, the Congress resolutions provide the best guide to the issues and factors the majority of participants in the struggle were perceiving. I have accordingly analysed the Congress resolutions to determine the *issues* and *scope of perception* on the part of the *Indian Nationalists.*
2. Joan V. Bondurant, *Conquest of Violence* (Berkeley and Los Angeles: University of California Press, 1967).
3. Daniel Argov, *Moderates and Extremists in the Indian Nationalist Movement* 1883-1920 (New York: Asia Publishing House, 1967), Foreword. Hereafter cited as Argov.
4. Michael P. Sullivan, "International and Community Conflict: Comparing Levels of Theory" (Department of Government, University of Arizona, 1968). Hereafter cited as Sullivan.
5. Kenneth Boulding, *Conflict and Defence: A General Theory* (New York: Harper and Row, 1962). p. 5.
6. Sullivan, p. 12.
7. Sullivan, p. 11.
8. Sullivan, p. 12.
9. James Coleman, *Community Conflict* (New York). The Free Press. 1957, p. 10. Hereafter cited as Coleman.
10. Coleman, p. 10.

11. Pattabhi Sitaramayya. *The History of the Indian National Congress* 1885-1935 (Bombay: Padma Publications Ltd., 1946), Vol. 1, p. 24. Hereafter cited as Sitaramayya.
12. Sitaramayya. pp. 24-25.
13. K.P. Karunakaran, *Continuity and Change in Indian Policies.* (New Delhi: Peoples Publishing House, 1964). p. 30. Hereafter cited as Karunakaran.
14. Argov, p. 56.
15. Argov, foreword. pp. x and xi.
16. Gurmukh Nihal Singh, *Landmarks in Indian Constitutional and National Development,* 1600-1919 (Delhi: Atma Ram and Sons, 1952). Vol. 1, p. 116 Hereafter cited as Singh.
17. Singh, pp. 117-118.
18. Sitaramayya, p. 25.
19. Karunakaran, p. 37.
20. Argov, p. 103.
21. Argov, p. 105.
22. Sir Verney Louett, *A History of the Indian Nationalist Movement* (London: Frank Cass and Co., 1968), p. 61.
23. Argov, p. 118.
24. Ram Gopal, *How India Struggled for Freedom* (Delhi, 1958), p. 168.
25. Argov, p. 118.
26. Argov, p. 122.
27. Singh, p. 167.
28. Singh, p. 168.
29. Argov, p. 130.
30. R.R. Sethi. and V.D. Mahajan, *Constitutional History of India* (Delhi: S. Chand and Co., 1956), pp. 64-66.
31. M.N. Das, Syed Wasti, and Stanley Wolpert all provide interpretations of Morley and Minto.
32. Stanely Wolpert, *Morley and India* 1906-1910 (Berkeley and Los Angeles: University of California Press, 1967).
33. Argov, p. 142.

5

Politics of Indian Revolutionaries —1905-1910

Politics and political behaviour have undergone radical changes. We have developed a kind of psyche which is alien. We seemed to have lost our moorings. A few sound studies have been undertaken on this subject, but separating soul from the body. Here an attempt had been made to examine and analyse politics of revolutionaries in terms of their methods, style and organisation in an integrated way. It is expected that the study of heroic behaviour of the Indian revolutionaries during the short period under study may help to restore the sagging political behaviour.

Struggle of political freedom in India was rare phenomenon in the history of mankind. It was a broadbased movement. Many streams of belief, thought and action flowed into this movement. Revolt against the foreign domination had been raised by warriors, poets and common man from time to time. History of India is replete with the heroic traditions of its people. In India every village had its real heroes who had sacrificed themselves for their country.

In 1905 constitutional methods of mendicancy stood exposed, Armed resistance, bombs and secret societies were being organised. Revolutionary literature in the form of books, pamphlets and news-papers flooded the whole country. *Yatras* and lectures were conducted to awaken the masses. Organisations advocating revolutionary methods to liberate India sprang up in India and abroad. Schools were opened to give rigorous training to the youth to prepare them to take to revolutionary methods to free their country from the British yoke.

India during the period under study was in ferment. Political power was vested in the alien Government and its various local institutions. Nationalist politicians naturally, therefore, were forced to come together outside the existing constitutional machinery.[1]

"A psychological battle between Curzon and the Congress continued for half a decade till finally the Viceroy was able to effect the crowning achievements of his rule, namely, the partition of Bengal. For the Congress 'the cause of Bengal was made India's cause'. The unrest which followed had a fervour of a revolution and could not keep the entire Congress on the constitutional path. While the philosophy of revolution added considerable strength to the movement in general, the question as to constitutional agitation or other methods divided the Congress leadership badly."[2]

Such a conflict among the national leaders can be traced back to 1893 in a series of articles contributed by the Aurbindo to Indu Prakash. In 1904 Tilak decried the methods of the Congress as mere 'croak once a year like frog'.[3] There was considerable difference of opinion as to whether the fight was to be non-violent or violent in character. B.C. Pal, Tilak, Lajpat Rai, and Aurobindo laid stress on the bloodless revolution in their utterances, but their secret activities indicated a different policy.[4]

Among the nationalist leaders of India Lala Lajpat Rai was the earliest exponent of militant nationalism in the country. He was the first spokesman of the doctrine of passive resistance.[5] He asserted in the Congress of 1905 that the method which was perfectly legitimate, perfectly constitutional and perfectly justifiable the method of passive resistance.

I must tell that the message which the people of England wants to send to you through me was the message that in our utterance, in our agitations and in our fight and struggle for liberty we ought to be more manly than we have been before. An Englishman hates or dislikes nothing like beggary. I think a beggar deserves to be hated. Therefore, it is our duty to show Englishman that we have risen to the sense of consciousness, that we are no longer beggars and that we are subject of an Empire where people are struggling to achieve that position which is their right by right of national law.[6]

Non-payment of taxes was held by Aurobindo as a national logical result of the attitude of passive resistance. He explained that dissenters in England offered that form of resistance to the Education Act of the Conservative Government and the no-rent campaign in Ireland and the fight of the American Colonist over the principle of 'no taxation without representation'. He exhorted the people to take recourse to boycott which involved no breach of legal obligation or direct defiance of administrative authority.[7]

Aurobindo classified organized national resistance into three categories. First, following the genius of Parnell, to make administration impossible by an organized passive resistance; secondly, making organized aggressive resistance in the shape of riots, assassinations, strikes and agrarian rising like the Russian movements; and thirdly, armed revolt, which is at once the old time-honoured method, which demands the least powers of endurance and suffering and the smallest and briefest sacrifices. Under the circumstances in India Aurobindo considered passive resistance the most natural and suitable weapon. He held that under certain circumstances a civil struggle became in reality a battle and that the morality of war was different from the morality of peace.[8]

The period under study is an important phase in the history of revolutionary activities in India. The rulers had realised that with the growth of education among the population, the question for political freedom had increased. Educated young men were not satisfied with their position as 'babus' and petty-officers. They resented the racial discrimination and were determined to end political and economic exploitation that had brought ruin to their country.

In the economic field, the rulers proved to be the worst exploiters. To raise a voice against any injustice was to invite repression. Anybody who criticised the official policies was denounced as an anarchist or a traitor. The British Government tried to divert this resentment into communal hatred among them. The Revolutionaries came to the conclusion that the achievement of complete political freedom could end the miseries that the British rule had brought.[9] They organised secret revolutionary societies in India. Teachings of the *Gita* and the *Mahabharat* became the source of inspiration to the younger generation. Sakti, in the form of Durga,

Bhawani and Kali was invoked to strengthen the determination of the nation to fight against the foreign domination. The devotees were required to take a vow before the image of the Goddess to fight for emancipation of the motherland.[10] However, it was realised, that in order to fight a successful battle against the British it was necessary to get modern weapons and organise the struggle on scientific basis.[11] In order to achieve this objective revolutionaries went to Japan, Germany, France, America and other foreign countries.[12] Funds were raised, studies of liberation struggles in other countries were undertaken and young revolutionaries were given training in the use of modern weapons.[13] Contacts with foreign governments were forged to seek their military help.[14]

We find revolutionaries establishing their links with the government of almost all the big countries including Japan and Germany.[15] There delegates met among others the Kaiser of Germany.[16] The Indian revolutionaries forged close contacts with foreign revolutionaries including the French and the Russian.[17] Although the Soviet Union had not yet come into being, Indian revolutionaries, interest in the Russian methods of struggle for liberation is evident. For instance, the *Kesari* of Poona exhorted the people "to adopt Russian methods of agitation in fighting with their rulers."[18]

Shayamaji Krishna Verma exhorted the people to rise in rebellion against the British. He wrote:

"It seems that any agitation in India now must be carried on secretly and that the only methods which can bring the English Government to its senses are the Russian methods vigorously and increasingly applied until the English relay their tyranny and be driven out of the country."[19]

A French revolutionary associated with London group of Indian revolutionaries emphasised the necessity of starting a powerful revolutionary journal which should contain articles explaining among other things.[20]

(a) How to work among the Indian soldiery with a view to drive a section of them, at any rate into the revolution when breaks out.
(b) How to arm the mighty Indian people to make them play the role of a nation in arms.
(c) How to manufacture arms, ammunition, hand grenades, and high explosives for conducting scientific warfare.

Indian revolutionaries working in other countries organised secret societies and started publication of revolutionary journals such as *Bande Mataram* of Geneva, *Ghadr of San Francisco. The Ghadr* was published by Yugantar Ashram and was started by Lala Hardayal. It was specially intended to appeal to the martial races of India and was posted to the Punjab in large numbers.

The revolutionaries started schools of physical training which were transformed into political societies whose object was the overthrow of the foreign rule.[21] Secret societies were formed. Manufacture of bombs and fire-arms was initiated. Russian, Italian and Irish methods of revolutionary terrorism were tried and assassination of indiviual officials was carried out. The idea was to punish those who came in the way of India's freedom, to strike terror into the hearts of the rulers and to arouse the Indian people politically.[22]

Revolutionary organisations for Indian freedom were set up in India and abroad. The *Mitra Mela* of Nasik was founded by Ganesh Vinayak Savarkar and his brother Vinayak Damodar Savarkar in 1900. It evolved into Abhinav Bharat Samiti in 1904. It studied the methods of the Russians and Italian revolutionaries and set up revolutionary organisations in Western India.[23] In 1902 Anushilan Samiti was established in Calcutta by Satish Chandra Bose with Pramatha Mitra as its president. Sister Nivedita inspired the members of the Samiti and provided them with revolutionary literature.[24] Ajit Singh and Sufi Amba Prasad organised a secret society called the Bharat Mata by 1906.[25] Secret revolutionary societies were also established at Gwalior and Satara.[26] The *Swarajya* and the *Karmayogin,* the two journals started at Allahabad in 1907 and 1909 respectively, spread revolutionary ideas during their short span of existence.[27] Hotilal Varma, Aligarh correspondent of Aurobindo's paper *Bande Mataram,* was sentenced to ten years' transportation for carrying on revolutionary propaganda.[28] The Telugu paper *Swaraj* and the Tamil paper *India* published from Beswada and Madras respectively preached the message of revolution in Southern part of the country.[29] Subramania Siva and Chidambaran stirred up Madras Presidency resulting in their arrest on 12 March and Tinnevelly riot on the 18th March, 1908.[30] Nilkanta Brahmachari, Shankar Krishna Aiyar and later in 1910, V.V.S. Aiyar and Vanchi

Aiyar created revolutionary atmosphere in almost the whole of South India. Government sources noticed revolutionary activities in Bihar, Orissa and Central Provinces also.[31]

The Indian revolutionaries had taken position in Europe, America and South East Asia.[32] The Indian Home Rule Society was established in London by Shyamaji Krishna Verma in Jan. 1905.[33] The *Indian Sociologist,* its monthly journal preached the ideal of complete independence for India.[34] Madan Lal Dingra, a member of the group, shot dead Sir William Curzon Wyllie, political A.D.C. at the India Office at a gathering at the Imperial Institute in London.[35]

In Paris Madam Bhikaji Rustomji Cama was the centre of Indian revolutionary activities.[36] In August 1909, during the International Socialist Congress at Stuttgart she moved a resolution in favour of India's freedom. She unfurled the Indian national flag during this conference.[37] She published a monthly paper *Bande Mataram* from Geneva with the assistance of famous revolutionaries like Lala Hardayal and Thirumal Achari. In 1910 another revolutionary Virendranath Chattopadhyay also joined her.[38]

In 1908, in British Columbia the Indo-American Association was started by Taraknath Das in the American continent.[39] An English bi-monthly paper *Free Hindustan* was published by Das which was later shifted to Seattle.[40] He preached the necessity of winning over the Indian army to the nationalist cause.[41] By 1910 Sohan Singh and his associates set up another organisation of Indian revolutionaries in the United States.[42]

Indian revolutionaries also established themselves in Japan and South East Asian countries during the above period.[43]

Politics in India had undergone a radical change during the first decade of the twentieth century. Almost the whole of India was politically awake. The people had at last begun to realize that no amount of resolutions, deputations, memorials and beggings of any sort were going to get them freedom. Martyrdom of Khudiram Bose and Madan Lal Dhingra, imprisonment of Tilak, deportation of Ajit Singh, Lajpat Rai, Har Dayal provided stronger impetus. The hearts of the people of India vibrated as one whole and pulsated in turn with one another. The distinction of caste or creed lost its significance. Harmony and goodwill among the Hindus and Muslims were preached and practised.

"How easily we are led to forget that for any nation or country true to itself and having a grain of self-respect in it, independence is the greatest blessing, the highest aim, the noblest aspiration and that no tempting gifts, favours or crumbs should allow us to betray the greatest human privilege—our love of Freedom".[44]

Secret societies were formed in order to overthrow and subvert the Government as "it was a secret society the Metarin which prepared the Greeks for that contest which culminated in the independence of their country. It was the secret society of the united club of Irishman which prepared the Irish for the great struggle of 1798, and finally it was the secret society of young Italy founded by Mazzini, which by evoking the sentiment of National unity and National independence helped very materially towards the consummation of Italian unity and Italian independence".[45] Revolutionaries made sacrifices and protests. They were clear in their minds that if in the process they were killed they will attain Heaven and if in the process they were killed they will attain freedom. They intentionally shed the English blood to protest against the inhuman transportation and hangings of their countrymen. Under the circumstances an open battle was impossible. They attacked by surprise and as canon could not be had they drew forth and fired the revolver. They offered their blood on the altar of Mother's deliverance. The only lesson required in India, they believed, was to learn how to die and the only way to teach that was by dying alone.

"The soul is immortal and if everyone of my countrymen takes at least two lives of Englishmen before his body falls the Mother's salvation is a day's work".[46] While thus dying for their country the revolutionaries prayed. "May I be reborn of the same mother and may redie in the same sacred cause till my mission is done and she stands for the good of humanity and to the glory of God."[47]

There is no doubt that revolutionary politics to oust the British India did not liberate India in the time and circumstances in which it was experimented. But there is no denying the fact that the memories of courage and sacrifices of Khudiram Bose, Madan Lal Dhingra, Vanchi Aiyar, Sufi Amba Prasad, Hoti Lal Verma and many others, during the period under study bring tears even today.

—Raj Kumar

References

1. Raj Kumar, *Annie Besant's Rise to Power in Indian Politics 1914-197*, 1981, p. 1.
2. M.N. Das, *India Under Morley and Minto*, London, 1964. p. 82.
3. Tilak to Naoroji 1904, Tilak Papers, Nehru Memorial Museum & Library, New Delhi.
4. "The New Movement" speech at Madras, April 1907, B.D. Pal, Swadeshi and Swaraj, p. 29; Daniel Argov, *Moderates and Extremists in the Indian Nationalist Movement*, London, 1967, p. 125.
5. *The Indian Review*, January 1907, p. 52; *The Punjabee*, 27 Janurary 1907.
6. Ibid., also Proceedings of the Congress, 1905, MMM & L.
7. Aurobindo Ghose, *The Doctrine of Passive Resistance*, Pondicherry, 1948, p. 17.
8. Ibid.
9. Home Pol. Deposit, July 1907, No. 7.
10. "Bhawani Mandir", a pamphlet supposed to have been written by Aurobindo Ghose in 1905. NAI, New Delhi.
11. *Yugantar*, October 1906.
12. J.C. Kar, *Political Trouble in India, 1907-1917*, Calcutta, 1917, p. iii.
13. The Maniktola Bomb Conspiracy Case NAI, New Delhi.
14. J.C. Kar, *op. cit.*, p. iv.
15. Ibid.
16. T.R. Sareen, *Indian Revolutionary Movement Abroad*, 1905-1920, p. 116.
17. Ibid. p. 117.
18. The *Kesari;* also see J. Kar, *op. cit.*, p. iii.
19. *The Indian Sociologist*, December 1907.
20. Ibid. September 1909.
21. Home Pol. Deposit, October 1910, No. 20.
22. Home Pol. Deposit June 1907.
23. Ibid.
24. Ibid.
25. Pardman Singh and J.S. Dhanki, *Buried Alive*, 1984, p. 4.
26. J.C. Kar, *op, cit.*, p. 29.
27. Justice Rowlatt (ed.), *Sedition Committee Report*, 1918, p. 131.
28. Ibid.
29. J.C. Kar, *op.cit.*, p. 13.
30. Ibid.
31. Justice Rowlatt (ed.), *Sedition Comittee Report*, 1918.
32. A.C. Bose, *Indian Revolutionaries Aclbroad*, 1971.
33. J.C. Kar, *op. cit.*, 171.
34. Ibid.
35. Ibid. p. 179.
36. Sareen, *op. cit.*, p. 70.

37. Foreign Department, External B, Confidential 1911, No. 62, NAI.
38. Biplabi Niketan, *Hundred Years of Struggle,* 1847-1947, p. 132.
39. "History-Sheet of Tarak Nath Das", CXI, Department, Emigration B, March 1912, Nos. 31-34, NAI.
40. Ibid.
41. *Free Hindustan,* March-April 1910.
42. Biplabi Niketan, *op. cit.* p. 133.
43. Ibid.
44. *On Liberty,* A leaflet dates 20 July 1913 issued by the Revolutionaries.
45. Ibid.
46. Statement of Madan Lal Dhingra.
47. Ibid.

6

Armed Struggle from the South-East

With the outbreak of the war neutral countries bordering on India, like China and Thailand, acquired an importance for anti-British operations. Both the countries by then had well-organised centres of Indian revolutionaries, and the latter were in close touch with the local German Legations as well as with the Ghadar leaders in U.S.A. The Ghadar exodus had started with the outbreak of the war, and hundreds of them were coming there every month from the U.S.A. and Canada on their way to India. This meant that there were in these countries large concentration of Indian revolutionaries eager for action, which was an opportunity that should not be missed. Besides, it was felt that arms for a revolt in India could be either secured locally in these countries or sent there from the U.S.A. with relative safety, to be ultimately smuggled overland to India. Moreover, the failure of attempts at igniting a revolt in India by sending home shiploads of almost unarmed revolutionaries had convinced the Germans and many Ghadar leaders that those returning home should better assemble somewhere close to the Indian frontier, from where a regular armed raid into India might be organised.[1] Both China and Thailand had obvious advantages as *points d' appui* for such raids into India and for smuggling arms across her long and practically unguarded frontier.

China in those days lacked a strong central government, and the governors of her southern provinces were virtually independent. In fact, a rebellion was expected in South China towards the end of 1914, and, since Yuan She-kai was known to be friendly with the British, the Germans and the southern governors looked upon one another as natural allies. Moreover Barakatullah and some other Indian revolutionaries in Japan were on friendly terms with Dr. Sun Yat-sen, and it was expected that his followers would have sympathy with India's aspirations. Even Yang Ch'eng, the Chinese Commissioner in Shanghai, was friendly towards the Germans and Indians there.[2] So, it was hoped, not unreasonably, that once arms were brought to China it would not be very difficult to carry those across the Indian frontier.

Then, early in November 1914, Satyendranath Sen and Vishnu Ganesh Pingley came from the U.S.A. with assurances of German assistance for their planned revolt. *En route,* they had discussions with Tahal Singh, had also met Dr. Sun for his advice and co-operation.[3] But it was soon realised that British control over China's sea-customs would make impossible large-scale shipment of arms to her ports.[4] Moreover, as was realised later, Dr. Sun with his base of authority and operations close to Hongkong, though generous with advice, was not willing to antagonise the British.[5] Still the Indians in East Asia began getting ready for concerted action, and, soon after Satyendranath and Pingley had left for India, Tahal Singh sent Atmaram Kapur, Santosh Singh and Shiv Dayal Kapur to Bangkok to make the necessary arrangements.[6]

In Thailand, the Germans and the Indians had already started working with certain positive advantages. Thai public opinions was definitely anti-British, at least in the early months of the war,[7] and Thai officials were expected to keep their eyes deliberately shut to Indian revolutionary activities. Even the Indian Muslims there had recently been stirred by the anti-British propaganda of Col. Niazi Bey, a pan-Islamic emissary from Turkey. He had come to Bangkok from Saigon towards the middle of August 1914, and had become an effective emotional link between the Indian revolutionaries and pan-Islamites there.[8]

The Germans there, too, were not sitting idle. Even before the war had actually broken out Dr. Hertzka, Press Attaché at the

German Embassy at Bangkok, had planned a propaganda offensive against Britain by offering handsome bribes to a few Thai newspapers. They also began publishing at Bangkok, from the beginning of October 1914, a German newspaper, the *Unshan.*[9] Almost at the same time Dr. Voretzsch, formerly German Consul at Hongkong, was sent there with DM 100,000 to take charge of the preparations in Thailand for organising a revolt in India.[10] Special arrangements were also made with three business houses for carrying on secret correspondence and financial transactions. Orders were also placed through various agencies, and the next few months saw an unprecedented increase in the number of shot-guns imported into Thailand.[11] Moreover, as stated before, it had been arranged by December 1914 that the returning Ghadarites from North America would first disembark in China, preferably in Shanghai, and then proceed *to* Bangkok via Amoy and Swatow.[12] Soon large numbers of intending invaders of India had assembled at Bangkok, and it was felt by many that instead of encouraging them to return to home in small batches they should be advised to wait in Thailand and organise themselves for a well-timed armed incursion into India. It is said that even tunnels were dug near Pakoh in the north-west of Thailand for secret collection of arms.[13]

However, the King and the Crown prince of Thailand were firm in their friendship for Britain,[14] and did not view Col. Niazi Bey's activities and these Indo-German intrigues with pleasure. So, when Britain requested the Thai Government to put a stop to Col. Niazi Bey's activities, he was forthwith deported on 18 November 1914.[15] Obviously, the anti-British elements had overplayed their cards. So, to allay the suspicion of the Thai Government, Dr. Voretzsch was transferred to Shanghai in January 1915.[16] henceforth it became the controlling headquarters of Indo-German conspiracies in East Asia, under the general supervision of the German Embassy at Washington. For the proper co-ordination of effort, the German Consulate in Shanghai used to be kept informed of all decisions arrived at in Germany or the U.S.A. as well as of the work being done in West Asia.[17] However, Thailand was then an immediate neighbour of India, and considerable preparations had already been made in collaboration with the Ghadarites for organising raids from there. So Bangkok remained the advance base of the planned Ghadar attack on India.

Hitherto these plans had been discussed and formed primarily by the Ghadarites and German officials, and the Indian Committee was not very interested in these endeavours. They were primarily interested in establishing contact with their comrades in Bengal, and, for the time being were mainly concerned with sending them shiploads of arms. But their attitude changed with the arrival of Barakatullah in Berlin on 9 January 1915.[18] He had been closely associated with the Ghadar group in the U.S.A., and knew of their plans and preparations. So, with his immense prestige, he could soon convince the Indian Committee of the desirability of adapting the Ghadar plan with their own so that the arrival of arms and the planned revolt in India could be properly synchronised with the armed expedition from Thailand to achieve the maximum effect. The German Foreign Office too looked upon the proposed armed incursion into India with favour. So Barakatullah had a meeting with Daus Dekker of Java in the third week of January,[19] and plans for an armed expedition into India from Thailand were slowly drawn up.

In Burma, too, which occupied an important strategic position in the context of this proposed raid, the activities of different groups of revolutionaries had already started bearing fruit. Rangoon, even before the war, was a centre of pan-Islamic activities, to which Tewfik Bey's visit in 1913 had lent fresh impetus. Even the new Turkish Consul there, Ahmed Mullah Daud (a local merchant), was known for his active sympathy for the pan-Islamites.[20] The Bengal revolutionaries, too, in the meantime, had extended their activities to Burma. Khirodgopal Mukherjee, an elder brother of Jadugopal Mukherjee, had gone to Burma in 1908, and had established a revolutionary base at Meiktila. Early in 1913, Jatindranath Hui too was sent to Rangoon for revolutionary work, and he soon established friendly contact with the Turkish Consul and the local pan-Islamites.[21] Then, with the outbreak of the war, hundreds of Ghadarites began passing through Burma, on their way to India, and these had visible effect on sections of the Indian army and armed police stationed there.

In November 1914, the 130th Baluchis had been moved to Rangoon from Bombay as a punishment. A month later, two pan-Islamic agents, Hakim Faim Ali and Ali Ahmed Siddiqui, also came from Istanbul. It cannot be said with certainty whether they had anything to do with the Baluch regiment. The latter, however, planned to mutiny early in 1915. But the authorities had prior information, and the planned rising was nipped in the bud on 21 January 1915.[22] At about this time, two revolutionaries from Thailand, Sohan Lal Pathak and Hassan Khan, also came to Rangoon, whence after some time they moved towards the Chinese frontier to establish contacts with the Indian soldiers and policemen posted there.[23] Muhammad Shah Jilani too was then active in Burma and Singapore forging an alliance between the Ghadarites and the pan-Islamites.[24] Unfortunately, not enough is known about their work in Burma.

At Singapore too the Malaya State Guides restive with disaffection, and had to be dealt with accordingly in December 1914.[25] when they refused to embark for East Africa. But the really serious outbreak took place there on 15 February 1915, when the 5th Light Infantry, composed mostly of Punjabee Muslisms, and a detachment of the 36th Sikh regiment posted there mutinied. They had been, for some time, exposed to sustained pan-Islamic propaganda, and two local Indian merchants, Jagat Singh and Kasim Ismail Mansoor—the latter was in secret correspondence with the Sultan of Turkey and his consul at Rangoon—were befriending many of them and inciting them to revolt.[26] Exaggerated reports about German victories in Europe and the exploits of the *Emden* near at hand—she shelled Madras on 22 September and Penang on 8 October 1914, torpedoing a Russian cruiser and a French destroyer anchored at the latter harbour—created the impression that the British Empire was falling to pieces. Even when the *Emden* was sunk, one of her officers Oberlieutenant Julius Lauterbach was kept in Tanglin barracks, Singapore, as a prisoner-of-war, and he lost no opportunity to stir up anti-British feeling among the Indian soldiers there.[27] The disaffected soldiers found their leaders in Jamadar Chisti Khan, Jamadar Abdul Ghani, and Subedar Daud Khan, and they broke into mutiny the day before the 5th Light Infantry was to have been despatched to Hong Kong.[28] They killed their British officers and freed about three hundred German prisoners. But the Germans refused to join them, and the leaderless mutineers were ultimately subdued or driven into the forests with fresh reinforcements and Japanese help, after four days of fighting.[29] One hundred twenty-six of them were tried, of whom thirty-seven were executed, forty-one transported for life, and the rest sentenced to various terms of imprisonment.[30] These naturally created an impression among the Indian revolutionaries and the Germans that Indian soldiers, especially those stationed in South-East Asia, were ready for revolt, and that the revolutionaries were only to cross into Burma in force to give the signal.[31]

Preparation for an attack from Thailand

However, it appears that by early March 1915 Herambalal Gupta had come to know of the preparation under way for an armed raid from Thailand and had felt that those concerned should have more arms and better leadership. So he requested Bernstorff to send another ship with eight thousand rifles, two thousand revolvers, and a few machine-guns for Indians at home and South-East Asia.[32] By the middle of March, he had also made contacts with Kurt von Reiswitz, the German Consul at Chicago, and through him with George Paul Boehm, Albert Wehde, Mueller, and Sterneck. Boehm and Sterneck as ex-servicemen were to accompany the proposed expedition as military instructors, while Wehde as its treasurer was to go with them, ostensibly, to purchase curios and objects of art for the Chicago Museum.[33] It was also suggested that Prince Myngoon, a descendant of the independent kings of Burma, then living in exile at Saigon, should also be approached to foment trouble when Indian revolutionaries would enter Burma in force.[34] On 9 April, Bernstorff recommended to the German Foreign Office that another ship with arms should be sent in time for the proposed expedition.[35] On 16 and 30 April 1915, Reiswitz paid 20,000 dollars each to Wehde and his friend, Wilson Will, to make the necessary purchases and arrangements.[36] However, it took them more than a month to complete their work at Chicago before leaving for San Francisco *en route* for East Asia.

As soon as it was decided that an armed expedition would be launched from Thailand, Santosh Singh sent Atmaram Kapur to India from Bangkok towards the beginning of March 1915. He first went to the Punjab but, after the betrayal of the planned rising on 21 February it was not possible for him to make any effective contact there. However, on his way back, he met Jadugopal Mukherjee in Calcutta and told him about the proposed expedition and preparations in East Asia.[37]

Soon after Atmaram's return, six Indian revolutionaries from Thailand secretly came to Burma in May 1915 to make contacts with the local armed police.[38] By then, six to seven hundred armed volunteers had been collected in Thailand. And it was expected that the Indian army and police in Burma, long subjected to pan-Islamic and revolutionary propaganda, would desert their alien masters or, at least, would not put up a stiff resistance when the armed volunteers would cross the frontier.[39]

However, reports has already reached the U.S.A. that Indian leaders in Thailand lacked unity and initiative, and that the progress of preparations there was far from satisfactory. So it was felt that a few efficient people should be sent there to infuse dynamism and to get everything ready in time.[40] In the meantime, Yodh Singh had reached New York on 24 or 25 April with some instructions from Berlin for Herambalal and Ramchandra. Herambalal was, obviously, impressed with him and, on the 30th, sent him to Ramchandra suggesting that he be sent to Bangkok to tone up the movements there.[41]

Boehm and his German associates connected with this expedition also reached San Francisco on 9 May, and on the 14th they sailed for Honolulu on their way to Thailand. Dhirendranath Sen (possibly an alias of Dhirendranath Sarkar) alone among the Indians accompanied the Germans in their voyage.[42] Only a few days before their departure, Jnanedra Chandra Som, alias Nripendranath Chatterjee, had left for Manila on 8 May with Ramchandra's message for Bagwan Singh.[43]

The day before Boehm and his group sailed from San Francisco, Jnan Sanyal had come there with Herambalal's final instructions. According to these they were first to proceed to Honolulu, and then act according to the advice of the local German Consul. Yodh Singh was to follow them a few days later.[44] But the German Consul there had no information about the expedition when they reached Honolulu, and they had to wait there for a few days till Sukumar Chatterjee brought for them fresh instruction from San Francisco.[45]

As desired by Ramchandra, Sukumar Chatterjee and Darisi Chenchhaya also agreed to accompany Yodh Singh to Thailand to activise revolutionary work there, and they all sailed from San Francisco on 22 or 23 May 1915 with coded letters for the German Consuls at Honolulu and Manila, as well as for Bhagwan Singh, who was then believed to be staying in the latter city.[46] On receipt of this letter the German Consul at Honolulu advised both the parties to proceed to Manila, which they reached on 19 June.[47] But unfortunately for them, Bhagwan Singh had already left for Japan only two days before.[48]

In the meantime, the Manila branch of the German firm, Behn, Meyer and Co., had advanced forty thousand dollars to Wehde—the money was actually paid by the German Consulate in Shanghai—who chartered the *Henry S,* belonging to a local German merchant, F. K. Schnitzler, for carrying arms to Thailand and India.[49] Her hold was filled with one hundred sixty four packages containing five thousand rifles, five hundred revolvers, and the requisite ammunition from two war-bound German vessels, the *Sachren* and the *Sueva.* It was decided that she would first go to Bangkok to disembark Boehm and five hundred revolvers, and then push forward to the appointed place near Chittagong[50] Dhirendranath and the Germans proceeded with the ship while Yodh Singh, Sukumar, and Chenchhaya, according to the original plan, left Manila on 26 June and reached *Amoy in* South China on 2 July.[51]

The *Henry S* sailed from Manila in the second week of July 1915 and set her course for Pontianak on the western coast of Kalimantan, then known as Dutch Borneo. But on the third day her engine broke down and she could reach Paleleh in the north of Sulawesi (then known as Celebes) only with difficulty. There the customs authorities scented something suspicious in the ship, and following a thorough search her entire cargo was confiscated.[52] The expedition was naturally given up. *Boehm* still tried to reach Bangkok but was captured by the British and confessed everything. Wehde and Dhirendranath, however, managed to return to Manila.[53]

In the meantime, Yodh Singh and his friends had reached Swatow on 4 and 5 July. There they met Thakur Singh and Balwant Singh, and Yodh Singh set out with them ahead of his two companions to reach Bangkok on 17 July. There they stayed with Shiv Dayal Kapur, who was the local treasurer of the planned expedition. Sukumar and Chenchhaya also reached Bangkok on 22 or 23 July. But the Thai Government had already been alerted by the British, and on 1 August 1915 most of the prominent Indian revolutionaries there, including the few new comers, were taken into custody. Other arrests were made later, and restrictions were imposed even on the free movement of Indians in Thailand with effect from 15 October 1915.[54] These virtually destroyed the chief centre of Indian revolutionary work in South-East Asia.

However, the Indians living at a distance from Bangkok escaped immediate arrest, and according to previous arrangements forty of them well-equipped with arms and thirty mules started from Chieng Mai, on 3 August, for the southern Shan States. They were to meet a party of armed Germans and Indians from Yunan at an appointed place in the Sino-Burmese frontier. But the former group lost their bearing among hills and forests, and failed to effect a meeting. So they returned to Thailand, and that was the end of attempts at organising armed expeditions into India.[55] Sohonlal Pathak and Narain Singh too were arrested near Maymo in Burma on 15 and 19 August 1915, respectively.[56]

Planned expedition from Sumatra

In the meantime, one Vincent Kraft of the 14th Corps of the German Army had forwarded to their Foreign Office, on 12 April 1915, a fresh proposal for helping the revolutionaries in India. He had long been in Indonesia, and believed that the mixed population of North-West Sumatra and the co-operation of the Sarikut Islam would make its easy for him to keep contact with the revolutionaries in India from there.[57] On 4 May he reinforced his earlier proposal with the suggestion that German vessels lying war-bound at Sabang in the North of Sumatra could be used for a surprise dash for the Andamans to liberate the political prisoners there, and then to land them with arms on the coast near Rangoon. He estimated that the entire venture would not cost more than DM 100,000. His proposals were accepted by the German Foreign Office, and he was engaged with effect from 15 May 1915 to organise the expedition.[58] After the necessary preparations he left Berlin for Java towards the end of June. The Germans had with them even the names of the political prisoners at Port Blair.[59]

In the meantime, the German Embassy at Peking had been informed of Vincent Kraft's plan, and a trusted Chinese, by the name of Li Chao, was sent to Sumatra, towards the end of May, to prepare the ground in advance for Kraft and to give him the necessary co-operation.[60] Deli in Sumatra was to be the base of this expedition.

Since sufficient arms were not available locally, it was decided that the *Djember* should bring fifty boxes of munitions from the U.S.A. As the two earlier attempts had been detected in the Pacific, it was considered safer this time to send the ship round the Cape of Good Hope. So the ship sailed from New York on 15 June for Deli, where it was believed seventy-six thousand rifles could be collected for the naval expedition. But, since the British were already on the alert in the Bay of Bengal, it was feared that the route of the ship might have to be changed from some Indian port, preferably Goa, on the Arabian Sea. So it was suggested that *Diaz*—who had already come over to Gemany from the U.S.A.—should go to Goa via Lorenzo Marquis ahead of the ship to warn the revolutionaries there of her possible arrival.[61] But, unfortunately it is not known what happened to the ship or how far *Diaz* could proceed towards India. It was rumoured in Berlin in those days, and many Indians connected with these arms-deals still believe that the ship was actually sunk by a British man-of-war in the Indian Ocean.[62]

In the meantime, Kraft had reached Medan on 11 July and Djakarta on the 25th,[63] a few days after the arrival of the *Maverick* without arms. A month later, Narendranath Bhattacharya and Phanindranath Chakravarty came from Calcutta to negotiate for more arms. They readily welcomed the plan to equip a few war-bound German ships for a dash for the Indian coast with arms. It was even decided that while one such ship would head for the Balasore coast another would raid the Andamans, release the political prisoners, and land them on the coast near Rangoon. A third ship was to come with arms from China and proceed to the island of Hatia,[64] in the main estuary of the Ganga. In course of a few weeks the necessary preparations were made for the planned naval expedition from Sumatra, and even code words for secret communication with Calcutta were arranged. But, from the very beginning, Kraft could not get on well with the Helfferich brothers or Erich Windles. In fact, they suspected him to be a British spy. These must have hampered their preparations, and almost at the last moment the planned expedition was given up.[65] Possibly, the Germans felt that such a blatant violation of Dutch neutrality would seriously antagonise the Dutch Government and jeopardise the larger war-time interest of Germany.

In the meantime, Champak Raman Pillai, who was in charge of the Indian Committee's contacts with the outside world through Holland, had thought out a fresh plan for resuscitating Indian revolutionary activities in East Asia. At Zurich, he was known to the Indonesian nationalist exile, Dr. Daus Dekkar, and the latter had come to Berlin, early in January 1915, at Barakatullah's request. Champak Raman Pillai at first requested him to arrange for the distribution of propaganda leaflets through Holland. Then in July he suggested that Daus Dekkar should go to Thailand to set up a centre of Indian propaganda. It was hoped that he would be able to ensure friendly understanding and co-operation between Indian and Indonesian nationalists. Champak Raman Pillai and Daus Dekkar jointly discussed their plans with Wesendonck, and on 8 September 1915 Daus Dekkar left Rotterdam for the U.S.A., on his way to Thailand. He met Ramchandra at San Francisco on 28 September, and reached Tokyo on 20 October. Bhagwan Singh was then away in Korea. However, he met Rash Behari Bose and left for Bangkok via Shanghai and Hong Kong. Coming on the heels of these setbacks the fiasco of Daus Dekkar's mission practically marked the end of Indian revolutionary efforts in South-East Asia.

References

1. "The situation created by the rise of the Ghadar Party in India, though serious, is not such as the Government of India cannot cope with, so long as party members continue to arrive in isolated groups....But a new and more difficult situation may arise if the Ghadar party after assembling in some adjacent country are in a position to collect sufficient of their members to make an armed incursion into India." British Minister, Bangkok to Foreign Minister Thailand in September 1915, quoted in *H.P. 1915 October 242-247. B.*
2. German Foreign Office to Bernstorff on 13-12-1914. DAA, Reel 397, files 1-11. Also, Ruedinger's statement, H.P. 1917 July 52 Dep. Also, German Consul, Canton to Berlin on 15-10-1914, DAA, Reel 398, files 12-31.
3. Jadugopal Mukherjee, op. cit., p. 419. Also, the statement of Khagendra Chandra Das, who had heard from Satyendranath Sen himself.
4. Note by Bernstorff, dated 18-1-1915, DAA, Reel 397, files 1-11. Also, Chakravarty to Berlin on 21-11-1916, cited in *San Francisco Chronicle,* 28-2-1918, p. 9.
5. See pp. 233-234.
6. Notes on the accused, Tahal Singh, Roll 6, Record Group No. 118.
7. British Consul, Chieng Mai to Chief Secretary, Burma on 17-2-1916, F.P. 1916 April 1. Also 1. British Charge d'Affaires, Bangkok to Foreign Secretary, Britain on 26-11-1914 H.P. 1915 June 60-88 B.

8. British Charge d'Affaires, Bangkok to Secy., Foreign and Political, India on 15-12-1914. H. P. 1915 June 60-88, Foreign (War) 1915 252-259.
9. *Ibid.*
10. Report from German Consulate, Canton, dated 15-10-1914, DAA, Reel 398, files 12-31.
11. Report from German Charge d'Affaires, Bangkok, dates 29-10-1914, DAA, Reel 397, files 1-11. Also, D.C.I. on 25-8-1915, H. P. 1915 October 43 Dep.
12. See 1230.
13. Shiv Dayal Kapur's statement, cited in *San Francisco Examiner,* 29-11-1997, p. 3, and in Brown, p. 18. Also, J. W. Spellman, op. cit., p. 39.
14. See footnote no. 7, p. 133.
15. D.C.I. on 26-1-1915 H. P. 1915 January 278-282 B. Also, British Charge d'Affaires. Bangkok to Secy. Foreign and Political, India on 15-12-1914, H.P. 1915 June 60-88 B.
16. Report of the German Charge d'Affaires, Bangkok, dated 17-11-1917 DAA, Reel 400, files 39-46.
17. Washington centre of the plot. German Consulate, Shanghai in charge of work in Asia. Actual work done in Thailand, Java and Iran. D.C.I. on 3-8-1915. H.P. 1915 August 552-556 B. Also, report from German Ambassador, Peking, dated 3-2-1915, DAA, Reel 397, files 1-11.
18. Openheim's note, dated 9-1-1915, DAA, Reel 397, files, 1-11.
19. Note by German Foreign Office, dated 18-1-1915, *ibid.*
20. Rowlatt, p. 121.
21. Jadugopal Mukherjee, op. cit., pp. 29, 30-40 and 383. Also, statement of Jatindranath Hui.
22. Rowlatt, p. 121.
23. *Ibid.*
24. D.C.I. on 30-3-1915, H.P. 1915 April 412-415 B.
25. Rowlatt, p. 121. They were strongly pro-Turkish in their sympathy. D.C.I. on 26-1-1915, H.P. 1915 January 278-282 B.
26. *Straits Echo,* 16-9-1915, and *Singapore Times,* 22 and 23 April 1915.
27. Lowell J. Thomas, *Lauterbach of the China Sea,* New York 1930, p. 109.
28. *Ibid.*, p. 111. Also *Singapore Times,* 19-3-1915, and *Singapore Free Press,* 25-3-1915. Also. R.W. Mosbergen. *The Sepoy Rebellion: A History of the Singapore Mutiny of 1915* (unpublished M.A. thesis of University of Malaya. 1954), p. 10.
29. R. W. Mosbergen, op. cit., pp. 20-21, 40-43, 66.
30. T. M. Winsley, *A History of the Singapore Volunteer Corps,* Singapore, 1937, p. 70.
31. Statements of Bhagwan Singh and Lala Sunder Das.
32. Report from Bernstorff, dated 25-3-1915, DAA, Reel 398, files 12-13.
33. Statement of George Paul Boehm (hereafter referred to as Boehm) on 17-11-1915, Roll 4, Record Group No. 118. Also, Bernstorff to German Foreign Office on 9-4-1915, DAA, Reel 398, files 12-31.
34. Note by Franz von Papen, dated 24-3-1915, DAA, Reel 398 files 12-31. Bhupendranath Datta, op. cit., pp. 22-23.

35. Note by Bernstorff, dated 9-4-1915, DAA, Reel 398, files 12-31.
36. U. S. vs. Jacobson *et al.*, in the District Court of the US S. Northern District of Illinois, Eastern Division, Roll 5.
37. See p. 251.
38. Chief Secy., Burma to Home Secy., India on 1-12-1915, H.P. 1916 March 619-665 A. A plot involving the Military Police was discovered in North Burma. *Ibid.*
39. Statement of an informer (possibly Kumud Mukherjee), H.P. 1916 February 201 A. Sikhs in Shan States were disaffected. D.C.I. on 30-7-1915, H.P. 1915 April 412-415 B. Even four Gurkha soldiers were peaching anti-British sentiment, Chief Secy., Burma to Home Secy, India on 17-12-1915, H.P. March 619-665 A.
40. Report by German Charge d'Affaireș Bangkok, dated 17-11-1917, DDA, Reel 400, files 39-46. Also , the statement of Indian informer, H.P. 1916 February 201 A.
41. Yodh Singh's statement, on 15-11-1915, Roll 4, Record Group No. 118.
42. Boehm's statement, op. cit.
43. Sukumar Chatterjee's statement on 13-11-1915, Rol, 5, Record Group No. 118.
44. Yodh Singh's statement op. cit.
45. Boehm's statement, op. cit.
46. Yodh Singh's statement, op. cit. Also, Sukumar Chatterjee's statement, op. cit.
47. Sukumar Chatterjee's statement, op. cit.
48. Yodh Singh's statement, op. cit.
49. German Charge d'Affaires, Bangkok, dated 17-11-1917 DAA, Reel 400, files 39-46.
50. Rowlatt, p. 84. Also, Boehm's statement, op. cit.
51. Yodh Singh's statement, op. cit. Also, Sukumar Chatterjee's statement, op, cit.
52. Rowlatt, p. 84. Also, Boehm's statement, op. cit. Also D.C.I. on 3-8-1915, H.P. 1915 August 552-556 B.
53. Boehm's statement, op. cit. Also, U.S. vs. Jacobson, Roll 5.
54. Yodh Singh's statement, op, cit. Also, British Minister, Bangkok to Secy., Foreign and Political, India in October 1915, H.P. 1915 October 242-247 B. Also D.C.I. on 10-8-1915. H.P. 1915 August 552-556 B.
55. Report from German Charge d'Affaires Bangkok dated 17-11-1917, DAA. Reel 400, files 39-46. Also D.C.I. on 7-9-1915, H.P. 1915 September 582-585 B.
56. Rowlatt, p. 122. Also, D.C.I. on 17-8-1915, H.P. 1915 August 552-556 B. Also C.I.D., Punjab to D.C.I. on 5-8-1915, F.P. 1917 June 1-46.
57. Vincent Kraft to German Foreign Office on 12-4-1915, DAA, Reel 398, files, 12-31. Also, Emil Helfferich's letter to author, dated 17-9-1956.
58. Home Secy., India to Secy. of State on 20-8-1915, H.P. 1915 September 484-503 and k.w.A. Also, D.C.I. on 17-8-1915, H.P. 1915, 552-556 B. Also, note by Erich Windels, data 6-10-1915, DAA, Reel 398 files 12-31. Report by Military Attachè, German Embassy, Washington, dated 31-5-1915, *ibid.*

59. D.C.I. on 25-8-1915, H.P. 1915 October 43 Dep.
60. Report from Military Attachè, German Embassy, Washington, dated 31-5-1915, DAA, Reel 398, files 12-31.
61. *Ibid.* Also Bhupendranath Datta, op. cit., p. 31.
62. Bhupendranath Datta, op. cit., pp. 25 and 169.
63. British Minister, Djakarta to Secy., Foreign and Political, India on 30-7-1915, F.P. 1917 June 1-46.
64. Rowlatt, pp. 84-85. The rumour that convicts would be liberated had reached India and the Andamans. Upendranath Banerjee, *Nirvasiter Atmakatha* (in Bengali), Calcutta, 1960, pp. 113-114.
65. M. N. Roy, op. cit., pp. 4-5. Also, Emil Helfferich's and Erich Windels' letters to author, dated 17-9-1956 and 1-11-1956 respectively.
66. Dr. Daus Dekkar's statement, Roll 6, Record Group No. 118. Also, Bhupendranath Datta, op. cit., pp. 29-31. Dr. Daus Dekkar was to get £600 *per mensem* for his work in connection with smuggling of arms. D.C.I. on 1-2-16, H.P. 1916 February 515-518 B. He even explained to the British the use of their secret code. Brown, p. 19.

7

The Indian Self-Government as Advocated by Annie Besant

It is often heard these days that we have lost our moorings—that we have developed a kind of psyche which is not our own and that there is a crisis of character from top to bottom.

Can history provide an answer to this? Is it that the system of government that we have adopted is alien and contributes to this stunting and dwarfing of our characters? In this exploratory quest of understanding, an effort has been made here to analyse the system of self-government that Annie Besant worked out with the help of our national leaders like Tej Bahadur Sapru, Sarojini Naidu, P.K. Telang, N.C. Kelkar, M.A. Jinnah, C.P. Ramaswami Iyer, Motilal Nehru and many others.

Annie Besant through her studies and experiences understood that Indians by nature were capable of guiding, shaping and controlling their own affairs and thus worthy[1] of establishing competent and effective self-government. She felt that destruction of India's village system was the greatest of England's blunders.[2] She advocated the establishment of village self-government as the basis of all effective reforms in the political field.[3] The decline of village life in India, she explained, created not only political but also economic and industrial problems.[4]

She did not envisage self-government for India by class conflict as in the west, but a self-government for social well-being by general consent and co-operation.[5] The existing democratic system, she felt, was defective in so far as it permitted a vote of equal weight to every individual.[6]

In her model of self-government for India, she tried to ensure that every one had a voice, with a share of power of guidance over things, in which knowledge experience and high character would be the credentials for power. The area over which that power extended would be proportional to the development of these characteristics in the one who sought to wield it.[7]

Annie Besant felt that welfare of a nation largely depended on the purity and independence of courts of justice. She therefore felt that all judges in India should be independent of the executive.[8]

She thought it worthwhile to consider whether in all elections in which suffrage was not universal, proportional representation should be adopted , so that minorities as well as majorities should be represented, and in proportion to their strength.

Suppose a Taluq Council was to consist of 30 members, it might be divided into 30 electoral areas, each area returning one member, and each elector having one vote; in such case, the 30 members may all represent one school of thought, though each in his own area had a bare minority, and all the 30 minorities remained unrepresented.[9]

In proportional representation, voting power was so distributed as to allow the minorities to club together by grouping the electoral area, or by allowing a man to vote in any area for any member within the whole electorate.

Thus, in Taluq with its 30 electoral areas, these might be grouped into six areas each returning five members, and each elector would have 5 votes which he may give to one member or distribute among the five; the minority put up one candidate or more, if strong enough and plump for him or them, while the majority scatter their votes.

Another way was to give each elector but one vote, allowing him to vote in any one of the 30 electoral areas, so that the entire minority vote for a single member, in whatever part of the Taluq they may live. Such a plan was far better for the representation of minorities than the forming of separate electorates for a favoured class, a method which invariably led to jealousy and injustice, breeding discontent and unrest.[10] Annie Besant was in favour of granting complete autonomy to the smallest units both at the village and the town levels, which she explained was the system prevalent before the advent of European trading companies and which gave India peace and prosperity throughout the ages. Indian policy, she therefore advocated, should grow out of its own ethos. She cautioned against any foreign adoptation in the evolution of Indian self-government.

Annie Besant worked out in detail a system of self-government for India. She began from the bottom with the village in the country and ward in the town as the units. She held that every adult of 21 years of age and of sound mind and free from crime must have his share of control and must have his voice in the management of affairs. The village electorate, she held, would be one of universal suffrage, and would elect the village council. The principle was that whatever belonged to the village should exclusively be controlled by the village council. She was in favour of annual elections. Members were required to be educated at least up to primary level.

The village needs would be made known and if necessary it would be represented by the Panchayat to a higher authority. The village would thus articulate through its panchayat, and would no longer be the dumb and often driven creature as it was then. She wanted the Panchayat to arrange lectures, organise discussions, amusements, games, etc. Thus village life would be lifted to a higher level, widened, and enriched by such organisations and each village, forming part of one of the group of villages would realise its unity with others, and become an organ of the larger corporate life. Thus she envisaged the revival of Indian village community-life.

The units in the town corresponding to the village unit in the country was the ward. The Ward Council, like the Village Council, would take up the smaller town matters which were often neglected because the Municipality was too heavily burdened to attend to them properly.

The second grade of the Council would be Taluq Boards in the country and municipalities in towns below a certain population, and the electors here should be Village and Ward Councils and residents in the area, over 25 years of age, and who had reached a certain standard of education, matriculation or equivalent.

She also suggested proportional representation, so that minority as well as majority should be represented and that in proportion to their strength.

The third grade of council would be District Boards in the country and municipalities in towns over a certain population, and here the electors would be second grade Council, and all men and women resident in the district or town over the age of 30 and educated up to the intermediate or equivalent standard. All the business, which concerned the whole district or town, would be under their control.

The provincial scheme would end in the provincial Parliament, elected by the Councils of the third grade and by all men and women over 35, resident in the province, and educated up to the graduate level. The Provincial Parliament would control the universities within the Province, and all that affected the Province as a whole. The provincial Government, she wrote, would be a Ministry, responsible to the Parliament, with a Governor appointed by the Crown as a link with the Empire, for a term of years as now and representing the Crown, receiving the resignation of a Ministry defeated in Parliament, calling on a leader to form a New Ministry and so on.

The main point to establish was that whatever the Council, it must consist of elected members only, that all governing bodies must draw their authority from and be responsible to the Councils of which they were the executives, and then only would self-government become a reality, and the destiny of India would be in the hands of her own people.

This scheme was based upon her clear understanding and proper appreciation of the past of India and modern democratic system. She was amply clear that restoration of happy and healthy Indian village community-life alone would help India find herself.

Appendix

T.S. Archives, Adyar

Ref:— Part II. Subject files (B II) Home Rule League.

No. 18. Papers relating to the *Reconstruction League* started by Home Rules to train the masses in the experiments of Self Government on their ancestral lines.

List of the Members:

Dr. Annie Besant D.L.
Post Box 904, Adyar, Madras.

Sir Victor Sassoon, Bait. M.L.A.

Ballard Estate, Fort, Bombay.

Sir Purshottamdas Thakurdas, Kt. C.I.C.M.L.A.
Ridge Road, Malabar Hill, Bombay.

The Hon. Ratansi D. Morarji
Vasantha Vihar, Mount Pleasant Road,
Malabar Hill, Bombay.

Dr. G.S. Arundale, M.A.D.L.
Post Box 904, Adyar, Madras.

A. Ranganatha Mudaliar Esq. M.L.C.
Adyar, Madras.

B. Shiva Rao Esq.
Adyar, Madras.

T.C. Srinivasa Iyengar Esq. M.L.A.
High Court Vakil, Madura.

A Rangaswami Aiyar Esq., B.A.B.L.
High Court Vakil, Madura.

N. Sri Ram Esq.,
Adyar, Madras.

The Raja Vasudeva Raja of Kollengode, Kt. C.I.E.
Kollengode, via Olavakot. (S.I.R.).

The Maharaja of Pithapuram
Dunmore House, Madras.

N.C. Kalkar Esq., M.L.A.
The "Kesari" Office, Poona.

Lala Lajpat Rai, M.L.A.
Hirendranath Datta Esq., M.A.B.L.
139, Cornwallis Street, Calcutta.
Pandit Iqbal Narain Gurtu, M.A.M.L.C.
Shanti Kunja, Banaras City.

P.K. Telang Esq. M.A.L.L.B.
Theosophical Society, Banaras City.

D.K. Telang Esq.
Theosophical Society, Adyar, Madras.

Jamobed N.R. Mehta
Chairman, Municipality, Karachi.

Sir Tej Bahadur Sapru K.C.S.I.
19, Albert Road, Allahabad.

Smt. Sarojini Naidu
Taj Mahal Hoel, Bombay.

M.A. Jinnah Esq., M.L.A.
Rukmini Gokhale
922, Sadashive Peth, Poona City.

A.R. Rangaswami Aiyar
Sivagunga.

Rangaswami Iyengar
Editor, Hindu.

Sir C.P. Ramaswami Iyer, K.C.I.E.

Pandit Motilal Nehru.

Mrs. Dorothy Jinarajadasa
Joint Organiser of Women's Section, Madras.

Mr. D. Shiva Rao
Chairman of the Provincial Committee of the
Trade Union Congress, Madras.

Dr. Pattabhisitaramayya
Editor, "Janmabhumi".

Dr. James H. Cousins.

Mrs. Margaret Cousins,
Joint Organiser of Women's Section, Madras.

—Raj Kumar

References

1. Annie Besant, *India Bond or Free?* (Adyar, Madras, 1939), p. 181.
2. Ibid., p. 28.

3. Ibid., p. 170.
4. Ibid., p. 172.
5. *New India,* 13 April, 1915.
6. *New India,* 17 March, 1915.
7. Ibid.
8. Annie Besant, *New India Political Pamphlets: Self Government* (Adyar, Madras, 1916), pp. 14-15.
9. Ibid., p. 10.
10. Ibid., p. 11.
11. Annie Besant, *The Congress Speeches of Annie Besant.* (Adyar, Madras, 1917) Bombay Congress, 1915, Self-Government.
12. *New India,* 10 April, 1915.
13. Ibid.

8

Quit India Movement

Nations survive only when individuals go out to seek and face death. The Quit India Movement of 1942 made an attempt in this direction. Freedom fighters from various provinces of India rose in revolt. It was no doubt a major event in Indian and British colonial history.

How this movement came to be called Quit India Movement? According to Pyarelal, Gandhi's Secretary, the phrase Quit India was coined by an American Press Correspondent during the course of his interview with Gandhi and it "caught on". The actual expression used by the Mahatma originally was "orderly British withdrawal".

Various reasons given for the outbreak of the Quit India Movement are:—

(a) Gandhi's desperation at the failure of the individual Satyagraha movement.

(b) Rejection of Cripps proposal.

(c) General demoralization in the Congress ranks.

(d) The growing danger of Britain acceding to the Muslim League demand for Pakistan.

(e) The presence of a large number of American troops in India.

(f) To assist Japanese operations against India.

The important Congressmen believed that India would meet the same fate as that of Singapore, Malaya and Burma. They thought that the Britishers would fight in India to the bitter end, destroying the cities and industrial centres in pursuance to the scorched-earth policy.

The decision to start a movement by the Congress at this juncture was due to the Japanese menace having drawn nearer and the disappointment produced by the visit of Sir Stafford Cripps. There was also a belief among the Congressmen that if liberty was not granted at the moment when the government was driven into straits of difficulties resultant of the fearful war, there would come no occasion in the future for the Government to transfer real powers.

The thinking of the Indian National Congress was no doubt governed by three factors during the war. First, the experience of World War I when the Congress had cooperated with the Government, but was rewarded by the Montford Reforms and the policy of repression, was too bitter for them to forget. Their memories were revived on the outbreak of World War II and they decided to demand not only a promise about the future independence but establishment of self-government in the present. The second dominating influence was the last twenty years' struggle with the Government which had produced lack of trust and a mood of non-cooperation. The third influence was the ideological faith that the war was a war between Nazism and democracy and so must it also be a war to liberate people from imperialism and colonialism.

Gandhi believed that the British would not be able to repel the Japanese invasion of India and at that time he probably also doubted whether Allies would ultimately win the war in the West. He may, therefore, have been convinced that after having turned India into a battlefield the British would ultimately leave India to the mercy of the Japanese as a conquered country. If this happened, his dreams and promise of Swaraj would be at an end. Against this prospectus, it may have seemed to him better and in the interest of India that almost any internal chaos should arise in the country, rather than that India should go down with the sinking ship without a chance of acting for herself. His view may well have been that, if India could only stand alone, the Congress could make overtures to Japanese in order to secure position of neutrality, in which event the Japanese would have no reason to attack Indian territory. Some such ideas may have also been at the back of his rejection of Cripps' offer. He thought no advantage in linking India's destiny with Allied victory which he rated as doubtful and thus involving India in what he believed to be a certainty of invasion for the sake of long-term promises which might not be fulfilled. Failing to secure satisfaction from Sir Stafford Cripps he resolved in the face of Japanese threat to take advantage of the opportunity of shaking off the British domination whether by agreement with the British Government or otherwise, in order that India might be left to work out her own salvation. He did not want the Japanese to come to India or to obtain independence with their help if it could be avoided. But if it came to the worst, the Japanese would probably give more suitable terms to the Congress if it had openly disallowed allegiance to "the Allied cause".

There was difference of opinion among the members of the Congress Working Committee regarding the advisability of launching the "Quit India" movement.

"Nehru, Rajagopalachari, Mrs. Sarojini Naidu and Bhulabhai Desai took the common sense view that the withdrawal of British at this stage must inevitably mean Japanese occupation. Rajendra Prasad, Kripalani and Vallabhbahi Patel followed Gandhi. Pant and Acharya Narendra Deo held that if given self-government, all problems would solve themselves." Though there was difference of opinion about Japan and the war, there was complete unanimity about hatred of British.

The All-India Congress Committee on August 8th passed the resolution put up to it by the Working Committee sanctioning a civil disobedience campaign under the leadership of Gandhi. In the early hours of the 9th morning Gandhi and the principal Congressmen were arrested, not only at Bombay but in other parts of the country as well. It had been decided before hand by Gandhi and the Working Committee that this was to be the signal for the launching of a campaign, and, should these arrests be made, the people were to embark upon civil disobedience in all its forms. Gandhi at the time of his arrest passed the word when he left his famous message "Do or Die. You can go to the farthest limits under 'ahimsa'."

The movement was greatly intensified owing to the intervention of the Congress Socialist Party, Forward Bloc and other revolutionary parties. Students played a very important role in this movement. There was to be a dictator for each province and in case of largger provinces like United Provinces (Uttar Pradesh), districts were grouped into zones for each of which a dictator was appointed (Agra, Kanpur and Benaras [Varanasi] were the important towns in Uttar Pradesh) as well as their successors in case they were arrested. For example,

Keshodeva Malaviya and later on Baba Raghav Das were in charge of the movement in United Provinces. There was a Committee of Action to assist each dictator and there were several departments—for propagada, information, finance, intelligence, volunteer, village, school and college, dak, ambulance, etc.—each under the charge of a member of the Committee. Technical instructions were circulated to destroy planes, tanks, locomotives, etc., with easily obtainable substances and by simple methods. For the trading of *azad dastas* or guerilla bands, a centre was set up outside the British territory at a place known as *Bakro Ka Tapu.* Sardar Nityanand Sinha of Bihar was the chief instructor at this centre while Dr. Rammanohar Lohia took over the charge of Radio and Publicity Department. Among the revolutionary groups working in different parts of the country, Siaram Dal and Parasuram Dal in Bihar, Hindustan Socialist Republican Army in Uttar Pradesh, Anushilan Samiti and Jugantar Group in Bengal were the most important ones.

The British Government had made full preparations to suppress the movement even before it was launched. The first stage planned was to initiate propaganda in India and outside to justify strong action against the Congress and actually it was completed by 3 August 1942. In the second stage, which was to commence with the ratification of the "Quit India" Resolution by the All-India Congress Committee, the Government proposed that all Provincial Governments should simultaneously proclaim the All-India Congress Committee and the Provincial Congress Committees unlawful, but not the Congress as a whole, under the Criminal Law Amendment Act. It was also planned that first Gandhi and all members of the Working Committee should be simultaneously arrested in Bombay, if possible, and secondly that a statement should be issued denouncing leadership of the Congress in strong terms and after that, all Provincial Governments should seize Congress Committee offices and funds and arrest all provincial leaders and organizers of real importance. Stage three contemplated action in case the measures proposed above failed to suppress the movement. This involved proclamation of the whole Congress unlawful and promulgation of Emergency Power Ordinance.

Government indulged in air shooting and flogging. The Viceroy suggested to the Secretary of State on 4 October 1942: "If you have any trouble in the debate (in Parliament) about shooting from air, it may be worthwhile mentioning that in many cases this action was taken against mobs engaged in tearing up lines on vital strategic railways in areas which ground-floor forces could not reach owing to interruptions of rail communication by sabotage and of road communication by destruction of road culverts and by extensive flooding. But this is not true of all cases in which firing occurred from aircraft. In any event, I think you may feel able to avoid the least suggestion of apology for air action.''

There was whipping of persons or caning particularly students by police. It was resorted to at places particularly in Nagpur, Hyderabad (Sind), C.P., Bombay and Poona. Exact number of persons killed during the Quit India Movement is not known. Number according to official records were 1028 killed and 3125 seriously injured. According to Jawaharlal Nehru the figure of the dead was 4000 to 10,000.

The "Quit India" Movement of 1942 is a landmark in India's struggle for freedom. The then Viceroy Lord Linlithgow wrote : "I am engaged here in meeting by far the most serious rebellion since that of 1857, the gravity and extent of which we have so far concealed from the world of reasons of military security." It was spread over almost all the provinces from the Himalayas to Cape Comorin. The violent upsurge of the masses and their readiness to sacrifice everything for the emancipation of the motherland, showed their grim determination to throw off the foreign yoke. It warned the British that they were not wanted in India and that "their belief that any section of the Indian people—the Muslims, the depressed classes or the States people—favoured continuance of their rule was a delusion." The complete breakdown of law and order in many parts of the country and the setting up of parallel independent governments by the people made them realize that they could not hold their sway over India for long. Churchill, the then Prime Minister, gloomily disclosed to the King that "the idea of the transfer of power in India had become an admitted inevitability in the minds of the British Party leaders". The King noted: "He (Churchill) amazed me by saying that his colleagues and both or all the three Parties in Parliament were quite prepared to give up India to the Indians after the war. He felt they had already been talked into giving up India. Cripps, the Press and the U.S. public opinion have all contributed to make their minds up and that our role in India is wrong and has always been wrong for India." The violent mass upsurge of 1942, the enthusiastic response of the people from one end of the country to the other, many instances of individual and collective heroism and bravery in the face of heavy odds and their untold sufferings and sacrifices hastened the British decision to quit India.

The movement was not limited to any one part of India, but interspersed over the whole of the country; its intensity and depth varied from place to place. It represented the most serious challenge to British rule in India since the rebellion of 1857. For the first time the Government realized that the Indian bureaucracy and police, the main bastions of its rule, were not as reliable as before, so far as their role in keeping the Indian people under British rule was concerned. Thus cracks had appeared in the edifice of the empire, and even the foundation was shaken. The national awakening and the sense of solidarity and unity shown by the people constituted a warning to the Government, which it could not ignore for long.

The Quit India Movement was both a Revolt and a revolution. The Revolt failed but the revolution succeeded. Let us conclude this essay by what Gandhi wrote in *Harijan* on 25 May, 1942.

"I waited and waited until the country should develop the non-violent strength necessary to throw off the foreign yoke. But my attitude has now undergone a change. I feel that I cannot afford to wait. If I continue to wait, I might have to wait till Doomsday. For the preparation that I have prayed for and worked for may never come and in the meantime I may be enveloped and overwhelmed by the flames that threaten all of us. That is why I have decided that even at certain risks, which are evidently involved, I must ask the people to resist the slavery."

—Raj Kumar

9

Tribals and Freedom Struggle

Jawaharlal Nehru, speaking retrospectively of the nature and range of tribal participation in India's freedom movement, observed:

> For half a century or more, we have struggled for freedom and ultimately achieved it. That struggle, apart from anything else, was a fresh liberating force....We must remember that this experience of hundreds of millions of Indian people was not shared by the tribal folk. Our struggle for freedom did influence the tribes in Central India to some extent but in the frontier areas of Assam, for instance, they remained almost unaffected by it. This was partly due to the inadequacy of the means of communication available to us in the old days. Of course, there were other reasons too.
>
> One of the reasons was that the city people were a little afraid to leave their familiar haunts and go into the mountains....Apart from our own lack of initiative, we were not allowed to go there by the British authorities then in power. That is why our freedom movement reached these people only in the shape of occasional rumours. Sometimes they reacted rightly and sometimes wrongly, but that is beside the point.[2]

Jawaharlal Nehru's views were typical of the nationalist appreciation of the tribal question, which was concerned with larger issues and which tended to play down the role of parochial (caste and communal) politics in the formation of movements.

By and large, the tribal people were isolated and backward, and their participation in the national politics, unlike the Harijan's was inconsiderable. They were almost the last of the Indian communities to be politicized. But research into the freedom movement in different parts of the country, which has been recently undertaken in terms of the social composition of regional movements, has revealed a rich pattern of the involvement of local communities in regional politics. Evidence suggests that like other communities, tribal groups participated intensely in local politics, but with a difference. There was an attempt on the part of the tribal community to seek integration into the regional and national systems and also to preserve its identity.

In contrast to the nationalist approach, which reacted understandably sharply to the separatist movements and assumed too much unity and uniformity in an essentially pluralistic situation, there was another line of thinking. The latter assumed that separatist movements in tribal India were typical of Indian conditions, and were the precursor of the Indian states' 'inevitable' process of disintegration. Here is a specimen of this line of thinking in what is otherwise a good piece of writing on the Jharkhand movement.

> Harrison, a perspicacious American commentator reminded us, as late as 1960, that the *unity* of India was based on tenuous foundations, foundations perpetually inclined to disintegrate and thus make room for a possible emergence of Communist take-over....
>
> ...it is pointless to harp on cultural similarities between the victim and the victor...nothing can be deduced about *inter-group relations, particularly power relations,* if we *begin* analysis via the concept of culture. The crucial questions to be asked in this context are: who can compel whom, when, in which respect, and how?
>
> Let us remember the facts: creation of Pakistan, separatism *par excellence;* carving out of Andhra; consolidation of Maharashtra; earlier, separation of Bihar and Orissa from Bengal in 1912, the birth of Orissa in 1936; now, the Punjabi Suba agitation and the birth of Haryana as a separate State; the DMK movement, muted for the time being; the demand for Jharkhand. If analysis succeeds in rising above the cloud of *cultural* confusion, the answer to the question 'who compels whom',

will emerge vividly.[3]

Within four years of the publication of this piece of prognostication, the Jharkhand party had merged with the Congress and the Jharkhand movement had become moribund.

This approach overlooks the fact that nation-building is a continuing process and that the search for identity by small, backward, and sensitive communities should not always be considered anti-national. In the present paper an attempt has been made to analyse the historical processes of integration during the pre-independence phase, their assimilation with regional movements, and their search for identity. It should be noted that the social milieu of tribal middle-India is entirely different from that of the north-east. In the first region, tribal people do not constitute the majority except in about eight districts and forty *talukas;* they live with other communities. The society and economy are composite in nature; interaction, and not exclusiveness, has been the important element in social formation. Therefore, in this region separatism has never developed into secessionism and the tribal demand for autonomy has been expressed in constitutional terms.

Documentation of processes of tribal politics has not been easy. The story of the tribal movement from the 1920s onwards exists piecemeal, often under misleading labels and such accounts as are available are not without a slant. It is not easy to piece together the fragments of the story from private papers and archival sources and field study, stay clear of the existing stereotypes that have conditioned our thinking on this subject, and seek an understanding in terms of the tribals' own perception of the issues at stake.[4]

Tribal politics in the pre-1920 phase could be described in terms of a series of revolts, sporadic, isolated and spontaneous. Led by tribes who were settling down as agrarian communities, they resisted erosion of agrarian and forest rights. Inspired by the primeval dream of freedom, the movements aimed at the total restructuring of the primitive system which was breaking down under the impact of the colonial economy. They were violent, and were ruthlessly crushed. Certain tribes, such as the Bhil and Minas, who had been uprooted and lived in conditions of turmoil, had adopted banditry as a form of social protest. Their leaders, officially described as 'pests', were in fact peasant rebels.

The phase of tribal polities, which began after 1920 and was generally free from such episodes, was marked by movements which could be sustained only by organization and through external stimuli. The latter were provided by the nationalist struggle which came to the tribal world in the 1920s through the message and personality of Mahatma Gandhi.

Among the tribes which responded to the movement and the Mahatma were the Santals, Oraons, Bhils and Gonds, all major tribes. Among them, the sections which responded particularly were those who had already been Sanskritized or sensitized to Vaishnavism. The leaders of these sects were Bhagats steeped in the Bhakti tradition, like Hindu peasants elsewhere, and they understood the idioms in which Gandhi's message was couched. The Bhil Bhagats, the Tana Bhagats among Oraons and the Sapha Hors among Santals, the Haribaba movement among the Hos (1930) and the Rajmohini movement among the Gonds saw in the freedom movement led by Gandhi an opportunity for the recovery of the tribal Raj and the rights as agrarian communities which they had lost, for continuing social reforms such as temperance, purification and education and for seeking social uplift and establishing an equation with peasant castes. Most of these Bhagat sects in their origin antedated the freedom movement. They received a fresh lease of life through Gandhi's reconstruction programme. Many Bhagats became faithful followers of the Indian National Congress and clung tenaciously to its programme in the most adverse circumstances. They became the standard-bearers of the freedom movement among tribes in the backward regions. Interestingly, most of the leaders of the movement among the Hos and the Bhils called themselves the *chelas* of Gandhi though the latter disowned at least one of them. The significance of the 'nationalization' of the Bhagat movements was considerable, even though the Bhagats were only a minority among their people.

While the tribes accepted the nationalist programme and joined the mainstream of the national movement they were also not unmindful of the demands of their situation. Swaraj meant not only freedom from British rule, but also freedom from the oppression of the *dikus,* money-lenders, *zamindars* and feudal-overlords. *Ram Rajya* was interpreted as a restoration of the tribal world of primitive freedom, of the golden age of the race, the memory of which had survived. Freedom of them meant the restoration of agrarian and forest rights.

The impact of Mahatama Gandhi and the mechanics of the reconstruction programme as it was conceived and implemented in the tribal areas need a little more elaboration. Recent research has revealed a much more extensive impact by the Mahatma on the tribes of the remote regions than has been assumed.[5] Gandhi *Baba* found his way into the tribal rituals and pantheon, but more suggestive appears to be his impact on tribal folklore in an isolated region like Bastaer—leaving aside, or course, the more exposed Halbas and Marias.[6]

An excellent case-study of the reconstruction programme (1922-47) among the adivasis of Vedachi (Surat)[7] shows how, with the Vedachi movement, the trend for social reform had already been initiated among the tribes. Even before the Gandhi movement began,

> ...a sort of religious movement had begun among the Kaliparaj (Adivasis). A goddess was moving about and was preaching to the people not to drink liquor toddy. In some districts of Gujarat this movement broke down. But the Choudaries stuck to the orders of the goddess.[8]
>
> The Gandhian workers built upon the movement of social and economic reform started by the tribal people themselves, which enjoined abstinence from liquor, toddy and meat, after the norms of the high caste Hindus. The Gandhians added a political dimension, and brought tribal and non-tribal communities together on the same platform.

The Adivasis who distrusted the non-Adivasis could see that the programme of political movement and their own had a good deal in common. The new movement was therefore acceptable to them. This movement helped in blunting the edge of the Adivasi distrust of the non-Adivasis and served the Adivasis and non-Adivasis to common good, programme and ideology enunciated by the non-Adivasis.[9]

The Vedachi movement popularized khadi spinning, introduced education, promoted thrift and debt relief and tenancy reform. It brought economic benefits and 'strengthened the property-owning strata' among them. In fact a 'small committed and dedicated stratum of educated and education-oriented Adivasis with new outlook and aspirations',[10] had emerged, ready to act as agents of change in their own society.

Much the same pattern of development resulted from the operation of the reconstruction programme elsewhere in India and from the rise of autonomous movements for social reform among the tribes. In 1938, Gula Maharaj, a Bhil reformer, who worked as an ordinary labourer, urged his followers to give up drink, in Tolada *taluka* of Bombay.[11] His influence spread far and wide in the Bhil country.

The political aspect of the tribal urge for reform was brought out through their participation in the Kisan Sabha and Praja Mandal movements. The tribes who responded particularly to these movements were the Bhils, Gonds, Kharwars, Oraons, Mundas and Khonds. Most of them had a notion of property, private or communal, in land, which had been threatened by the colonial system and feudal exploitation. The agrarian issues which excited them were the demands for *begar* or *veth* (compulsory labour without payment), *rasad* or *mogan* (free supply of provisions for visiting officers), and exactions other than rent (*awabs*). Rent by itself was not a burning issue, because its incidence was very low in unsettled tribal areas (the exception being the Gangpur agitation against the enhanced rate of rent which lasted from 1939 to 1942); nor did eviction of tribal peasant exist on large scale. By the 1920s the process of the reclamation of tribes to 'civilization' had been almost completely implemented everywhere, and aided by economic factors, tribes in many parts of the country had settled down as agricultural communities which resented feudal exactions. The Kisan movement in Bihar and the Praja Mandal agitation in Orissa, although led by non-tribal people belonging to castes which were traditionally antipathetic towards the tribes, evoked support from the latter. The Khonds participated in the Praja Mandal agitation in 1939 which sought to secure agrarian and forest rights. The Kisan movement on the periphery of Chotanagpur agitated against feudal imposts. The Rajasthan Seva Mandal, and particularly its radical wing, organized the Bils and Jats against their feudal lords in the 1920s.

The leaders of the freedom movement in the tribal regions of the Central Provinces and the Bombay Presidency oriented their strategy to involve forest communities. Manufacturing salt was not as easy as violating the forest regulations. The no-rent payment campaign affected settled peasant communities, but the forest satyagraha in the 1930s involved the tribes, viz., the Korkus (Betul), Gonds (Mandla) and Kolis (Bombay). The forest satyagraha stemmed from the discontent caused by the restrictions on grazing rights, erosion of the traditional rights to take fuel and fodder from forests, and the oppression of forest officials. The leadership of this movement came from outside, but the tribal response was most enthusiastic. The incidents always turned violent despite the exhortations to remain non-violent, in characteristic tribal fashion. A Congress report said: 'The Gonds went in a mass to break forest laws. Here unfortunately the illiterate Gonds could not maintain the spirit of non-violence, and were successfully provoked by the police to some act of violence.' The Bhils acted similarly in 1922 and the Kolis in 1931 in Bombay.

While the tribals showed a penchant for protest movements, they had no interest in the sedate constitutional politics of the local and district boards in the 1920s and the 1930s. The Bhils and Gonds remained indifferent to the elections to these bodies, and had to be nominated to them. Even so, they were not interested in their deliberations and activities. In fact, this indifference born of ignorance was considered sufficient reason for perpetuating their backwardness through their exclusion from the operations of the Government of India Act of 1935 and for delaying their recognition as a *minority* in Indian politics.

By the 1940s tribal involvement in the freedom movement had become widespread, even though there was less manifestation of unrest than in 1930-2. Several regions of tribal middle-India, which had not been affected by the Civil Disobedience movement, felt the impact of the 'Quit India' movement. A typical example was found in Koraput. Lakshman Naik, a Bhumia, who had given up hunting and become a vegetarian under the influence of Gandhian ideology, offered satyagraha in 1939-40. He organized resistance to payment of taxes and led a march of the Bondo highlanders on 31 August 1942. They picketed liquor shops, and there was a scuffle in the course of which a forest guard was killed. Lakshman Naik was implicated in this case and hanged on 19 March 1943, even though he was universally believed to be innocent.[12]

It was not always the politics of the non-violent movement and social reform that interested the tribal people. The Koyas and Jatapus of the Agency area (Rampa) of the Madras Presidency participated in a rebellion or *fituri*[13] (1922-3) and guerilla warfare was waged by Alluri Sriram Raju (1898-1923) who sought to ovethrow the British Raj and set himself up as the Raja. A Kshatriya, he had acquired the reputation of a sanyasin, astrologer and magician which attracted the rural folk. Influenced by the non-cooperation movement, he preached temperance and the wearing of khadi which did not go down with the hill people. While there were factors of agrarian discontent arising from the restrictions on *pod* or shifting cultivation, extraction of forced labour and ill-treatment of coolies, the movement was essentially political designed to achieve independence. Raju, with the support of the Doras, the upper crust of tribal society, was able to establish a mass base for his movement. He took 'scrupulous care not to antagonise the people' and in turn enjoyed their support. He denounced the British officers and the police establishment but there were no 'incidents' involving the 'Indians'. The agrarian issue, which was relegated to the background, did not manifest itself in any attack on the money-lenders or the traders. The movement was suppressed, but Raju's martyrdom helped to strengthen the freedom movement in the Telugu region.

The north-eastern tribal region remained relatively free from the political influences of the kind that bore upon the tribal situation in middle-India. However, there were two exceptions. The movement launched by Jadunang[14] (1929-32) and the Riang movement led by Ratanmani, were structurally closer to the tribal movements in middle-India. Jadunang, like the leaders of tribal social movements elsewhere, started as a reformer and religious leader. He acquired a reputation as a mystic, healer, soothsayer and prophet. He preached monotheism, which alone could provide a base for unity among the tribes worshipping a multitude of spirits and deities. Gradually, his movement, which had turned revivalistic, developed political overtones, Jadunang had seen Gandhi when the latter visited Cachar in 1927 and even composed a song in his honour. This was the only apparent link with the national movement, but its impact appeared to be deeper. Jadunang called upon the people to disobey unjust laws, stop payment of taxes and refuse to render forced labour. The British Raj, it was rumoured, was coming to an end, and a Naga Raj under Jadunang would be established. (This has been the refrain of all tribal movements in middle-India, too.) Jadunang was captured and hanged on 29 August

1931. Rani Gaidinliu, who took over the leadership, established an even stronger link with the national movement. She was arrested and Jawaharlal Nehru sought to secure her release. He described her as the 'brave child of her hills, with the free spirit of the mountains in her, whose story India ought to know and to cherish.[15]

Like Jadunang, Ratanmani[16] started as a reformer and a *guru* among his people. 'The Riangs',[17] he would say, 'are simple and foolish. They do not know God and religion. Seeing this I decided to propagate the name of God among my people. Now many are reciting the name of God. They are thirsty for the message.'

He preached a form of Shaivism which brought him into conflict with the religion of the establishment, Vaishnavism. It did not take long for this religious movement to turn political (1942-3). Though it professed loyalty to the Maharaja of Tripura, the distant feudal lord, it demanded that the intermediate feudal structure consisting of the rais or the headmen be reformed, that they should be elected rather than nominated by the Maharaja, and that they cease to impose fines and collect taxes. Ratanmani set up an alternative government. He declared that he was a friend of the poor and it was therefore right to protect them against injustice. His followers disobeyed and defined traditional leaders, the rais and choudhuris, who exercised judicial powers and oppressed the people. Meanwhile, a famine had ravaged the land. Ratanmani's disciples set up a few grain depots in their villages to distribute grain. There were two instances in which the property of the Choudhuris was looted. The authorities apprehended resistance to the recruitment of the Riang youth for the army.

Over-zealous intelligence officers, alarmed at the possibilities of Japanese invasion, reported that Ratanmani and his followers had organized 'a revolutionary party consisting of 10 to 12 thousand workers...had committed treason and equipped with arms and ammunition, were robbing the rich of their valuable property'. They were also charged with forming a heinous conspiracy to dethrone the Maharaja, and place Ratanmani on the throne. Later reports, however, denied the existence of any fifth columnist conspiracy and dispelled the impression that Ratanmani was pro-Japanese. There was nothing to indicate the existence of any link with the freedom movement or with the I.N.A. With the Japanese knocking at the gate, the government felt that it could not afford to allow the movement to continue. It was put down by the army. Ratanmani was arrested; he was stated to have died of cholera in December 1943. A large number of his followers were hauled up and compelled to wear the sacred thread and to shave their heads in token of their reconversion to Vaishnavism.

We have briefly discussed the impact of the freedom movement on the tribal region and the attempts by small tribal movements to seek to identify themselves with it. There was also the countervailing process of the tribes moving away from the mainstream of national politics to seek a political identity of their own. The process of political separatism started as the era of constitutional reforms after the First World War dawned. Like some other communities, the tribes demanded special privileges. In the east, a Naga club was set up to formulate demands to be placed before the Simon Commission. Its political aspirations as reflected in the memoranda, did not go beyond the demand for the withdrawal of Nagaland from the framework of proposed constitutional reform and for continuation of direct British rule for the Nagas. This was not accepted, despite intensive lobbying by the British administrators in London. However, the Nagas did not give up. In the early 1940s they formulated a plan for the establishment of a Crown Colony.[18] This too did not make any headway.

The unfolding of these two developments—viz., tribal identification with the nationalist movement and the quest for a separate identity—suggests that political separatism in the north-east was not a force to be reckoned with until the beginning of the Second World War. Elsewhere in tribal India, a group of Bhils at the beginning of the Second World War demanded regional autonomy, but this was never followed up and no organization was set up to achieve it.[19]

A real movement for 'political separatism' developed in Chotanagpur.[20] This was the most advanced of the tribal regions in point of literacy, political consciousness and industrial progress. The major tribal communities were concentrated in a geographically distinct region; they were not split up like the Bhils and Gonds into different political and territorial systems. Christianity came in a big way to Chotanagpur; there was no other region of tribal India which witnessed such a spread of Christianity. As Christianity developed, it performed many roles; it gave to the tribes a sense of identity; it gave them a history and a myth; it created the notion of private property rights in land; it promoted education and medical care, and it also emphasized separateness from the rest. The Chotanagpur tribes had a tradition of militant and organized struggle, going back over a hundred years. The struggles were organized around land and not forests, as elsewhere. The incidence of proletarianization was small when compared with that among the Bhils. The tribal system had survived relatively intact in this region. There was also a rich corpus of anthropological literature to draw upon in order to create a new sense of history which could legitimize the tribal search for identity. Sarat Chandra Roy, the father of Indian anthropology, was not merely an anthropologist, but also the first active protagonist of the demand for tribal autonomy. He gave the first eloquent expression to the tribal demand for separation. Lastly, Chotanagpur was exposed to the operation of many interests. The Bengalis formed a sizeable professional and land owning community, and the Muslims were significant in trade and the professions. The Bengali-Bihari controversy over employment in the late 1930s and Muslim League politics affected the development of the tribal separatist movement.

We shall briefly describe the two phases through which the separatist movement developed. The first phase from 1916 to 1938 was dominated by the activities of the Chotanagpur Improvement Society. It was led by teachers and catechists and sought to secure employment for educated tribals, reservation in the services and legislative bodies and the formation of a sub-state joined to Bengal or Orissa. Though it sought to spread its activities among the villages, it remained essentially an urban, elitist movement. Nevertheless, it was able to focus the attention of the authorities on tribal problems. The Simon Commission and the government responded by seeking to solve them within the framework of the existing political structure.

During the period there was also a development of 'revivalism' among the tribes, very much on the lines of the Indian renaissance, stressing a return to the golden age and formulating an individualistic approach to self-reform and service of the community.

The second phase, from 1938 to 1947, saw the rise of a militant movement under the Adivasi Mahasabha. The immediate cause of the formation of the Mahasabha was the experience of the first elections held in 1937 under the Government of India Act of 1935. The Congress had swept the polls. This persuaded Christian and non-Christian tribals to close their ranks and form a joint body. The Chotanagpur Improvement Society merged with the Adivasi Mahasabha. Two other sources of influence on the Mahasabha were the Bengali-Behari controversy and Muslim League politics. The Bengalis felt that their interests in Bihar were not safe and, therefore, they could combine with the tribes to form a separate state. The Muslim League in the mid-1940s toyed with the idea of forming a corridor passing through the tribal areas to link East and West Pakistan. It sympathized with and gave financial support to the Adivasi Mahasabha. The Mahasabha was led by professional political workers, some of them highly educated and articulate. It became a Chotanagpur movement extending over both urban and rural areas, and involving tribes other than those of Ranchi. It demanded the formation not of a sub-state, but a complete separation from Bihar. A series of violent incidents occurred during this period to underline the militant nature of the movement. But by 1947 the militancy had failed to pay off. The Sabha was routed by the Congress in the first elections held in 1946. The link with the Muslim League was broken and the Bengali-Bihari controversy tapered off.

To conclude, tribal involvement in regional politics was deeper than is generally known; it was also more diverse, as it centred round specific issues concerning land and forests; its manifestation was often violent, despite the valiant attempts by the Bhagats to remain non-violent. Further, there was the process of Sanskritization. All this made for integration into the regional system. The process of integration, however, did not extend to the national level; tribal problems never figured in the resolutions passed at the Congress sessions; and few Indian leaders, with the exception of Mahatma Gandhi and Rajendra Prasad, showed any keen awareness of the tribal issue until the early 1940s. Tribal isolationism was the backlash of a sense of neglect and fear of losing identity; it was the characteristic response of backward communities at a certain stage of their development. In the typical social milieu of middle-India separatism did not develop into secessionism; ethnic separatism was only a passing phase until the movement developed a regional base.

—K.S. Singh

References

1. This paper, originally presented under the title 'From Movement to Party: A Study of the Tribal Politics in Middle India, 1920-63', at the Nehru Memorial Museum and Library on 29 March 1973, has been substantially revised with a new title. The latter part of the original paper dealing with tribal separatism has been developed into another article, 'From Ethnicity to Regionalism: A Study in Tribal Politics and Movements in Chotanagpur from 1900 to 1975', S.C. Malik (ed.) *Dissent, Protest and Reform in Indian Civilization* (Simla, 1977).
2. See J. Nehru, 'The Tribal Folk', in *The Tribal People of India* (New Delhi, 1955), p. 3.
3. P.C. Ganguly, 'Separatism in the Indian Polity: A Case Study', in M.C. Pradhan, R.D. Singh. P.K. Misra and D.B. Sastry (ed.), *Anthropology and Archeaology: Essays in Commemoration of Verrier Elwin,* 1902-64 (London, 1969), pp. 104-5.
4. The material for this paper, except where otherwise indicated, has been taken from the author's manuscript on 'Tribal Society' prepared under the Jawaharlal Nehru Fellowship award.
5. See the author's two papers on Gandhi's impact on the tribes, 'Haribaba Movement in Chotanagpur, 1931-32', in the *Journal of the Bihar Research Society,* vol. XLIX, Jan-Dec. 1963, and 'Mahatma Gandhi and Adivasis', *Man in India,* Jan-March 1963.
6. Hiralal Shukla, *Baster Ke Van Vasi: Geeton men Gandhi* (Raipur, 1969).
7. I.P. Desai and B.L. Choudhary, *History of Rural Development in Modern India,* vol. II (New Delhi, 1977).
8. Ibid., p. 47.
9. Ibid. p. 54.
10. Ibid. p. 139.
11. See S.V. Thakar, *Bhilla Sadhu Sri Gula Maharaj Charitra Wa Karya* (Pune, 1938), in Marathi.
12. Nityanand Das, 'Martyr Lakshman Naik: A Hero of the Freedom Movement', *Adivasi,* vol. IX, no. 1, 1967-8, p. 22-8.
13. Rampa disturbances, See Hapell's report, G.O. no. 572, 23 July 1923, Public Deptt., Govt. of Madras (Hyderabad Archives).
14. See *Jadunang: A Freedom Fighter of Manipur, A Commemorative volume on the occasion of the 41st death anniversary of Jadunang, 29th August, 1971,* (Imphal, 1971); A. Kumar Nag, *Rani Gaidinliu: Study of the Jadunang Movement of the Nagas* (Silchar, 1976); and R. Mahadevan, 'Zeliangrang Naga Uprising of 1930-32: a brief summary', *Proceedings of the Indian History Congress, Thirty-fifth Session* (Calcutta, 1978), p. 253-9. The Anthropological Survey of India has conducted a field study of this movement, which will be published in a volume on contemporary tribal movements edited by the author of this paper.
15. J. Nehru, *Unity of India* (London, 1948), pp. 187-8.
16. See File No. 226-P(S) 43, 1943, Political Deptt., Political Branch, 'Criminal activities in Tripura State of Ratanmani Naotia' (National Archives of India);

T.M. Das Gupta, 'Riang Vidroh 1943' *Tripura Prasanga* (Govt. Printing Press, May 1977), p. 36-50; and T.C. Sen, *Tripura in Transition* (1923-1957), (Agartala, 1970). Tarit Mohan Das Gupta contributes an eyewitness account.

17. The Riangs are a small tribe; according to the Census of 1951 they numbered 38, 556. See also B. Mukherjee, 'The Riangs', *Bulletin of the Department of the Anthropological Survey of India,* vol. VIII, January 1959.
18. Asoso Yonuo, *Rising Nagas* (Delhi, 1974), pp. 132-40.
19. A.N. Dyakov, *The National Problem in India Today* (Moscow, 1966), p. 167.
20. For a detailed discussion, see the author's article, 'From Ethnicity to Regionalism', op. cit.

10

Muslim Nationalism and Freedom Struggle

It goes without saying that even after three decades of India's partition (1947) we do not yet have a definitive study of the foundations of Muslim nationalism which led to it. Indeed, as far as Indian scholars are concerned, they have consistently avoided even the use of the term 'Muslim Nationalism', and have preferred to use in its place 'Muslim Separatism' or 'Muslim Communalism'. It seems to the present author that the movement which ultimately ended with the partition of India and the birth of Pakistan has as much claim to be called a nationalist movement as the one which led to the achievement of India's independence. Only its basis was different. While the movement for independence was based on a territorial approach to nationalism, seeking to embrace in its fold all who inhabited the country regardless of their race or religion, the movement for partition was based on a communal approach and sought to embrace in its fold all who professed the Islamic faith and were hence supposed to belong to the Muslim community. At this stage the problem of defining nationalism can be raised, but this need not really hold us up. In the wide world there have been all varieties of nationalism and it is no one's case that the boundary of a nationalist movement always coincides with the boundary of a country, particularly when that country has been under foreign rule for a long time and been riven by differences among various groups based on region and/or religion. It is, of course, true that the leaders of Indian nationalism did not recognise any other movement as a nationalist movement, but three decades after the achievement of independence we can take a dispassionate view and recognise that along with Indian nationalism, the forces of Hindu nationalism and Muslim nationalism also operated during the period of struggle for independence. Indian nationalism was able to defeat Hindu nationalism, but was defeated by Muslim nationalism.

What is, however, important is not which term we use to describe the movement which led the struggle for India's partition and the birth of Pakistan, but how we explain its emergence and the strength it acquired in a comparatively short span of time. For success in this endeavour it is necessary to take a total or comprehensive view of the Indian situation in the second half of the nineteenth century. Such a view must include both the socio-economic position of the Muslim masses as well as elite at that time and the factor which shaped their outlook. While the importance of the former has been generally recognised,[1] among the latter importance has so far been given mostly to British colonial policy and to some extent also to the upsurge of Hindu revivalism and nationlism,[2] the ethos of Indian nationalism,[3] and the strategy adopted by the Indian National Congress.[4] Some have seen the struggle for power between the Hindu and Muslim elites as the main factor behind the rise of Muslim nationalism.[5] The various phases of the interaction between the Congress and the Muslims have also been dealt with in a number of studies.[6] Beyond this, while some attention has been given to the role of historical writings in fanning the flames of communalism,[7] so far as the actual subject of those writings is concerned that has either been ignored or distorted. Yet since Hindus and Muslims had lived together in India for several centuries before the second half of the nineteenth century and since the Muslim elite has always shown special regard for historical traditions and history-writing, it should not require much argument to convey the point that such traditions would have had some role to play in shaping its mind. We shall take up soon the works of those who have misinterpreted or distorted the history of Hindu-Muslim interaction prior to the second half of the nineteenth century, but we must first deal with those who tend to ignore this history completely and assume that the emergence of Muslim nationalism can be explained without any reference to it.

Since it is a part of a general tendency to pay almost exclusive attention to socio-economic factors, plus, of course, the role of colonialism to explain major developments in modern Indian history on the assumption that this is in line with the tenets of Marxian historiography, it may be pertinent to recall here that Lukacs, one of the most perceptive theoreticians of such historiography, has to say on this point:

> It is not the primacy of economic motives in historical explanation that constitutes the decisive difference between Marxism and bourgeois thought, but the point of view of totality. The category of totality, the all-pervasive supremacy of the whole over the parts is the essence of the method which Marx took over from Hegel and brilliantly transformed into the foundations of a wholly new science.[8]

In a commentary on the ideas propounded by Lukacs it has been observed:

> In a mechanical conception there is a clear-cut line of demarcation between 'determined' and its 'determinants'. Not so within the framework of a dialectical methodology. In terms of the latter: although the economic foundations of capitalist society constitute the 'ultimate determinants' of the social being, these 'ultimate determinants' are at the same time also 'determined determinants'. In other words, Marx's assertions about the ontological significance of economics become meaningful only if we are able to grasp his idea of 'complex interactions' in the most varied fields of human activity...'Economic determinations' do not exist outside the historically changing complex of specific mediations, including the most spiritual ones.[9]

We may also recall in this connection the following observation of Gramsci:

> The claim, presented as an essential postulate of historical materialism, that every fluctuation of politics and ideology can be presented and expounded as an immediate expression of the structure, must be contested in theory as primitive infantilism, and combated in practice with the authentic testimony of Marx, the author of concrete historical and political works. Particularly important from this point of view are *The 18th Brumaire* and the writings on the Eastern Question, but also other writings....[10]

In *The Eighteenth Brumaire of Louis Bonaparte* we come across the following, oft-quoted lines by Marx:

> Men make their own history, but they do not make it just as they please; they do not make it under circumstances chosen by themselves, but under circumstances directly encountered, given and transmitted from the past. The tradition of all the dead generations weighs like a nightmare on the brain of the living.[11]

The same point has been recently emphasised in a quite competent formulation of Marxist methodology for understanding politics:

> At any rate, the enduring and pervasive importance of traditional ways, in a multitude of areas, is not in doubt, even in circumstances of very rapid economic, social and political change. Some of these ways are so deeply woven into the texture of life that they can survive more or less indefinitely without visible means of support and under conditions of extreme adversity.[12]

Enough has been said, it is hoped, to establish the point that it will be impossible to understand the foundations of Muslim nationalism in pre-independence India without having a proper understanding of the historical traditions of the Indian Muslims, more particularly of their elite.

II

We must at the same time guard against the tendency among many Indian as well as Pakistani historians to explain the emergence of Muslim nationalism on the basis of a centuries-old conflict or, at any rate, antipathy between two antagonistic cultures or ways of life. Among the Pakistani historians perhaps the most forceful exponent of this view is Hafeez Malik who asserts that the pattern of relations between the Hindus and Muslims ever since they came into mutual contact has been one of conflict. Assuming the existence of two nations in India since the medieval times he remarks:

> It is true that the people who now comprise India and Pakistan have lived together for the last twelve hundred years. However, it was not by mutual consent, nor do they share memories of a common heritage. On the contrary... Hindus and Muslims have different traditions and historical backgrounds. Both have

independent histories of which each is proud. When their histories began to overlap in India, each nation interpreted the events and movements through its own glasses. This is a process which has continued down to the present day. Each nation has its own heroes who are honoured. More often than not the heroes of one are the foes of the other.[13]

Ishtiaq Husain Qureshi is another firm upholder of this view. He refers to the hope that since Hindus and Muslims had lived together they would have a common desire for national unity, and that Muslims would be reconciled to the role of a religious minority and identify themselves fully with the Indian nation, and remarks: "Such hopes were built upon the most deplorable ignorance of the psychology of the Muslim community, of the thinking of its leaders and masses, and of the history of its origins, developments and integration." As a result of this ignorance, he further adds, "When history asserted itself and the Muslims claimed to be a nation, many were surprised and not a few even scandalized."[14] Elsewhere he writes that the hope of Hindus and Muslims joining together in a common nationhood was based on "the fallacious assumption that the Muslims of the sub-continent had everything in common with the Hindus except their religion. The situation in fact was that the two peoples had little in common."[15]

Although Khalid B. Sayeed (now a Canadian citizen) presents a more balanced picture of the factors responsible for the creation of Pakistan and lays particular stress on their "multiplicity". He also goes on to affirm that "perhaps a dominant or decisive cause of Pakistan is that there has never taken place a confluence of the two civilisations in India—the Hindu and the Muslim. They may have meandered towards each other here and there, but on the whole the two have flowed their separate courses—sometimes parallel and sometimes contrary to one another."[16]

K.K. Aziz adopts a somewhat similar approach,. While commenting upon the period of Mughal rule he remarks: "Persian became the language of the court and, in conjunction with the Hindu languages, gave pitch and point to Urdu. Islamic forms of architecture mingled with the Hindu tradition and flowered into the glorious Indo-Islamic art of the builder."[17] Unlike Malik and Qureshi, he does not assert that the Muslims had been a nation in India ever since the beginning of the period of the so-called Muslim rule here, but admits that the idea of a separate Muslim nationality in India developed much later during the period of the Indian nationalist movement.

As he puts it:

> The formulation of the idea of a Muslim nationality in India started with a relatively small nucleus. Then its influence slowly spread until it reached millions of people. The idea originated with a few individual leaders in various realms of mental and intellectual activity: a Sayyid Ahmed Khan here, an Ameer Ali there, a Shibli at one time, an Iqbal at another. Gradually the different strands of Muslim life and culture in the sub-continent were synthesized. The image of Muslim India took shape, an image which was simultaneously the cause and the effect of an increasingly coherent intellectual life. The ideals of a culturally united community and of a socially consistent society were accepted by the masses. They were also persuaded of the fact that they shared the same historical background. Thus were laid the foundations of a separate nationalism.[18]

However, while discussing the cultural factors he also characterises the Hindu-Muslim interaction as "a clash of two civilizations".

> The Hindu-Muslim conflict was not merely religious. It was the clash of two civilizations, of two peoples who had different languages, different literary roots, different ideas of education, different philosophical sources, and different concepts of art. Such a yawning cultural gulf was enough to destroy any affinity which the two peoples might have had and to bring to nought all efforts at unity. When this cultural variance was combined with diversity in social customs and modes of livelihood the emergence of a united Indian nationalism was doomed without redemption.[19]

Aziz Ahmad sounds a dispassionate note in his preface to his book dealing with Muslim society and culture in India during the medieval period:

> Hindu and Muslim religions, civilisations and ways of life coexisted together for well over a thousand years, undergoing alternating or simultaneous processes of mutual attraction and repulsion. Neither the attraction nor the repulsion constitutes the whole story, which is interwoven in an infinite pattern of points and

counter-points.[20]

However, in the very next sentence he moves on to refer to the "long story of divided co-existence of Hindus and Muslims in India, leading to divided existence as India and Pakistan in the twentieth century..." It must be said to his credit that he sets before himself as motto Herbert Butterfield's famous observation: "The historian seeks to explain how the past came to be turned into the present, but there is a very real sense in which the only explanation he can give is to unfold the whole story and to reveal the complexity by telling it in detail."[21] This he faithfully follows, but does not hide his own view according to which "The history of medieval and modern India is to a very considerable extent a history of Hindu-Muslim religio-cultural tensions, interspersed with movements or individual efforts at understanding, harmony and even composite developments."[22] This is, of course, slightly different from the views of Malik and Qureshi.

The same can be said about the views of another leading Pakistani historian, S.M. Ikram. Although he recognises that for practical purposes, "the gradual crystallisation and realisation of the idea of Pakistan is related to the period of the British rule", he argues with the view that "the ground for Muslim separatism was prepared when Islam entered the sub-continent, and all efforts to provide a bridge between the Hindus and the Muslims failed."[23] Elsewhere, he quotes an observation of a leading Indian historian to the effect that between the Hindus and Muslims, "the social and religious differences were so acute and fundamental that they raised a Chinese wall between the two communities, and even seven hundred years of close residence (including two of common servitude) have failed to make the least crack in that solid and massive structure, far less demolishing it." Apparently accepting this view Ikram comments: "It was this dividing wall which led, in 1947, to the partitioning of the sub-continent."[24]

The Indian historian referred to by Ikram was, of course, R.C. Majumdar,[25] but before we come to analyse his views, we may refer to K.M. Panikkar, perhaps the first among India's leading historians to propound the theory of clash between the two communities on the basis of religion and culture In a well-known book published in the same year which witnessed both India's independence and partition, he remarked:

> The main result of the introduction of Islam as a religion into India was the division of society on a vertical basis. Before the thirteenth century, Hindu society was divided horizontally, and neither Buddhism nor Jainism affected this division. They were not unassimilable elements and fitted in easily with the existing divisions. Islam, on the other hand, split Indian society into two sections from top to bottom and what has now come to be known in the phraseology of today as two separate nations came into being from the beginning. Two parallel societies were established on the same soil. At all stages they were different and hardly any social communication or intermingling of life existed between them.[26]

Another leading Indian historian, Tara Chand, had analysed the nature of Hindu-Muslim interactions during the medieval period earlier, at a time when the Indian nationalist movement was engaged in propagating the theory of the existence of a composite culture in India, based largely on a positive interchange between Hindus and Muslims, and lent strong support to that theory. He wrote:

> The Muslims who came to India made it their home. They lived surrounded by the Hindu people and a state of perennial hostility with them was impossible. Mutual intercourse led to mutual understanding. Many who had changed their faith differed little from those whom they had left. Thus after the first shock of conquest was over, the Hindus and Muslims prepared to find a *via media* whereby to live as neighbours. The effort to seek a new life led to the development of a new culture which was neither exclusively Hindu nor purely Muslim. It was indeed a Muslim-Hindu culture. Not only did Hindu religion, Hindu art, Hindu literature and Hindu science absorb Muslim elements, but the very spirit of Hindu culture and the very stuff of Hindu mind were also altered, and the Muslim reciprocated by responding to the change in every department of life.[27]

In the wake of India's partition, however, the author of these lines perhaps realised that they presented too romantic a view of the interaction of Hindus and Muslims during the medieval period. In an article written over a decade after partition he almost swings to the other side and seeks to find a philosophical basis for the event. He writes:

While the Hindu mind was primarily concerned with what is true, the Muslim was exercised over what is right. The Hindu emphasised the private and personal aspects of religious experience, the Muslim its incorporation in the collective body of the faithful. The Hindu was inclined to gloss over the shortcomings of his social customs, the Muslim was annoyed with them. On the other hand, the intolerance of the Muslim and the memory of the past distressed the Hindu. The Hindu felt no kinship with the Arab past which the Muslim hugged to his bosom. The Muslim did not feel at home in Vedic India. While consciousness of group developed, and the element of territoriality was present in both, the content of the two did not quite coincide and fuse.[28]

The historian who became most famous for his opposition to the theory of the emergence of a composite Indian culture during the medieval period was R.C. Majumdar. In this he was helped by some of his critics who labelled him a communalist historian. Whatever that may be , he consistently held on to his view and gave expression to it in a number of his writings. At one place he admits that Hindus and Muslims did influence each other in various ways, but asserts that this merely affected the externals and did not touch the hard core of their separate cultures. As he puts it:

> Of course, it would be nothing short of a miracle if two communities could live side by side for seven centuries without being affected in the least by mutual contact. As a matter of fact we find the common people of both communities sharing each other's primitive beliefs and superstitions, reverence for saints and popular festivals, folksongs, popular pastimes and some minor social customs and etiquette, including dress which did not encroach upon the religious faith of either. Individuals of both the communities learnt each other's language and literature and even composed books. There was a slight degree of reciprocal influence in civil architecture. The evolution of the Urdu language and introduction of some new musical tunes exhibit such influence at its highest. Most of these, however, were very trivial, and concerned the externals without affecting in any way the essential elements of culture. Where such elements were affected, as, for example, the liberal religious

thoughts and beliefs propagated by the Sufis and religious leaders like Kabir and Nanak, the number of persons who adopted them formed a microscopic minority, less than two per cent, who never made any impact on the people at large, and this religious liberalism slowly ebbed away without leaving any deep impression on either community.

Apparently, Majumdar considers religion as constituting the hard core of culture in medieval times and this created the main dividing line between the two communities. He continues:

> The steel frame of religion and society, which sustained the fundamental structure of medieval culture and civilisation, remained unchanged both among the Hindus and the Muslims. The worship of images which formed the most cherished element in the religious beliefs of the Hindus was an anathema in the eyes of the Muslims, and the long tradition of ruthless desecration of temples by them for nearly a thousand years formed a wide gulf between the two. The method of congregational prayer among the Muslims was a thing unknown to the Hindus, and the ceremonial worship of the Hindus to the accompaniment of music, both vocal and instrumental, was not only alien to the Muslims but positively distasteful and irksome to them.[29]

Indeed, according to Majumdar, the gulf created by religion was so wide that "the Hindus entertained a much greater degree of hostility or repugnance to Muslim than to British rule". It is this which explains the paradox of so little Muslim impact on Hindus culture compared to the impact created by the British on the same culture in spite of the much shorter duration of the latter's rule. "The exigencies of subjection to Muslim rule might force the Hindus to learn Arabic and Persian and adopt court-dress and etiquette, but very little of Islamic culture that was not demanded by absolute necessity for livelihood or personal safety would appeal to them. A man does not seek to learn anything from those who are repulsive to him."[30] And such repulsion was mutual. That is why "neither the Hindus nor the Muslims imbibed, even to the least degree, the chief characteristic features of the other's culture which may be regarded as their greatest contribution to human civilisation." Thus the Hindus continued to combine "catholicity in religious outlook with bigotry in social ethics", while the Muslims continued to display "an equal bigotry in religious ideas with catholocity in social behaviour."[31] Even in Bengal, where Hindus and Muslims shared a common language, "they differed in almost everything except language."[32]

In a recent study Professor Niharranjan Ray has presented a much more sophisticated analysis of Hindu-Muslim interaction during the medieval period than R.C. Majumdar, but his conclusion is in some respects quite similar to the latter's. He affirms that at certain levels of relationship Hindus were imbued with hatred against the Muslims, "but this was not because the Muslims were alien or foreign (the converts, who formed by far the largest number of the community, certainly were not), but because in Islam the Hindus had found for the first time a religion and a way of life that admitted of no compromise, were militant and aggressive in its (sic) behaviour pattern and aimed at controlling the entire area of man's life including the political and the economic."[33] He does not deny that at certain levels the elites of the two communities came into mutual contact, but, partly echoing Majumdar emphasises that "at this level the basis of relation between the two communities was one of mutual interests dominated by political and economic, that is, pragmatic considerations, not that of any attempt at mutual understanding." Again, like Majumdar, Ray thinks that the adaptations to each other's cultures resulting from such contacts did not touch the fundamentals of these cultures but were confined to the external aspects of life and, besides, did not have any wide impact. He writes:

> We have thus the curious examples of feudal Hindu princesses married to Muslim kings, emperors and nobles, pursuing their own religious rites and performances and living their own way of life in their own apartments in Muslim *harems,* yet sharing the bed of their Muslim husbands and bringing forth their offsprings to inherit their power and property, all but unaffected by the faith and the way of life of their husbands. It must, however, be recognised that because of such close association the Hindus and the Muslims were both obliged to adopt and adapt themselves to certain external features of life and patterns of social behaviour from each other's repertory of culture, the Hindus more than the Muslims, for various reasons without doubt. But this was mostly confined to matters of food and dress, civil manners, courtly etiquettes and fashions, tastes, and predilections, fort and palace

architecture and certain arts like court-painting and court-music, both meant for the delectation of feudal tastes and sensibilities. The impact of this composite culture was nowhere very wide and never penetrated very deep because of the hierarchical gradations in which both Hindu and Muslim societies were organised and of the tight bureaucratic and aristocratic character of the Hindu and Muslim nobility.[34]

Needless to add, British historians have generally emphasised the antithetical character of Hinduism and Islam and their mutual repulsion. According to F.W. Thomas, Islam represents the "very antithesis of Hinduism."[35] Murray Titus writes: "For twelve long centuries Islam has been in contact with Hinduism in India. For twelve centuries each community has been confronted by the other."[36] Perceval Spear has emphasised that in Hindu-Muslim interaction in India "the principle of repulsion has been more obviously at work than the principle of attraction."[37] In a more dispassionate vein he writes:

> The two bodies remained distinct for nine centuries, yet with so much intimate contact there was bound to be some mutual influence.... Some of it was important but on neither side was it fundamental ....
>
> There was much give and take, but no fusion or synthesis. In daily life there was much day-to-day tolerance and consideration, but behind it all was a permanent tension between the two ways of life. Indo-Persian culture spread a mantle of elegance, over the whole of Indian aristocratic society, but Hinduism and Islam remained apart.[38]

III

These are all eminent authorities. Yet the present author finds it difficult to accept the theory of a perpetual conflict between Hindus and Muslims during the medieval period because of their differences in religion and culture. Indeed, the contrary can be proved on the basis of information and analysis provided by some of the protagonists of the 'Chinese Wall' theory themselves. We propose to do so with reference to the works of one Pakistani (S.M. Ikram) and one Indian (K.M. Panikkar) historian.

To begin with Ikram, we learn from his account that Amir Khusrau (c. 1253-1325), the most distinguished writer of the early

Sultanate period, famous for his Persian poetry, was "also among the earliest writers of Hindi poetry." We are further told that it were the Muslim rulers of some of the regional kingdoms "who were responsible for many of the first translations of the Sanskrit classics into the provincial languages." Among the examples are the translation of the *Ramayana,* the *Mahabharata* and the *Bhagavata Puran* into Bengali under the patronage of Sultan Husain Shah (r. 1493-1518). In Kashmir Zain-ul-Abidin (1420-1470) patronised the study of "Hindu literature and philosophy". It was at this time that *Rajataranjini* was translated into Persian. The state records of Golkunda and Bijapur were maintained in Marathi. The interaction in the field of music, begun at the time of the Arab conquest of Sind, continued during the period of the Sultanate and became "even more fruitful when the rich heritage of Persia and Central Asia was added." All this resulted in the creation of a new form of music in North India, "quite different from the traditional Indian music, which maintained its hold in South India." There was a parallel development in the field of architecture, the greatest artistic achievement of the Sultanate period. "As with the musicians, the creativity of the Muslim architects was nourished by the mature styles of both the existing Islamic and Hindu traditions."[39]

When we come to consider the interaction in the field of religious faith and practice, the task according to Ikram, becomes more complicated, partly because of lack of evidence, for the religious movements of medieval India have left few records, and partly because of the uncertainty "whether a pattern of behaviour and belief in both religions has a common origin in one, or if it grew up independently in both cultures." The exact nature of relationship between the Hindu and Islamic mystical movements for instance, becomes very difficult to delineate because of this factor. The same applies to an evaluation of the role of Islam in the emergence of the Bhakti movements. All the Bhakti movements cannot be described as sympathetic to Islam. The movement started by Chaitanya (1485-1533) in Bengal was certainly not. But this could not be said about the movements associated with Kabir, Guru Nanak or Dadu. Kabir, whose dates are uncertain but who is generally supposed to have flourished in the middle of the fifteenth century, was "probably the most influential" among the religious leaders of the period covered by the Sultanate. He denounced polytheism, idolatory and caste, but was equally unsparing in his denunciation of Muslim formalism and also made no distinction between what he considered sane and holy in Hinduism and Islam. "He was a true seeker of God, and did his best to break the barriers that separated Hindus from Muslims." Similarly, Guru Nanak (1469-1539) aimed at uniting Hindus and Muslims "through an appeal to what he considered the great central truths of both." Dadu (1544-1603) was another important religious leader "through whose teachings Islamic ideas found wide currency among non-Muslims". As far as Namadeva (late fourteenth or early fifteenth century) and Tukaram (1598-1649) the two famous poet-saints of Maharashtra are concerned their songs clearly suggest that they were to reacting in any hostile fashion to Islam."[40]

If Islam influenced Hinduism, Hinduism too influenced Islam. This process had begun even before the establishment of the Delhi Sultanate. This is proved by the probable Hindu element in certain forms of Islamic mysticism, and the intellectual interchanges that had taken place after the conquest of Sind in the seventh and eighth centuries." During the Sultanate changes of a different order took place. While traces of Hinduism in Muslim religious practices, particularly among the lower classes, may be taken as an illustration of "incomplete change from the old way of life", in social life "Indian Islam retained certain characteristic features of Hindu society which, if not religious in themselves, certainly had been given religious sanction". Thus there developed among the Muslims something similar to the caste system among the Hindus "with converts clinging to some memory of their former status in a hierarchical society, while what may be called Muslim castes developed as Indian Muslims (of the upper classes) classified themselves as Sayid, Shaikh, Mughal, or Pathan." The structure of caste in the Muslim society was, of course, never as rigid as among the Hindus. Whatever that may be, this did not exhaust the Hindu impact on the social life of the Muslims. The latter, for instance, adopted from the former the custom of early marriages and objection to widow remarriage. The same was the case with certain ceremonies connected with births, deaths and marriages.[41]

Nor was there a Chinese wall between Hindus and Muslims in the economic and political fields. During the Arab occupation of Sind Hindus had been appointed to high administrative positions. Hindus also occupied high military positions at the court of Mahmud of Ghazni famous in history as an inonoclast. During the early days of the Sultanate, the high administrative and military positions were occupied only by Turkish nobles and Muslims of Indian origin were also kept at a distance along with Hindus. As the situation became less rigid later on and Muslims of Indian origin began to secure high administrative positions, Hindu nobles also followed them. In some of the regional kingdoms they were even appointed as ministers. Though the number of Hindus in high administrative and military positions was much smaller than that of Muslims, they generally outnumbered the latter in the lower positions. In trade and commerce they continued to maintain their dominant position.[42] Although the Sultan was supposed to be the defender of the faith, the Delhi Sultanate was not a theocracy and the rulers took decisions on vital matters with reference to the needs of the situation and not to the principles of the *Sharia.*[43] The Hindus did have to pay *jizya*, but they were exempt from *Zakat*, which the Muslims alone had to pay. Besides, the Hindus who paid *jizya* were exempt from military service.[44]

The friendly interaction between the Hindus and Muslims reached its high water-mark under Akbar, the great Mughal (1556-1605). He abolished *jizya,* imposed a ban on cow slaughter and employed Hindu nobles to some of the highest offices in the State, though of course Muslims continued to be employed to such positions in much larger numbers. In the fields of architecture, painting, music and literature the close collaboration between artists and writers of the two communities continued to grow. One of Akbar's famous generals, Abdur Rahim, following in the footsteps of earlier Muslim poets of Hindi like Jayasi and Kabir, made a significant contribution to Hindi poetry and also extended his patronage to a number of Hindi poets.

The trend set by Akbar was continued by his two successors Jehangir and Shahjahan (1605-1657), and indeed reached its climax during the last years of the latter's reign when his eldest son Dara Shikoh (the translator of the *Upanishads* into Persian) had the upper hand. In the meanwhile, however, a reaction has set in and this reached a climax with the accession of Aurangzeb (1658-1707), famous for his championship of orthodoxy. But even during the period of his rule while the *jizya* was reimposed after a lapse of about a hundred years and the Hindus were subject to discriminatory customs duties

(5 per cent as against 2 per cent for Muslims), the general policy of collaboration between Hindus and Muslims in the political and cultural fields was continued. Thus Hindus continued to be appointed to the highest positions in the State; both on the civil and the military sides. Indeed there were more Hindu officers under Aurangzeb than under any other Mughal emperor.[45] Trade and commerce also continued to be generally in the hands of Hindu merchants.[46] It is revealing of the spirit of the times that next to Persian, which was the court language, "the language which received the greatest patronage at court was Hindi." Akbar began the practice of appointing a Hindi *Kavi Raj* (poet laureate) along with the Persian *Malik-ul-Saura* and this was continued even by Aurangzeb.[47]

It is doubtful whether Aurangzeb issued a general order calling for the destruction of all Hindu temples. Originally such orders applied to a few specific cases. At a later stage he did try to "enforce strict Islamic law by ordering the destruction of newly built Hindu temples. Later, the procedure was adopted of closing down rather than destroying the newly built temples in Hindu localities." Often such orders remained unimplemented. That numerous Hindu temples were built in certain areas, e.g. in Bengal, during the period of his rule shows that Aurangzeb's "alleged ceaseless campaign of temple destruction obviously could have been neither thoroughgoing nor universal."[48]

We need not dilate further on this point. What has been written above, based on information supplied by Ikram, should be enough to show that while there is evidence to show occasional tension and conflict between segments of the elites of the Hindu and Muslim communities, there is no evidence of the existence of a Chinese wall between them based on differences of religion and culture. On the other hand, there is abundant evidence of close collaboration between the two in various fields of human endeavour. Such evidence naturally affects Ikram's own conclusion. He, of course, keeps clinging to the Chinese wall theory wherever possible and points to instances of conflict here and there between Hindus and Muslims, but as there is not much material on this point he fails to produce such instances in any large number. Even so, he makes the following observation on the nature of the Hindu-Muslim interaction during the period of the Sultanate:

> More striking than the amount of interaction that took place in the first three centuries of Muslim rule was the fact that there was not more. The impression one gains is that there was never a very conscious attempt to create understanding except on the part of Kabir and Nanak, and that the contact between the two great religions were, on the whole, remarkably superficial as far as the total life of the country was concerned.[49]

Yet as Ikram proceeds further and surveys Indian life and culture during the Mughal period, he finds himself overwhelmed by facts which point to a contrary conclusion. It is a tribute to his integrity as a scholar that he makes no effort to resist this conclusion, although it obviously contradicts Majumdar's Chinese wall theory which he has adopted:

> Any generalization about Indian history is dangerous, but the impression one gains from looking at social conditions during the Mughal period is of a society moving towards an integration of its manifold political regions, social systems, and cultural inheritances. The greatness of the Mughals consisted in part at least in the fact that the influence of their court and government permeated society, giving it a new measure of harmony.

Again, in his final summing up, he emphasises the importance of the Indian component in Islam's culture heritage. Surveying "the ten centuries of Muslim rule" he identifies four main strands "that have given Indo-Islamic culture its characteristic texture": the Islamic religious inheritance including aspects rooted in Arabic tradition, the Turkish origin of many of the rulers, the impact of Persian culture, and the indigenous environment in Afghanistan as well as India. Then he pens the final epitaph of the Chinese Wall theory in these words:

> There has been a tendency to overlook this indigenous component, but its influence is deep-rooted and all-pervading. The predominantly non-Muslim environment in which Indo-Muslim culture developed, and the heritage of an ancient civilisation did not leave Islam untouched. Furthermore, the vast majority of the Muslims were... Hindu converts, which shows (itself) not only in numerous usages and practices carried over from the ancestral Hindu society, but also in unconscious reactions and mental attitudes. The vigorous Islamic revival of later centuries has tended to overshadow the indigenous element.

> While the Turkish rulers and aristocracy contributed much in the sphere of government, law, dress, and food, and the Persian element was prominent in literature, fine arts, mysticism, and philosophy, essentially the two basic components which gave the civilisation its peculiar flavour were the Indian and the Islamic.[50]

IV

What has been said about Ikram applies with equal force to Panikkar. Although as shown above, he sees the existence of two separate nations in India almost from the beginning of the thirteenth century with "hardly any social communication or intermingling of life" between them, while actually describing the political and social conditions in India during the medieval period, he himself provides profuse evidence of close contact and collaboration between the two. Thus he writes about the conditions of Hindus under the Delhi Sultanate:

> We shall get a very inaccurate and altogether false view of the situation of the Hindus during the first period of Islamic Empire in Hindustan (1210-1370), if we depend on the court chronicles and analysts of Delhi. Historians like Barani were principally anxious to picture their heroes as the patrons of Islamic orthodoxy and virtue. The stories of temples desecrated, idols broken and Hindus converted or massacred which they relate, must, therefore, be read in the light of their desire to show to an orthodox Islamic world, for which they wrote, the glory of these monarchs and their zeal in dealing with the *Kafir*.[51]

Proceeding further Panikkar tells us that although in the period of conquest Hindus had undoubtedly to suffer, they being deprived of political power in large areas, their religion held in contempt and their temples destroyed, after the first flush of conquest was over "the structure of economic life in the country forced even the most jealous and fanatical of kings to moderate this policy." Thus the cultivating classes remained largely Hindu as the invaders had not brought cultivators with them. Nor did trade and commerce change hands to any considerable extent and the Hindu *bania* continued to occupy an important place in the social structure. Even in the field of religion an ethos of toleration and mutual respect developed quite early. There is indeed ample evidence that "even under the most bigoted kings, like Allauddin Khilji and Firoz Tughlaq, the Hindu religious leaders received honour and recognition." Also the Hindus, from the very beginning of the Sultanate, provided the bulk of the lower bureaucracy, though, of course, the Muslims occupied the higher positions. "The *patwaris,* the accountants, the treasurers and others in the districts were invariably Hindu, while the governors and district officials were Muslim."[52] Writing about the architectural achievements of the Sultanate period, Panikkar observes: "The Indo-Muslim style is a complete harmonisation of the artistic spirit of Hinduism and Islam and nowhere does it become more clear than in the mosques at Ahmedabad and Jaunpur. The architects were no doubt Muslims but the mortar-builders and craftsmen continued to be Hindus."[53] In the filed of literature he underlines the encouragement given to local talent by Muslim rulers and notes that Maladhar Basu's Bengali translation of the *Bhagavata* was undertaken at the order of Nusrat Shah and Kavindra Paramashwar's translation of the *Mahabharata* at that of Paragal Khan, a general of Hussain Shah.[54] And what could be greater evidence of Amir Khusro's love for Hindi than his declaration that it was "in some ways ruler and more flexible than Persian."[55] In the field of religion we are told that Islam had a great impact upon Hinduism:

> One thing is clear. Islam had a profound effect on Hinduism during this period. Medieval Hindu theism is in some ways a reply to the attack of Islam and the doctrines of medieval traders, by whatever names their gods are known, are essentially theistic. It is the one supreme God that is the object of the devotee's adoration and it is to His grace that we are asked to look for redemption. All Bhakti cults are, therefore, essentially monotheistic, not in the exclusive sense that other devotees cannot worship the same Supreme Being under other names, but in the affirmative sense that whether known as Siva, Krishna or Devi, they all symbolise the one and the Eternal.[56]

In his survey of the Mughal period Panikkar naturally finds much greater contact and collaboration between Hindus and Muslims. Thus we are told that the Mughal school of painting, famous all over the world, was "pre-eminently an Indian school and Hindus and Muslims alike contributed to the artistic achievement of the period." Out of seventeen top artists mentioned by Abul Fazal, he adds, thirteen were Hindus.[57] Fatehpur Sikri is described as "an example of the mingling of Hindu and Muslim conceptions". We are further told that "the dress, social amenities, etc. which the Mughals introduced ceased to be foreign and were accepted by the higher classes everywhere."[58] But if Hindus were influenced by Muslims, they also influenced the latter:

> Kabir and Nanak, two vital figures in medieval Hindu religion, were both influenced by the rigid monotheism of Islam and in both of them there is a mingling of Sufism and Bhakti. In no one was this more remarkable than in Dara Shikoh, the unfortunate son of Shahjahan. Deeply versed in the mysteries of Sufism, Dara was an adept in yogic practices and in the doctrines of the Hindu saints.... In fact, the influence of Hinduism of Indian Muslims seems to have been quite considerable. The translation of Hindu classics into Persian proceeded apace. Not a few of the leading Muslim scholars of the period seem to have known Sanskrit well, for we have Badauni's own statement that he was commissioned by Akbar to make a fresh translation of *Rajatarangini.*[59]

In the political field the Mughal period, according to Panikkar, witnessed the emergence of a "national monarchy." After noting Akbar's marriage with a Hindu princess, his appointment of his wife's nephew, Man Singh, to a high position in the State and his abolition first of the pilgrim tax and then of the pool-tax (*jizya*) in 1563, Panikkar remarks: "The national monarchy had come into existence, and though political power was the immediate entourage of the court with its predominantly foreign nobility, no longer could the Hindus in the empire feel that they were only the tax-payers, foreigners in their own land." The appointment of Man Singh was followed by that of others, notably Todarmal and Birbal, who were both of middle-class origin. This policy of career open to talent converted the Mughal empire "from a foreign government into a national State."[60]

Though Jahangir was the candidate of the orthodox faction at the court, he generally followed his father's policy. The same was true of Shahjahan in spite of the fact that he had been responsible for the demolition of a few temples. A change came with the accession of Aurangzeb. "To him Akbar's policy of a national state seemed to be the very negation of Islamic ideas." Even before his accession to the throne he had shown his hostility towards the Hindus by the desecration of the Chintamani temple at Ahmedabad. In 1669 he issued his first general order "to demolish all temples and schools of the infidels". This marked the beginning of "an active policy of temple demolition" and some of the most famous temples at Banares, Mathura and Somnath "fell to his destructive enthusiasm". This was followed by the reimposition of the *jizya* in 1679 after the lapse of more than a hundred years. Such a policy naturally created great unrest among the Hindus. The national State now ceased to exist.[61]

Panikkar's lively imagination now leads him to the portrayal of the spirit of Hindu independence which, we are told, had not been crushed as a result of three hundred years of fight and which was embodied by the kingdom of Vijayanagar in the south particularly after Akbar's policy in the north had "deprived Hindu nationalism of its hereditary leaders." However, by the middle of the seventeenth century the central authority of the Vijayanagar kingdom had collapsed, "and Hindu political independence had no visible national head. It is to this vacant position that Shivaji, under the inspiration of Ramdas, now aspired." But it was not only against Shivaji and the Marathas that Aurangzeb had to fight. The Rajputs and the Sikhs were also up in arms against him. "The loyalty of the Hindu population, so sedulously built up by his three immediate predecessors, existed no longer."[62]

We need not pause here to point out the obvious weakness of this formulation. There was never in existence any organization of all or even most of the Hindu States and simply because a rebellious armesisting state had a Hindu ruler, that could not be described as a symbol of Hindu resistance, for several other rulers, who were not Hindu, but belonged to the faith of head of the Mughal empire, were also engaged in similar activities. Aurangzeb's religious policy must surely have been extremely unpopular among the Hindus, but it is important to remember that the rebellions in Rajasthan and Maharashtra had already begun before the reimposition of the *jizya*. Whatever that may be, Panikkar, while contradicting himself helps us to retain a sense of perspective about the nature of political alignments and motivations in India as late as the last quarter of the eighteenth century and makes it clear that religious affiliation was not the main factor behind them:

> In 1794, Poona witnessed a strange and impressive ceremony. The Peshwa, the actual head of the great Maratha empire, was invested, in circumstances of solemn ceremony, with the insignia of certain dignities conferred on him by the emperor of Delhi. The

> insignia were received with the tokens of the highest respect, and with suitable formalities indicating the gratitude of the recipient of such imperial favours. The "emperor", whose Khilat was thus received was a prisoner of a servant of the Peshwa, was the sovereign not even of his palace whose sanctity an Afghan adventurer had violated....The poor emperor of Delhi counted for nothing; but the tradition of Akbar, the idea of the national State had survived, so that the head of the Maratha confederacy, which ruled without question most of Hindustan as an independent sovereign power and who held the person of the emperor as a prisoner, was honoured to accept a title from him... The empire by ceasing to be a fact had become an accepted idea.[63]

The final *coup-de-grace* to the theory of two nations existing in India right from the beginning of the thirteenth century is delivered in these words:

> Before the nineteenth century, Islam in India was not separately organised. The Hindus and Muslims lived together, professing their different religions. The political power of Islam was a sufficient guarantee for the religious faith and the necessity for the Muslims to organise separately was never felt. The Muslim officers freely entered the service of the Hindu rulers, and even at Panipat, where the Maratha forces met the Afghans, the Hindu side had numerous Muslim soldiers and captains, and it was Ibrahim Gardee's artillery that played the greatest havoc on the Afghan forces. The Maratha governor of Lahore in 1758 was Adnam Beg. In the same way, when Babar invaded India, the Afghans allied themselves with the Hindus to resist the invader.[64]

V

If any one were to make an effort to describe the social and cultural life of Hindus and Muslims in the various parts of India as late as the nineteenth century, he would find ample evidence of a lot of sharing together by the members of the two communities. The pattern of life in eastern Bengal, one of the areas where Muslims were in a majority, has been quite elaborately described by a distinguished historian of Bangladesh, which was a part of Pakistan when he wrote his book. According to him while Hindus participated in Muslim festivals, Muslims participated in Hindu festivals without any hesitation and indeed with great enthusiasm.[65] Bengali Muslim writers, while they used Persian and Arabic words, wrote in as Sanskritised a style as their Hindu contemporaries. Besides, they adopted "themes, modes, images and ideas" from Sanskrit in much the same way as the latter did.

> Some Muslim writers wrote on purely Hindu themes, as for example did *Shaykh* Faydullah whose ballad on the glorification of *Goraksha* abounds with the mystic beliefs and practices of the Natha cult of Bengal. The works of 'Abd *al-Shukur* and Sayyid Sultan are similarly imbued with the ideas of the Saiva cult and mystic tantrism. Other typical examples of this class of literature are furnished by 'Alaul, who composed hynus in honour of goddess Kali.
>
> Even while dealing with Muslim themes, some continued to throw upon Hindu mythology. In *Nabi Vansa* (Geneology of Prophets), Sayyid Sultan goes to the length of including Brahma, Vishnu, Siva and Krishna—all Hindu gods—in his list of prophets.[66]

As usual, literature reflected the social reality. As a result of long association and the liberal policy of some of the great Muslim rulers, there had evolved certain "common objects of worship." This was particularly true of the common people "who mutually applied to the deities or saints of the other community when they imagined that supplications to their own had been ineffectual." Buchanan found this practice common even among the Brahmins and Mullahs in some parts of Bengal and Bihar.[67]

Thorburn's finding in the Punjab, the next important area of preponderant Muslim population, was not very different from that of Buchanan in Bengal. In Western Punjab about the entire population consisted of Muslims and in Central Punjab Muslims considerably outnumbered Hindus and Sikhs put together. In Eastern Punjab Hindus outnumbered Muslims by over three to one. Here Muslims had been converted to Islam only two or three hundred years ago. According to Thorburn they retained many of their ancient Hindu customs and superstitions and were "very lax Mohammedans." In Central Punjab also there was "little active antipathy" between Muslims, Hindus and Sikhs.[68] In Eastern Punjab, where the main agricultural tribes were Jats and Rajputs, we are further told, it mattered little whether they were Hindus or Muslims: "both are socially and politically one people, ancient tribal custom and the ties of blood being stronger than the separatist teachings of a half-learnt religion." In Central Punjab the Islamic faith of the Muslims generally was "of a more decided type than it is in the eastern districts."

> Upto the present time, however, the whole rural population of the Punjab, east of the Jhelum meridian (that is, in central and eastern districts), whether Hindus or Musalmans, may be regarded, for all administrative purposes as one people. They are untainted with religious animosities. They live side by side as peaceful cultivators, in happy indifference to the petty jealousies which superior knowledge stirs up in the heads of their Hindu and Muslim brethren in the towns.[69]

Sleeman's account of his travels in the kingdom of Oudh in 1849-50, when it was still under the rule of the Nawab, presents a somewhat similar picture of relations between the Hindus and Muslims in the social and cultural field in an area where the Muslims constituted a small minority of the population, but occupied a dominant position in government and politics. Thus Sleeman expresses his surprise at the fact of Hindus as well Muslims going to the shrine of a Muslim general of Sultan Mahmud of Ghazni at Bahraich: "Strange to say, Hindoos as well as Mohammedans make offerings to this shrine, and implore the favours of this military ruffian, whose only recorded merit consists of having sent a great many Hindoos to hell, in a wanton and unprovoked invasion of their territory."[70] He saw the same thing at another place at the shrine of his general's father and noted: "All our Hindoo camp followers paid as much reverence to the shrine as they passed as the Mohammedans."[71] While passing through Bharwara, he noted how the members of a particular Rajput tribe, though divided by religion, lived together "in tolerable harmony; and eat together on occasions of ceremony, though not from the same dishes."[72]

It must also be remembered that Muslims as well as Hindus were divided among themselves socially by several barriers. The divisions among Hindus based on caste are well-known. What is not generally remembered is that this does not involve division into merely four, but innumerable castes. Besides the caste groupings and their status in society varied from area to area. A person belonging to a particular caste might mean something to people in his own area, but might be entirely meaningless in another area. But Muslims were also subject of numerous divisive factors. There was, for instance, the doctrinal divisions between Sunnis, who formed the bulk of the Muslim population in India and such minority sects as the Shias and the Bohras. Besides, Muslims also were not free from the working of the caste system and the ideal of Islamic brotherhood remained an ideal only. Pakistani scholars, in spite of their interest in stressing the concept of Islamic solidarity, have also accepted this. Thus, for instance, they agree that the upper class Muslims were divided into four main groupings: Shaikhs, Syeds, Mughals and Pathans. Inter-marriages between members of different groupings were rare and this was one of the main reasons why most of the marriages took place among close relations. These four were regarded as constituting the *Ashraf* of the respectable community. Many of them were the descendents of administrators, scholars, preachers and soldiers who had come from Central Asia, Arabia, Persia, or Afghanistan. But many more claimed such descent and prepared geneological tables as this conferred respectability. The various converts from Hindu groups like the Rajputs also maintained their own separate castes. Then there were the bulk of Muslims, converts from people belonging to so-called lower Hindu castes. They more or less continued their old social status also as Muslims. As Mallick puts it:

> The ideal of brotherhood and equality, on which much stress is laid in Islam, was modified by Indian Muslims in imitation of the Hindu community. The proud distinctions of caste and the reverence shown to Brahmins did not fail to attract the notice and the admiration of the Muslim conquerors. The Shaykhs and Sayyids had an inmate holiness assigned to them, and the Mughals and Pathans copied the exclusiveness of the Rajputs. By the beginning of the nineteenth century the doctrine of caste seemed to have gained "a complete practical ascendancy" over the Muslims of some parts of India and occasioned a vast number of subdivisions, the members of which did not intermarry and often did not eat in a company.[73]

VI

What has been said above should help to exorcise the ghost of a perpetual Hindu-Muslim confrontation, based on their different approaches to religion and culture, throughout the medieval period. People belonging to the two faiths maintained their separate identities and did not merge themselves into one particular religious faith but otherwise there was considerable intermingling between the two communities and the two influenced the social and cultural moorings of the other to a considerable extent. This, of course, does not mean that there was no conflict between particular Muslim and Hindu rulers or that the principle of secularism was firmly established in medieval Indian politics. On the contrary, such conflicts were endemic and religious slogans and symbols were freely used in them. The religious faith of the ruler determined the nature of the state which he headed, but persons from other faiths, could, in normal times, freely pursue their religious beliefs and be freely employed in its service. There was no parallel to the Clarendon Code in medieval India.[74]

It is time now to turn to the problem posed at the beginning of the paper and see whether and in what way the legacy from the past constituted one of the foundations of Muslim nationalism in pre-independent India. If we have to succeed in doing so we must begin by taking note of the fact that Islam at the very beginning succeeded in inculcating among its followers a strong sense of belonging to a community and a community which was not merely religious but also political.

Montgomery Watt writes:

> Our investigations have shown one area in which Islam had great success in integrating the political life of its adherents. That was in the formation of the *ummah* or Islamic community, which, while it had a religious basis, was also a political body. The success was not merely in founding such a body, but in managing to attach to it some of the valuable attitudes which, in the case of the pre-Islamic Arabs, had been attached to the tribe. One such attitude arising from the feeling of brotherhood between the members of a tribe, led to a strong feeling of brotherhood between the members of a tribe, led to a strong feeling of brotherhood among the members of the Islamic community....[75]

Indeed from very early times Muslims began to look upon their community as a charismatic community, destined to establish the kingdom of God on earth. It is this faith in the community which lay behind the crucial role assigned to consensus (*ijma*) in the maintenance and development of the *Shariah.* Adds Watt : "The best explanation of this recurrence of consensus seems to be that it arises out of an intense belief in the community, a belief that the community is in some way supernatural, is a divinely instituted and divinely ordered community, in brief, that it is a 'charismatic community'".[76]

The strong feeling of belonging to the community was also the main factors behind the keen Muslim interest in history, which developed quite early. As Hamilton Gibb points out:

> The historical arguments contained in the Koran, the natural pride taken in the extensive conquests and the rivalries of the Arab tribes no doubt contributed to this. But the remarkable feature that, apart from the philologists, the collectors of the historical tradition were almost exclusively theologians and *muhaddiths* suggests that a deeper reason existed. For in the theological view history was the manifestation of a divine plan for the government of mankind; and while the historical outlook of the earlier generations might be limited to tracing it through the succession of prophets which culminated in Muhammed, all Islamic schools were agreed that it did not end there. In the Sunni doctrine, it was the Islamic community, the *ammaṭ Allah,* with which the continuation of the divine plan on earth was bound up; consequently the study of its history was a necessary supplement to the study of the divine revelation in Koran and *hadith.*[77]

W.C. Smith draws attention to the fact that the Islamic era—I.A.H. (622 A.D.)—does not begin with Muhammed's birth or with the time when he began to receive revelations but with the rise to power of the nascent Muslim community after the Prophet's shifting from Mecca to Medina. Smith writes further:

> ....for the Muslim, community and history are "special". For him they are, as far no other, religiously significant. The Quran, of course, is in Muslim eyes holy, or "sacred". One would be going only slightly too far to stay that his society and its history partake of an almost sacred character also. Here is a community that has explicitly undertaken to live in accordance with God's plan. Since it has been in existence, to become a Muslim means to join that community; and to take part in the enterprise of

fulfilling God's good pleasure on earth. The enterprise is hardly less important than the revelation. The privilege and duty and experience of taking part in it are central to the Muslim's faith.[78]

Both the sense of community, based on allegiance to Islam, and the sense of power, based on the assumption that Muslims must have authority to enforce *Sheriah* and regulate their lives according to the injunctions of the Prophet, were reflected in the treatment prescribed for non-Muslims. They were to be treated as *dhimmis,* to be protected as subjects by the Muslim state but not to be treated as equals. They were to pay *jizyah* in order to meet the cost of protection; those who undertook or were asked to offer military service were exempt from it.

As Arabs and later Turks, after their conversion to Islam, expanded in various directions and established their rule over a far-flung empire, encompassing territories in both Asia and Europe. The Muslim elite acquired a faith in something like an imperial destiny and a feeling that they belonged to a conquering race and had a right to rule over the non-Muslim people and spread Islam among them. Wars and conquests, even when really motivated by other reasons, were justified by reference to the need for spreading Islam. As Professor Mujeeb puts it:

> There was never any doubt in the minds of the Muslims of their right to spread over the earth. An objective view of this attitude would require a consideration of the historical forces underlying their expansion from the seventh century onwards. The Muslim Turks who established their rule in India were off-shoots of nomadic tribes forced to exploit opportunities of conquest and migration. There are several instances in pre-Muslim Indian history of the conquest of parts of northern India by tribes squeezed out of their homelands, and the irruption of Muslim Turks was a continuation of this process. The urge and the courage required for the conquest and occupation of alien and unknown lands cannot be the result of philosophical detachment or defeatism. Conquerors have always had some deep conviction that justified their policies. The Muslims Turks found the moral justification for their advance into India in the injunction to propagate Islam. As this could not, in the opinion of kings and warriors, be achieved without the subjugation of

the non-Muslims and the occupation of their territory, the propagation of Islam became identical with war and conquest.[79]

This brings us to the questions as to how these early traditions or modes of thinking of the Muslim elite, particularly their sense of community and sense of power, which constituted the bedrock of Muslim nationalism, were affected by their political experience in India. There can be only one answer to this question, namely, that these traditions were further strengthened. The rulers knew that although they had risen to power on the basis either of military prowess or hereditary right, they could rule only so long as they remained Muslims and retained the support of the court nobility which was in the beginning exclusively and later predominantly Muslim. Their identification with the interests of Islam provided the main moral prop or legitimation or mystification of their rule. This role was performed by the *Ulama,* a section of whom also worked as historians. A well-known authority on this subject points out with reference to the period of the Delhi Sultanate:

> The ideal temporal ruler of Islam which the Muslim historians of the Delhi Sultanate wished to show forth in their histories is that in which the Muslim world shall be seen to be governed by a partnership of pious scholars and pious Sultans... In short, the world in which 'religion and kingship are twins', the world where the continuity of the life of the Muslim community is symbolised not by the supremacy of the *khilafat,* now in the post-Mongol period, a chimera, but by the supremacy of the *Sharia.* In order that the faithful shall see that, despite the rise of military adventures to power, history has not escaped the providence of god and that in yielding obedience to sultans the community has not deviated from the right path into error, history shall present the picture of sultans obeying the Holy Law and showing due deference to the *ulma* and *mashaikh* or of Sultans ensuring by their justice and equity such a degree of peace and stability that the learned may quietly pursue their appointed task of better educating the community in the precepts and practices of true Islam. And if history does not present a picture of obedience to Islam by the rulers of the day, then it should present a picture of the evil consequences of disobedience.[80]

The pious sultan was expected not merely to uphold the dignity of the *ulma* and remove hindrances to the propagation of the 'true faith' by the latter, but also facilitate their task by humbling and humiliating the Hindus if not completely exterminating them. The following extract from the *Tarikh-i-Firuzshahi* (fourteenth century) by Zaiuddin Barani will illustrate this point:

> The obligation to be the refuge of the faith cannot be fulfilled until they (the kings) have utterly destroyed infidelity and unbelief, polytheism and idolatory for the sake of God and the protection of the true religion. If they cannot wholly extripate polytheism and infidelity because they have taken root and (exterminate) the infidels because of their large number, it will not be less meritorious if, for the sake of Islam and of affording refuge to the true faith, they use their efforts to insult and humiliate and to cause grief to and bring ridicule and shame upon the polytheistic and idolatrous Hindus, who are the bitterest enemies of God and the Prophet of God... They should not, for the sake of true glory of Islam and the honour of the true faith, permit even a single unbeliever and polytheist to live as a respectable person...or be set in authority over a community or a group, a province or a district.[81]

It is a tribute to the sense of realism and wisdom and generosity of the Turkish rulers that they did not pay heed to such outpourings, openly asserted their right to do what they considered best for the state, regardless of the injunctions of the *Shariah* or the preachings of the *ulma,* and beginning with the fifteenth century appointed Hindus to high positions in the government till a stage arrived when even the highest offices under the monarch were not barred to them. Akbar is justly famous for his liberality in this respect, but, contrary to the general impression, under Aurangzeb Hindu nobles continued to occupy the highest positions; as they had done earlier; if anything their number increased.

But whether the ruler was an Akbar or an Aurangzeb the vast majority of the nobles in the higher ranks always remained Muslim. And even though Akbar defied orthodox Muslim opinion to some extent, particularly by abolishing the *jiziah,* holding discussions at the court with representatives of various religious faiths and permitting the performances of Hindu religious rites by his Rajput wife, even he could not afford to defy it beyond a certain point. As Professor Mujeeb points out: "We must assume that Akbar was not a statesman who would deliberately undermine the basis of his own authority. He must have known that he could rule only as a Muslim and as the leader of a minority that was in power."[82] Besides, "the identification of Muslim orthodoxy and Muslim political power was too close and too real and they would stand or fall together."[83]

Indeed, depending on the exigencies of the situation even Akbar felt constrained to appeal to the orthodox Muslim sentiment in the most blatant terms. Thus he proclaimed the fall of Chittor as the victory of Islam over infidels and issued a *fathnama* which declared:

> As directed by the word of God, we, as far as it is within our power, remain busy in *jihad* and owing to the kindness of the supreme Lord, who is the promoter of our victories, we have succeeded in occupying a number of forts and towns belonging to the infidels and have established Islam there. With the help of our bloodthirsty sword we have erased the signs of infidelity from their minds and have destroyed temples in those places and also all over Hindustan.[84]

This is not to question the overall liberal direction of Akbar's religious policy, based on *Sulh-i-kul* (Peace with all), but only to underline the strength of Muslim orthodoxy at that time and the constraints under which he was working. After his death, "orthodoxy gradually got the upper hand and maintained its position in spite of Dara Shikoh's liberal and mystical predilections."[85] This trend, of course, reached its climax under Aurangzeb who reimposed *jiziah* in 1679 after a lapse of about a hundred years. But even if Dara Shikoh had defeated Aurangzeb and ascended the throne, it is doubtful if orthodoxy could have been effectively challenged.[86] Perhaps it was this realisation about the nature of Mughal rule which accounts for the fact that in spite of marked differences in the religious outlook of Dara Shikoh and Aurangzeb there was not much difference in the number of Hindu nobles supporting Dara Shikoh (24) and Aurangzeb (21).[87]

After the disintegration of the Mughal empire, orthodoxy acquired an even stronger hold over the mind of the Muslim elite in India. Now it began to be stressed that Islam must be cleansed of all impurities that had crept into it and that Muslims must again acquire supreme political power in India. This is best illustrated by the teachings and activities of Shah Waliullah (1703-1762), generally regarded as one of the greatest thinkers and religious leaders produced by the Muslim community in the Indian subcontinent, in the eighteenth century. He wrote to one Muslim potentate after another in the hope that the latter would restore Muslim power and thereby facilitate the preservation of the supposed Muslim way of life. Failing to secure a proper response in India, he finally wrote to Ahmad Shah Abdali inviting him to invade India and liberate the Muslims from the rule of the non-Muslims (Marathas and Jats.).[88] His attitude towards the Hindus can be understood from his categorisation of human beings in the ideal society of his conception. According to him there would be three classes of men in such a society:

> First, those loyal, outwardly and inwardly, to the Faith; second, those who out of compulsion would conform to the Faith and not dare oppose it; third, the humiliated Infidels, whom the Imam (the Leader) would keep so subdued and humbled that they would be kept employed in cutting the crops, threshing corn and other labours in exactly the same way as draught animals and beasts of burden.[89]

The so-called Wahhabi movement of the nineteenth century "marks the practical culmination of the religio-political thought of Shah Waliullah".[90] Its leader Sayyid Ahmad Shahid or Barelvi (1781-1831) was a disciple of Shah Waliullha's son and successor Shah Abdul Aziz and recognised by the latter's family as the person best suited to lead the twin movement of purification of Islam and the revival of its political power. It is significant that he spent a good deal of energy finding a territory that could be called *dar-al-amn* and from where he could lead a *jihad* in strict accordance with the *Shariah,* finally setting down at a place across the north-west frontier of India. As he explained his action to his followers :

> While in India I thought of a place of peace where I could take Muslims and organise *jihad*. In spite of its extent of hundreds of miles, I could not find a place to which I could migrate. There were many who advised me to carry on *jihad* in India, promising to provide me with whatever was necessary by way of material, treasure and weapons. But I could not agree to this, for *jihad* must be in accordance with the *Sunnah*. Mere rebellion was not intended.[91]

It may be noted that the Wahhabi rebellion was first directed against Sikh rule in the Punjab and only later against the British rule in India though, of course, it is also true that it was anti-British in its aims from the very beginning; the objective in both cases was, of course, the restoration of Muslim rule in India.[92] It is also significant that the campaign or the purification of Islam meant in practice really freeing it from Hindu influences.

W.C. Smith observes:

> The relevant point here is that the accretions which the reformers set themselves to removing from the Muslims' religion, were mostly borrowing from Hinduism, or superstitions degradations shared with Hinduism. When a religious reformer appeared in a village, he attacked with unrestrained zeal those aspects of the Muslims' religious practice that they shared with the Hindus, and he emphasised with the ardour of intense conviction the 'fundamentals' of Islam—i.e. the points at which it differed from other faiths. Lower-class Islam emerged from the reform 'purer' but more communalist.[93]

Contemporaneously there arose a somewhat similar movement in Bengal, known as the *Faraizi* movement led by Haji Shariatullah (1781-1840) and his son Dudu Miyan (1819-62). The movement of Muslim peasants led by Titu Mir (1782-1831) in West Bengal was more directly connected with the movement led by Sayyid Ahmad Barelvi in north India. Both these movements in Bengal aimed at focussing attention to peasants' grievances, but the Muslim orientation was also clearly there, though the rebels led by them also attacked Muslim landholders and the latter too were hostile to them. To quote Smith again: "The movement made use of a religious ideology, as class struggles in pre-capitalist society have often done; but through religious, it was not simply communalist." He further adds:

> The "Wahhabi" movement, therefore, did not set lower-class Muslims against lower-class Hindus in open conflict, nor did it divert lower-class Muslims from economic issues to a false solidarity with their communal 'friends' but class enemies. None-the-less it did encourage communal attitudes especially in religious thinking, and left a considerable section of the Muslim masses more susceptible to later communalist propaganda than they might otherwise have been.[94]

Enough has been said, it is hoped, to substantiate the point that Muslim nationalism did have historical roots. To point to these roots, however, is not to assert that these made inevitable the emergence of that nationalism. That was the end result of the conjunction with those roots of a number of other factors: the socio-economic background, the cultural environment, the force of Hindu revivalism and nationalism, the British colonial policy and the ethos and strategy of the Indian nationalist movement. All these factors in combination constitute the foundations of Muslim nationalism and must be studied together in order to understand its emergence. If the decisive weight of the other factor did not favour this emergence, the legacy from the past would not by itself have led to it. For in the historical tradition of every country or community there are elements of all types. Which elements of a particular tradition or historical legacy become important would depend on the conjunction of all the factors. But this does not mean that we should ignore the study of historical traditions, for they do shape people's minds and are themselves dialectically related to the other factors which influence their selection.

—Bimal Prasad

References

1. See R. Palme Dutt, *India Today,* (Bombay, 1949; first published 1940), pp. 420-446, W.C. Smith, *Modern Islam in India* (London, 1946), pp. 157-194; and A.R. Desai, *Social Background of Indian Nationalism* (Bombay, 1976, first published, 1948), pp. 392-398. See also P.C. Joshi, "The Economic Background of Communalism in India", in B.R. Nanda, *ed., Essays in Modern Indian History* (Delhi, 1980), pp. 167-181.
   Professor Bipan Chandra, also follows the same approach. See his paper "The Role of Religion in the Rise and Growth of Communalism in Modern India" (mimeographed), presented at the seminar on Mohamed Ali in Indian Politics held at Jamia Millia Islamia (New Delhi) in October 1979. It is part of a larger study which is expected to be published soon.
2. See N.B. Krishna, *Problem of Minorities* (New York, 1938) and Beni Prasad, *The Hindu-Muslim Questicns* (Allahabad, 1941).
3. See Bipan Chandra, "The Hindu Tinge in Indian National Leadership and the Growth of Communalism in Modern India", paper presented to the seminar on Mohamed Ali in Indian Politics, organised by the Jamia Millia Islamia in October 1979; mimeographed.
4. See Bipan Chandra, "Indian National Movement and the Communal Problem" in the same author's *Nationalism and Colonialism in Modern India* (New Delhi, 1979), pp. 252-274, (First published in *Secular Democracy* Annual

Number, 1973); C.H. Philips, *India* (London, 1949), pp. 131-142, and *The Partition of India, 1947* (Leeds, 1967); Bimla Prasad, "The Emergence of the Demand for India's Partition", *International Studies*, vol. 9, no. 3, 1968; and B.B. Misra, *The Indian Political Parties* (Delhi, 1976), pp. 420-442.

5. See Prabha Dixit, *Communalism—A Struggle for Power* (New Delhi, 1974); Paul R. Brass, *Language, Religion and Politics in North India* (Delhi, 1975), pp. 119-234; and Francis Robinson, *Separatism among Indian Muslims* (Delhi, 1975.)
6. See Rafiq Zakaria, *Rise of Muslims in Indian Politics: An Analysis of Developments from 1885 to 1906* (Bombay, 1970); Mushirul Hasan, *Nationalism and Communal Politics in India 1916-1928* (New Delhi, 1979); Uma Kaura, *Muslims and Indian Nationalism, 1928-1940* (New Delhi, 1977); C.H. Philips and Mary Doreen Wainwright, eds., *The Partition of India: Polities and Perspectives, 1935-1947* (London, 1970); and Shila Sen, *Muslim Politics in Bengal*, 1937-1947 (New Delhi, 1976); E.W.R. Lumby, *The Transfer of Power in India*, 1945-47 (London, 1954); V.P. Menon, *The Transfer of Power in India* (Bombay, 1957); and H.V. Hodson, *The Great Divide* (London, 1969). There are a few general works which cover the entire period of the nationalist movement: Ram Gopal, *Indian Muslims: A Political History, 1858-1947* (Bombay, 1959); P. Hardy, *The Muslims of British India* (Cambridge, 1972); B. N. Pandey, *The Break-up of British India* (London, 1974); and V.V. Nagarkar, *Genesis of Pakistan* (Bombay, 1975.)
7. Romila Thapar, Harbans Mukhia and Bipan Chandra, *Communalism and the Writing of Indian History* (New Delhi, 1977, 2nd ed., first published 1969).
8. George Lukacs, *History and Class Consciousness* (London, 1971), p. 27.
9. Istvan Meszaros, "Contingent and Necessary Class Cons ciousness", Meszaros, ed., *Aspects of History and Class Consciousness* (London, 1971), p. 87.
10. Antonio Gramsci, *Selections from the Prison Notebooks* (New York, 1973), p. 407.
11. Karl Marx and Frederick Engels, *Selected Works* (Moscow, 1970), p. 96.
12. Ralph Miliband, *Marxism and Politics* (Oxford, 1977), p. 47.
13. Hafeez Malik, *Moslem Nationalism in India and Pakistan* (Washington D. C. 1963), p. 294.
14. Ishtiaq Husain Qureshi, *The Muslim Community of the Indo-Pakistan Subcontinent, 610-1947* (The Hague, 1962), p. 6.
15. Ishtiaq Husain Qureshi, *The Struggle for Pakistan* (Karachi, 1969), p. 10.
16. Khalid B. Sayeed, *Pakistan: The Formative Phase* (London, 1968, 2nd ed.) pp. 11-12.
17. K.K. Aziz, *The Making of Pakistan; A Study in Nationalism* (London, 1967), p. 18.
18. *Ibid.*, p. 209.
19. *Ibid.*, p. 143.
20. Aziz Ahmad, *Studies in Islamic Culture in the Indian Environment* (Oxford, 1964), VII.
21. *Ibid.*

22. *Ibid.*, p. 73. See also the same author's *Islamic Modernism in India and Pakistan, 1857-1964* (London, 1967).
23. S.M. Ikram, *Modern Muslim India and the Birth of Pakistan (1858-1951)* (Lahore, 1965; 2nd ed. first pub. 1950), p. 1.
24. S.M. Ikram, *Muslim Civilisation in India*, ed. Ainslie T. Embree (New York, 1965; 2nd printing), p. 294.
25. See R.C. Majumdar, *Glimpses of Bengal in the Nineteenth Century* (Calcutta, 1960). p. 48.
26. K.M. Panikkar, *A Survey of Indian History* (London, 1971; first published 1947), pp. 143-144.
27. Tara Chand, *Influence of Islam on Indian Culture* (Allahabad, 1963; first published 1936), p. 137.
28. Tara Chand in Humayun Kabir, ed., *Abdul Kalam Azad* (Bombay, 1959), p. 238.
29. R.C. Majumdar, "Impact of Islam on Hinduism", Horst Kruger, ed., *Kunwar Mohammad Ashraf* (Delhi, 1969), pp. 266-267.
30. *Ibid.*, pp. 268-269.
31. R.C. Majumdar in R.C. Majumdar, ed., *The Delhi Sultanate*, vol. VI of *The History and Culture of the Indian People* (Bombay, 1960), pp. 616-617.
32. R.C. Majumdar, "The National Movement 1833-1905", in N.K. Sinha, ed. *The History of Bengal, 1757-1905* (Calcutta, 1967), p. 189.
33. Niharranjan Ray, *Nationalism in India* (Aligarh, 1973), p. 53.
34. *Ibid.*, pp. 55-56.
35. F.W. Thomas, *Mutual Influence of Muhammedans and Hindus in India* (Cambridge, 1892), p. 12.
36. Murray Titus, *Indian Islam* (London, 1930), p. 176.
37. Percival Spear, *India, Pakistan and the West* (London, 1958), p. 88.
38. Percival Spear, *India: A Modern History* (Ann Arbor, 1961), p. 10.
39. Ikram, *Muslim Civilisation in India*, pp. 116-121.
40. *Ibid.*, pp. 123-130.
41. *Ibid.*, pp. 130-131.
42. *Ibid.*, pp. 97-109.
43. *Ibid.*, p. 88.
44. *Ibid.*, pp. 95-96.
45. *Ibid.*, p. 199.
46. *Ibid.*, p. 226.
47. *Ibid.*, p. 243.
48. *Ibid.*, pp. 198-199; p. 232.
49. *Ibid.*, p. 131.
50. *Ibid.*, p. 295.
51. Panikkar, op. cit., p. 139.
52. *Ibid.*, pp. 139-140.
53. *Ibid.*, p. 137.
54. *Ibid.*, p. 138.

55. *Ibid.*, p. 145.
56. *Ibid.*, pp. 144-145.
57. *Ibid.*, p. 184.
58. *Ibid.*, p. 187.
59. *Ibid.*, p. 188.
60. *Ibid.*, pp. 168-169.
61. *Ibid.*, pp. 171-175.
62. *Ibid.*, pp. 176-181.
63. *Ibid.*, pp. 206-207.
64. *Ibid.*, p. 248.
65. Azizur Rahman Mallick, *British Policy and the Muslims in Bengal, 1757-1856* (Dacca, 1961), pp. 4-5.
66. *Ibid.*, pp. 5-6.
67. *Ibid.*, pp. 21.
68. S.S. Jhorburn, *Musalmans and Money-Lenders in the Punjab* (Edinburgh, 1886), p. 2.
69. *Ibid.*, pp. 13-14.
70. P.D. Reeves, ed., *Sbeeman in Oudh* (Cambridge, 1971), p. 69.
71. *Ibid.*, p. 288.
72. *Ibid.*, p. 240.
73. Mallick, op. cit., pp. 22-23.
74. See S.R. Sharma, *The Religious Policy of the Mughal Emperors* (Bombay, 1962; 2nd ed.).
75. W. Montgomery Watt, *Islam and the Integration of Society* (London, 1970; 4th impression), pp. 174-175.
76. *Ibid.*, p. 204.
77. Hamilton A.R. Gibb, *Studies on the Civilisation of Islam* (London, 1962), p. 115.
78. W.C. Smith, *Islam in Modern History* (Princeton, 1957), pp. 15-16.
79. M. Mujeeb, *The Indian Muslims* (London, 1967), pp. 67-68.
80. P. Hardy, "The Muslim Historians of the Delhi Sultanate: Is What They Say Really What They Mean?" *Journal of the Asiatic Society of Pakistan* (Dacca), vol. IX, No. 1, June 1964, See also the same author's *Historians of Medieval India* (London, 1960).
81. Mujeeb, *op, cit.*, p. 68.
82. *Ibid.*, p. 258.
83. *Ibid.*, p. 264.
84. Iqtidar Alam Khan, "The Nobility under Akbar and the Development of His Religious Policy, 1560-80", *Journal of the Royal Asiatic Society, 1968.* See also the same author's "A Note on the Conception of Akbar's Religious Policy", Debiprasad Chatto padhyaya, ed., *History and Society*, (Calcutta, 1978), pp. 455-466.
85. Mujeeb, *op. cit.*, p. 247.
86. *Ibid.*, p. 363.

87. See the table entitled "Supporters of the Contending Princes in the War of Succession, 1658-59" In M. Athar Ali, *The Mughal Nobility under Aurangzeb* (Bombay, 1966), p. 96.
88. See Khaliq Ahmad Nizami, "Shah Waliullah Dehlavi and Indian Politics, in the Eighteenth Century", *Islamic Culture*, 1951, pp. 133-145.
89. Irfan M. Habib, "The Political Role of Shaikh Ahmad Sirhindi and Shah Waliullah", *Enquiry*, No. 5, 1961, p. 53.
90. Aziz Ahmad, *Studies in Islamic Culture in the Indian Environment*, p. 210.
91. Mujeeb, *op. cit.*, p. 395.
92. See Qeyamuddin Ahmad, *Wahabi Movement in India* (Calcutta, 1966).
93. W.C. Smith, *Modern Islam in India*, p. 161.
94. *Ibid.*, p. 162. See also A.R. Mallik, *op. cit.*, and Muinuddin Khan, *The Faraidi Movement* (Karachi, 1965).

11

Subhash Chandra Bose—His Role in India's Freedom Struggle

Of all the stalwarts of India's freedom struggle, Subhash Chandra Bose came least under the influence of Gandhiji and his teaching. Subhash Bose stepped into the void in Bengal's political leadership created by C. R. Das's premature death in 1926, carrying with him the tradition of differing from Gandhiji, even on principles. If C.R. Das had broken away from Gandhiji on an item of comparative insignificance, *viz.* that he did not adopt Gandhiji's programme for the boycott of the legislatures, Subhash Bose went much further: for him the elimination of British imperialism from India was an objective of such vital importance that the means adopted receded into the background as a matter of relatively little interest.

Early in life he was greatly influenced by the teachings of Ramakrishna and Vivekananda and later of Aurobindo. Until politics and Indian freedom became an all-absorbing passion with him, he has moved in his youth by an intense interest in the varieties of religious experience.

''Why do I believe in Spirit?'' Subhash asked, analysing his philosophical faith, and himself provided the following answer: "Because it is a pragmatic necessity. My nature demands it. I see purpose and design in nature; I discern an increasing purpose in my own life. I feel that I am not a mere conglomeration of atoms. I perceive, too, that reality is not a fortuitous combination of molecules.

The world is a manifestation of Spirit, and just as Spirit is eternal so also is the world of creation. Creation does not and cannot end at any point of time. This view is similar to the Vaishnavite conception of Eternal Play (*Nitya Leela*). For me, the essential nature of reality is LOVE! LOVE is the essence of the Universe and is the essential principle in human life."

He went to Cambridge for higher education and passed the Indian Civil Service examination in 1920. But all the time he was preparing himself for a prominent role in the struggle against foreign domination in India and for a life of sacrifice and dedication. His high rank in the ICS examination came as a surprise to him, but he had already made up his mind not to accept the position in the Service and become part of the British bureaucracy in India. In deference to his family's wishes (including that of his brother Sarat Bose) he joined as a probationer and continued for seven months but he was continuously trying to persuade his family to let him resign. The sacrifices of C.R. Das and the example of Aurobindo Ghosh, whom he expected back in politics in a few years, were prominently before him. He took the final step in April 1921 and resigned from the Service.

At the Calcutta session of the Congress in December 1928, over which Pandit Motilal Nehur presided, the Independence League, with S. Srinivasa Iyengar, Jawaharlal Nehru and Subhash Bose as its main exponents, was a source of much concern to both Gandhiji and Pandit Motilal Nehru. Following a vigorous debate on the endorsement of the Nehru Report, a vote was taken on the issue of Dominion Status versus complete independence, the result of which seemed to be in doubt until the final stage of the counting. The opposition, led by Subhash Bose in favour of complete independence, seemed formidable, and the large number of votes cast against veteran leaders like Gandhiji and Motilal Nehru showed the rising strength of the extremist opinion. On a quip by Dr. Pattabhi Sitaramayya, in declaring the result, that in the process of voting some dead members had apparently come to life, Gandhiji delivered one of the sharpest rebukes I have heard him utter on standards of behaviour in public life.

There was, in fact, little in common between Gandhiji and Subhash Bose beyond their whole-hearted devotion to the cause of India's freedom. Non-violence—an article of faith with the one—was only a weapon for the other, to be used or discarded according to the necessities of the situation. Through the thirties, until the eve of the second World War, Subhash Bose found points of contact with the left-wing of the Congress. He was bitterly opposed to the 1935 British-imposed Constitution and to acceptance of office under any conditions.

In one respect, however, he was cast in a mould different from that of Jawaharlal Nehur. The latter's keen awareness of the danger to world peace from the growth of Fascism and Nazism in Europe left Subhash Bose completely unimpressed. No ideological inhibitions handicapped him in his search for collaborators to overthrow British Imperialism. On a visit to Europe just before the commencement of the Second World War, he made an unsuccessful attempt to secure Hitler's support for India's freedom movement. The Nazi leader was at that time in no mood to challenge the British Empire or even to weaken its hold on any part of the world. In *Mein Kempf* he had written with unconcealed scorn of his Indian admirers as "those Oriental mounted banks each one of whom claims to represent all his countrymen".

It was inevitable that Subhash Bose, with the heavy sacrifices that stood to his credit and with his radical views, should have the honour that had earlier gone to Jawaharlal Nehur—namely, the Presidentship of the Congress. The Haripura session (1938) was his acknowledged right, as it were. But Gandhiji was not happy about some of the behind-the-scenes activities reported to him from Bengal. The terrorist movement was showing signs of renewed life, dramatised by the unsuccessful attempt by a girl at point-blank range on the life of the Governor of the Province, Sir John Anderson with his background of experience of the Sinn Fein movement in Ireland, was firm in dealing with the Bengal terrorists.

Meanwhile, with another session of the Congress approaching at Tripuri in 1939, Subhash Bose was looking forward to a renewed term as its President. This time, however, the members of the Working Committee (including Sardar Patel, Dr. Rajendra Prasad and Acharya Kripalani) made public declarations against the proposal. Gandhiji let it be known that Dr. Pattabhi Sitaramayya was his choice for the Presidentship. Nevertheless, Subhash Bose won a keenly fought contest by the small margin of 95 votes. Gandhiji's reaction was prompt and characteristic: Subhash Bose (he said) was not only entitled to congratulations on his triumph; but he had earned in addition the right to nominate his own Working Committee to form a homogeneous Cabinet. It was clear that Subhash Bose's victory was at the cost of the support of many of his former colleagues and—most significant of all—of Gandhiji. On the outbreak of the Second World War, he was one of the first against whom action was taken under the Defence of India Rules. After spending some time in detention he decided to warn the authorities that a fast unto death was imminent, unless his release was effected without delay. The Bengal Government took the risk (small as it appeared) of complying with his request, maintaining close surveillance on his movements and activities.

The mystery surrounding his escape from India, despite elaborate security restrictions in the early part of 1941 (apparently through Peshawar and Kabul to Berlin) has never been satisfactorily explained. This time he evoked a positive response from the Fuhrer who saw possibilities of developing new pressure against Britaid and her Allies. Subhash Bose spent some time in Germany organising the Indian prisoners of war captured by the Germans, and gained valuable experience in the process.

With Japan's entry into the war, and after Pearl Harbour and her spectacular success in South-East Asia, it was felt that he would be more useful in this region and could take over from Rash Behari Bose* the responsibility of building up a new front against the British. After an adventurous submarine voyage of about 30 days in October 1943, Subhash Bose established the provisional Government of Azad Hind. The rapidity of Japan's advance through Malaya and Burma had led him to the belief that the initiative in the war was passing into the hands of Germany and its partners and that he could, with their assistance, play a valuable role in the release of India from British control.

On assuming the command of the Indian National Army which he had formed in Malaya, he issued a proclamation in the course of which he observed:

---

* Rash Behari Bose left India in 1915, married a Japanese girl and became a Japanese citizen. He however continued to work for India. It was owing to his effort that a conference was held at Tokyo in March 1942 leading to the resolution to form an Indian National Army.

> This is for me a matter of joy and pride, because for an Indian there can be no greater honour than to be the Commander of India's army of liberation. But I am conscious of the magnitude of the task that I have undertaken and I feel weighed down with a sense of my responsibility. I pray that God may give me the necessary strength to fulfil my duty to India under all circumstances however difficult or trying they may be. I regard myself as the servant of 38 croers of my countrymen who profess different religious faiths.... It is only on the basis on undiluted nationalism and perfect justice and impartiality that India's army of liberation can be built up. We must weld ourselves into an army that will have only one goal, namely the freedom of India and only one will, namely to do or die in the cause of India's freedom. When we stand, the Azad Hind Fauj has to be like a wall of granite; when we march, the Azad Hind Fauj has to be like a steam-roller.

In the course of a few weeks, Subhash Bose secured recognition for his provisional Government from several Powers: among them were Japan, Germany, Italy, and other regimes allied to them. From Nippon he received the assurance of "whole-hearted co-operation, so that the struggle for liberating India would ultimately be crowned with success". Thailand expressed through her Prime Minister "full sympathy with the high aspirations of the freedom-loving Indians".

The war with Britain, he had warned his troops, would be long and hard. At last, on 18th March, 1944, the I.N.A. crossed the Burma border and stepped on Indian soil in Manipur. It was a great moment in his life. The fight for India's liberation had actually commenced. With pride he addressed his soldiers:

> Inspired by the righteousness of our cause, we have encountered the numerically superior and better equipped but heterogeneous and dis-united forces of the enemy and defeated them in every battle. Our units, with their better training and discipline and unshakable faith in India's freedom have established their superiority over the enemy whose morale deteriorated with its defeat... With their blood sacrificed, these heroes have established traditions which the future soldiers of free India shall have to uphold.

Just when an advance on Imphal was about to begin, Nature in one of her most perverse moods baulked the I.N.A. of possible victory. Rain, torrential and unseasonable, converted the region into a quagmire. Retreat became inevitable and, under circumstance of increasing difficulties—shortage of supplies, harassment by American bombers etc—the I.N.A. fell back first on Mandalay, then on Rangoon and finally made for Bangkok.

The rest is a sad story of disillusionment and of hope turning to dust and ashes just as it was near fulfillment. Desertions became frequent and Subhash Bose felt compelled to issue an order for summary trial and death in all cases of cowardice and treachery. News reached him in August 1945 of Germany's collapse in Europe. Where could he turn next for help? Perhaps Russia, he thought, since until then it has remained neutral in the war against Japan. Moscow could be sounded tactfully through Japan, though he had misgivings about the response in view of his friendly relations with Hitler. He did not have to remain in suspense for long. With Japan's difficulties multiplying after Germany's collapse, Russia declared war against Nippon.

Every circumstance thus seemed to conspire against Subhash Bose. No longer was he an asset to the Japanese but a heavy liability. But even in adversity his courage did not desert him. In the final stage there were recriminations about the composition of the Indo-Japanese War Council. Other difficulties too were arising, and the Japanese, fighting for their own survival, had no thought to bestow on India's liberation.

The end came with tragic suddenness. A group of Japanese approached Subhash Bose and some of the close lieutenants somewhere in Malaya. A plane was in a near by field (they assured him) ready to take off and he could have a seat. What was the destination? The reply was vague. Could one of his lieutenants accompany him? No, the plane (he was informed) was full, though actually some seats went empty. Taking faith in the future for his guide, he accompanied them, alone. A few days later a Japanese naval officer announced to his anguished friends, "Netaji is dead." So that no doubt might linger as to his meaning, he added, "His Excellency Subhash Chandra Bose is dead."

So a meteoric career ended, leaving behind a memory which will linger in the hearts of all his admirers and followers. Subhash Bose will be gratefully remembered by his countrymen for passionate love of freedom and his dauntless courage.

The celebrated trial of three officers of the Indian National Army at Delhi's historic Red Fort in 1946, ending in their acquittal, was a vindication of Subhash Bose's heroic effort.

The three accused placed on trial for "waging war against the King" were Capt. Shah Nawaz Khan (1/14 Punjab Regiment); Capt. P. K. Sehgal (2.10 Baluch Regiment); and Lieut. Gurbaksh Singh Dhillon (1/14 Punjab Regiment)—all of them Indian Commissioned Officers. The defence was conducted by a number of lawyers led by Bhulabhai Desai.

B. N. Rau suggested two distinct lines of defence in a memorandum which he prepared for Bhulabhai Desai. The first was that, broadly speaking, when circumstances offer no choice except between two evils, it is not a crime to choose the lesser of the two. For instance, under Section 81 of the Indian Penal Code, the captain of a ship running down a boat containing two passengers in order to avoid running down another boat containing 30 commits no crime.

The situation in which these officers found themselves in 1942 and 1943 was most abnormal in character. Japan was advancing with lightning rapidity. Malaya had been evacuated. Singapore, regarded as almost impregnable, had surrendered under circumstances that were not fully disclosed. Burma was being evacuated. Even Madras was almost evacuated (in April, 1942) in panic. There were also rumours of plans for the evacuation of various other parts of India. Charges of discrimination during evacuation had been made because of special arrangements made for Europeans.

The question therefore arose: who was to protect Indian lives and Indian property in areas evacuated or about to be evacuated? Protection was sorely needed from enemy violence and looting and—in Burnma and Malaya—also from unruly elements of the local population. But there was another, even more pressing, need. Japan was threatening to send a large number of Indian prisoners of war to starvation and death in the South-west Pacific region unless they formed an I.N.A., and she had actually carried out the threat on some occasions. This kind of mass murder had to be stopped.

The I.N.A. had, therefore, to be formed for these two main purposes: (1) to prevent mass deportation and marooning of Indian POWs; and (2) to protect Indian lives and property in the territories evacuated or about to be evacuated by the forces of the Crown. But obviously such an organisation could not function—Japan would not have allowed it to function—unless it kept up at least an appearance of collaboration in her war effort. A minimum degree of collaboration was, therefore, found necessary—both in word and deed—hence the speeches and slogans. But even so, it may be noted that: (a) every opportunity was given to those who, on any ground, did not wish to go into action on the Japanese side, and (b) even in the speeches made, POWs joining the I.N.A. were told that they might have to fight against Japan if necessary. It is thus clear that collaboration was to be kept down to the minimum possible.

It must not be imagined—it would indeed be disingenuous to pretend—that (1) and (2) were the only motives that influenced the organisers. But they were the only motives of *legal significance.* The conduct of the accused was to be judged, not in the light of the circumstances existing in 1946, but in the light of those existing at that time.

The second line of defence suggested by B. N. Rau was as follows. The charges against the accused were under the Indian Penal Code, but that Code must be read subject to the principles of international law whenever possible. For example, a Japanese, normally caught bombing any part of India, would be chargeable under the Indian Penal Code; but obviously if this was done during a war, he would be treated as a POW and so not chargeable.

After citing a number of cases (such as MacLeod vs. the United States and MacLeod vs. Attorney-General for New South Wales), it was argued that if, under the recognised principles of international law, the accused were POWs, the Indian Penal Code did not apply to them. Phillimore, a great legal authority, cited the case of General Lee in the war between England and the rebellious American colonies in 1776. General Lee was released because the American contention that he was entitled to be treated as a prisoner of war ultimately prevailed. Phillimore himself apparently considered Lee's temporary detention to be a 'melancholy example' of unwarranted severity.

There was another reason why the act could not be described as voluntary. The prisoners *believed* that their duty of allegiance to the Crown had ceased when they were formally handed over to the

Japanese by Col. Hunt. They *thought* that they were from that time subject to the orders of the occupying Power. They might have been wrong in so thinking; but if they had honestly thought so, the point had a bearing on the question of *mens rea;* it would show that they had not *intentionally* committed any breach of allegiance to the Crown and that they had merely carried out what they considered to be the lawful order of the occupying Power.

There is a widespread notion—not confined to laymen—that protection by the Crown and allegiance to the Crown go hand in hand, so that when one ceases, so does the other. In a statement to the Press, Sir Hari Singh Gour had once said: "The theory of allegiance to the Crown postulates fulfillment of the Crown's duty towards its subjects of safety and protection, both of person and property. When on account of its defeat in war this protection is no longer possible, international law takes the course of *inter arma silent leges*— war suspends the law," The I.N.A. accused also believed so, particularly after Col. Hunt handed them over to the Japanese, and therefore their collaboration with Japan—so far as it went—was not a voluntary breach of allegiance to the King. If the accused were not 'deserters', the only ground for regarding them as beyond the pale of international law disappears and they were entitled to be treated as prisoners of war and not as ordinary criminals. Assuming for the moment that these young officers were technically rebels, nevertheless, the circumstances were so peculiar that a general amnesty might well have been declared, especially after the war had been brought to a successful close.

Rebellion is an ugly word, but let us not forget that Washington was a rebel—fortunately for him, a successful one. At one time, the British view was that the Boer War was also a rebellion, since the Transvaal Republic was under the suzerainty of the Queen; in this view, General Smuts was a leader of the rebels. De Valera was a rebel. Micheal Collins and his associates, with whom Lloyd George's Government (which included Sir Winston Churchill) concluded a treaty in December 1921, were all rebels. Papinean was the leader of a rebellion for self-government in Lower Canada in 1835. The revolt failed and Papinean became a refugee in the U.S.A.; but Canada obtained self-government in the end and Papinenan's great-grandson died in action fighting on the Allied side in 1917, earning the M.C. for gallantry in 1915. In the American Civil War, the Confederate Army was an army of rebels, but after it had surrendered there was an amnesty; not a single officer or man was tried or punished.

It is of minor significance which of the above arguments finally prevailed with the court—the legal arguments or the appeal to statesmanship. The three accused were acquitted by the court at the end of the lengthy and sensational trial whose outcome was a fitting commemoration of the role of Subhash Bose in India's freedom struggle.

12

Shyama Prasad Mookerji and Freedom Struggle

Born at Calcutta on 6 July 1901, Dr. Shyama Prasad Mookerji inherited a rich tradition of erudite scholarship, fervent nationalism and fearlessness from his illustrious father, Sir Ashutosh Mookerjee. His mother, Shrimati Jogamaya Devi, was a typical Hindu lady, devoted to her husband, family and *Dharma.* Being an upper-class Brahmin family with a high social status, the Mookerji house in Bhowanipur, Calcutta, was known as much for its "Poojas" as for its cultured and scholarly atmosphere. It was the *rendezvous* of literary and political luminaries of Bengal who gathered there to get guidance and inspiration from Sir Ashutosh, who as the Vice-Chancellor of the Calcutta University and a Judge of the Calcutta High Court occupied a unique position in the life of Bengal.

Shyama Prasad Mookerji, together with his elder brother, Rama Prasad, and younger brother, Bama Prasad, was brought up by Sir Ashutosh with filial care and affection, tempered with severe discipline and austerity befitting Brahmacharins. He got his early education at the Mitra Institution, from where he passed his Matriculation examination at the age of sixteen with a scholarship and joined the Presidency College, Calcutta, in 1917. He stood first in the University in Inter Arts examination in 1919 and passed the B.A. examination with Honours in English, securing a first class first in 1921. But for his M.A., he took Indian Vernaculars instead of English. This was in keeping with Sir Ashutosh's policy of giving Bengali and other Indian languages their rightful place in the University education which was till then dominated by English alone.

The high idealism which characterised Shyama Prasad Mookerji's entire life began to find expression through actions and words from his student days. Writing to Professor Percival in London on 2 September 1920 for an article for the Presidency College Magazine, of which he had been appointed the Editor, he requested him to "bless me from your innermost heart that I may live a pure and manly life". "Pure and manly life" was the ideal he set before himself while still in his teens, and he lived up to it right till the end of his crowded life in 1953.

While studying for his M.A. he was married, in April 1922, to Shrimati Sudha Devi who bore him four children—two sons and two daughters—before she died in 1934. Shyama Prasad refused to marry again and decided to devote the rest of his life to the service of the nation with single-minded devotion.

He did his B.L. in 1924, once again standing first in the University, and was called to the English Bar in 1927 from the Lincoln's Inn, England, which he joined in 1926. But he never practised law. The death of his father in 1923, whom he had been assisting from his student days in the work of running the Calcutta University, brought him into the educational field even while he was still a student. He was known to have the closest insight into the educational plans and policies of Sir Ashutosh. The well-wishers of the University, therefore, considered his association with the University administration as essential for its healthy growth on the lines laid down by Sir Ashutosh. He was elected to the University Senate and Syndicate in 1924 and became its youngest Vice-Chancellor in 1934.

He began his political career in a small way as early as 1929 when he was elected to the Bengal Legislative Council as a Congress candidate from the University Constituency. It was in a way a necessary adjunct to his educational work. He was supposed to act as a watchdog of the Calcutta University in the Legislature. He resigned his seat in the Council in response to the Congress call for boycott of Legislative Councils, but soon after re-entered it as in dependent to be able to safeguard the interests of his University. The training that he got in parliamentary life and the insight he acquired into the working of the Muslim League and the Congress mind during this period stood him in good stead in later life and helped him to chalk out his political course with an open mind.

He was again returned from the University Constituency to the Bengal Legislature in 1937 when it was first constituted on the basis of the Communal Award. In a house of two hundred and fifty, Hindus had been given only eighty seats for which mostly Congressmen were returned. The rest was divided between the Muslims and the British interests which both had been given heavy weightage. The Muslim members were divided between the Muslim League and the Krishak Praja Party led by Fazlul Haq. Had the Congress Party formed a coalition with the Krishak Praja Party, Bengal could have got a non-Muslim League stable Government. But the British interests wanted the Muslim League to form the government. The Congress leadership also played the game of the British and the Muslim League by refusing to form a coalition with the Krishak Praja Party. This came as a rude shock to Shyama Prasad, who was amazed at the utter bankruptcy of statesmanship in the Congress and its cowardly policy of appeasing the Muslim League at the cost of the wider interests of Bengal and the country as a whole.

The Muslim League Ministry, as soon as it was formed, decided to strike at the educational strucuture which Sir Ashutosh and Shyama Prasad had so assiduously built up by passing the Secondary Education and the Calcutta University Bills. After having failed to persuade the Congress leadership to change its suicidal policy of allowing the Muslim League a safe spell of power, he decided to go ahead single-handed to topple the Muslim League Ministry. The way he rallied round himself non-Congress and non-Muslim League nationalist forces in Bengal, ousted the Muslim League Ministry and formed the coalition ministry with Fazlul Haq as Chief Minister in which he became the Finance Minister, established his position as a practical and far-sighted political leader.

During the same period he came under the influence of Veer Savarkar who after his release in 1937 refused the Congress offers of power and position and put new life in the Hindu Maha Sabha, of which he was elected the President. The pure nationalism and patriotism of Veer Savarkar coupled with his realism came to Shyama Prasad as a refreshing contrast to the utopian idealism and pseudo-nationalism of the Congress. He joined the Hindu Maha Sabha and became its acting President in 1939.

Soon after he joined the Bengal Cabinet, Gandhiji started the Quit India Movement and the British Government let loose a reign of terror in the country. The rapid advance of the Japanese armies through Burma added new dimensions to the situation. The British government, instead of taking the people into confidence, began the policy of scorched earth in the Eastern region of the country. Since all the Congress leaders were in jail, there was no one to take up the national cause against the British. Shyama Prasad, even though he was a member of the Government, decided to take up the cudgels with the British government on behalf of the nation. His correspondence with Lord Linlithgow, in which he urged upon him to release the leaders, trust the people and permit the raising of a National Defence Force to meet the Japanese threat, is a classic example of persuasive firmness in the national cause. Having failed to persuade the Central Government, he decided to quit the Bengal Cabinet and lead the nationalist forces against the British unshackled by the strings of office.

The man-made famine of 1943 brought the humanitarian in Shyama Prasad to the forefront. The massive scale in which he organised the relief work and the ready response that his appeals for funds evoked in all parts of the country went a long way in saving lakhs of lives from the clutches of sure death.

No sooner had the people overcome the rigours of famine than the shadow of partition began to overcast the sky. The Muslim League, encouraged by the British and fortified by the appeasement policy of the Congress, decided to have its full pound of flesh in the form of Pakistan before the British left India for good. Shyama Prasad Mookerji organised a countrywide campaign against the partition of the motherland. But the ground slipped under his feet when the British Cabinet Mission, before which he was arguing against partition, confronted him with the Poona resolution of the Congress Working Committee which said that the Congress would not coerce any unwilling part to remain in India. It came as a shock and surprise to him. He had supported the Congress in 1946 elections because he was assured by Sardar Patel that the Congress would never accept Partition. He never knew till then that the Congress Working Committee had already conceded the right of the Muslim majority provinces to opt out of India.

Thereafter Shyama Prasad Mookerji bent his energies to partition Pakistan. Had Congress and Muslim League had their way, the whole of Punjab and the whole of Bengal would have gone to Pakistan. It was primarily due to the efforts of Shyama Prasad Mookerji that half of Punjab and half of Bengal was saved for India. That explains Dr. Mookerji's famous retort: "*Congress partitioned India and I partitioned Pakistan.*"

Shyama Prasad was invited by Gandhiji to join the first National Government in August 1947. He accepted the invitation in the hope that he would be able to influence the policies of free India in its formative period and safeguard the interests of crores of Hindus who had been left back in Pakistan much against their will.

His performance as Minister for Industries and Supplies in the first Government of free India was truly prodigious. He laid the firm foundations of the industrial development of the country by setting up the Chittaranjan Locomotive Factory and the Sindri Fertilizer Factory.

But on broad matters of policy, particularly regarding Pakistan, his differences with Pandit Nehru came to the surface quite early. The Nehru-Liaqat Pact of 1950 brought those differences to a climax. Having failed to prevent that ignominious pact being signed, Dr. Mookerji decided to leave the Cabinet and organise opposition to Nehru's policies from outside the Government. He thus became the first member to sit in the opposition in the Parliament-cum-Constituent Assembly of India.

The statement he made in Parliament about his resignation on 19 April 1950 has proved to be prophetic. It is the most realistic assessment of Indo-Pak relations that has ever been made. The reasons he enumerated why the Nehru-Liaqat Pact would not solve any problem are as valid today as they were in 1950.

The history of Indo-Pak relations since then, the fate of the Tashkent Agreement and the continued genocide of Hindus in Pakistan are eloquent testimony to his foresight and realism.

After quitting the Cabinet, Dr. Mookerji concentrated his energies on creating a political platform through which the ideology and policies he stood for could be projected. He had already said goodbye to the

Hindus Maha Sabha because it refused to accept his suggestion to open its doors to all Indians, irrespective of caste and creed. The Bharatiya Jana Sangh was the concrete result of his efforts. He became its founder- President in October 1951 and spent the rest of his life in building up this organisation as a nationalist democratic alternative to the party in power.

He was returned to the first Lok Sabha from North Calcutta in the first general election held in 1952. Jana Sangh could return only two other members. But Dr. Mookerji was not the man to despair. He brought together a number of small parties including the Ganatantra Parishad of Orissa, the Akali Dal of Punjab, the Hindu Maha Sabha and a number of independents to form the National Democratic Party in the Parliament, of which he was elected leader. This made him the virtual Leader of the Opposition in the Parliament and alternative Prime Minister of the country.

His role in the Parliament as Leader of the Opposition earned him the title "*lion of Parliament*". Parliament has yet to see his equal as a parliamentarian.

Soon after he entered the Parliament, the secessionist activities and policies of Sheikh Abdullah drew his attention. He decided to take up the cause of Jammu and Kashmir Praja Parishad which had been demanding that Jammu and Kashmir state be fully integrated with the rest of India and that it should have the same flag, constitution and President as the rest of the country. During his visit to Jammu in August 1952, he told a mammoth meeting: " I will get you the Indian Constitution or lay down my life for it." His words proved prophetic. When he decided to visit Jammu again in May 1953, to study on the spot the situation created by the reign of terror let loose by Sheikh Abdullah against the people of Jammu, the Government of India first decided to arrest him at Gurdaspur in Punjab but later changed its mind and allowed him to enter the State to be arrested there so that the Supreme Court of India, which till then had no jurisdiction over Jammu and Kashmir State, might not set him free. It was part of a conspiracy to remove him from the earthly scene. The way he died as a prisoner at Srinagar and the refusal of Pandit Nehru to hold an inquiry about his death in spite of the universal demand for it strengthened the doubts that he did not die a natural death. He thus became a martyr to the cause of Indian unity.

Dr. Shyama Prasad had a well-built stately body and an alert and analytical mind. He was an intellectual giant. His habits were simple He usually wore dhoti and kurta. He led an austere life and was an embodiment of simple living and high thinking.

He was a nationalist to the core of his heart. "Country comes first" was his watchword. His approach to all problems, internal and external, was uninhibited by any consideration of left or right. He stood for a reciprocal policy towards Pakistan, closer cultural and economic relations with the countries of South-East Asia and bilateral arrangements with other countries including the U.S.A. and the U.S.S.R. on the basis of mutuality of interests.

In the economic field he stood for market economy but did not rule out the entry of the State in the economic field in exceptional circumstances.

His views regarding education and language were clear-cut. He wanted to reorient the entire system of education with stress on vocational education and greater attention to moral and national content in the curricula. He was a great advocate of regional languages and accepted Hindi as the official language without any reservations. He continued to take a keen interest in the educational and cultural life of the country even when he became totally engrossed in politics. As President of the Mahabodhi Society, he acted as a link between India and the Buddhist world. His vistit to Burma and Cambodia in 1952 with the remains of Sariputta and Maha Moggalana was a great essay in revival and strengthening of cultural ties with these countries.

His death created a void in the cultural and political life of the country as a whole and particularly of Bengal which still remains to be filled.

[Shyama Prasad Mookerjee—A Phase of the Indian Struggle, Calcutta, 1942;—Educational Speeches, Calcutta; —Awake Hindusthan, Calcutta, 1944; Balraj Madhok—Dr. Shyama Prasad Mookerjee: A Bigoraphy, Delhi, 1954; Uma Prasad Mookerjee (Ed.)—Shyama Prasad Mookerjee: His Death in Detention, Calcutta, 1953; Shyama Prasader Kaekti Rachana, Calcutta, 1363; B.S.; V.P. Varma—Modern Indian Political Thought, Agra, 1964; The Statesman and The Amrita Bazar Patrika, 24 June 1953.]

—Balraj Madhok

13

The Last Phase of the Freedom Struggle—the R.I.N. Mutiny

1. The Nation in Ferment

With the end of war in Europe in April 1945 India's struggle for freedom entered a new phase. The war brought about tremendous advance in anti-imperialist consciousness. The INA trial had stirred the masses. Huge popular demonstration demanded the release of the INA prisoners. There were strikes and widespread unrest throughout the country.

The war had changed the balance of power in the world. Fascism had been routed. Socially radical regions were emerging in Eastern Europe, France, Italy and China. South-East Asia was being swept by an anti-imperialist wave. The United States of America and the Soviet Union emerged as big powers. Both supported India's demand for freedom.

The war had shattered the economic and military power of Britain. Labour Party replaced the Conservatives. The new government supported the Congress demands. There was decisive shift in British policy, due also to international dimension in the world-wide weakening of imperialist forces. The British Indian government could no longer rely on the Indian personnel of its civil administration and armed forces to suppress the national movement.

Patriotic ideas had entered the ranks of the professional Indian army, the chief instrument of the British rule in India. There were widespread strikes in the Indian Air Force. The Indian Signal Corps at Jabalpur went on strike. The police and the bureaucracy were showing signs of national leanings. They could no longer be safely used to suppress the national movement. The police force in Bihar and Delhi went on strike. Mass pressure was building up. The confident and determinant mood of the Indian people was by now obvious. They could no longer tolerate the humiliation of foreign rule. They could no longer rest till freedom was won. There were numerous agitations, strikes, hartals and demonstrations all over the country. Lakhs of people demonstrated in the streets to demand the release of INA prisoners. There were mass demonstrations. Bombay observed complete hartal and general strike in factories and offices.

Men in the armed forces seemed to have been realising the wretchedness of their position and the anxiety of their countrymen to finally put an end to the foreign rule. In 1930 during the civil disobedience movement, the Garhwali soldiers had refused to fire on their countrymen.[1] Thus men in armed forces time and again defied the orders of their foreign rulers. They were gradually realising that they too had a role to play in the struggle for freedom.

During the Second World War one hundred and fourteen members of the 21st Indian Cavalry had refused to fight the imperialist war abroad. Consequently four of them were hanged and one hundred and ten imprisoned.[2] Following August 1942 movement there were revolts in the armed forces which were suppressed. Nineteen mutinies have been reported in the Royal Indian Navy alone between March 1942 and April 1945.

Jawaharlal Nehru rightly said that the RIN episode had opened an altogether new chapter in the history of the armed forces in India.[3] It marked the end of the period when Indian servicemen could be used for the suppression of the Indian liberation movement. They joined hands with their countrymen in their fight for freedom from the foreign bondage.

Wavell told C-in-C and the Home Member to be prepared for trouble and possibly for a fresh struggle with the Congress as in August 1942, in view of the obvious intention of the Congress leaders to stir up mass struggle.[4] On 2 November, 1945 the Viceroy noted that wild speeches by Nehru and Patel threatened a mass movement. The Home Member had advised the Viceroy to warn Nehru about his speeches.[5] Wavell met Nehru on 3 November, 1945 and told him that no government could continue to tolerate indefinite incitement to violence or threats to its officials. Wavell wrote that Nehru practically admitted that he was preaching violence and said that he did not see how violence could be avoided, if legitimate aims could not be attained otherwise. Wavell noted: 'Nehru seems to me to have reached the state of mind of a fanatic and is quite incapable of considering any views that do not coincide with his own. I think he knows he is heading for trouble but feels he can rouse the country sufficiently to make it difficult for us to suppress it'.[6]

The situation in India was growing from bad to worse. The colonial rulers realised that nationalist press was virulent and saw a prospect of violent suppression with weaker and demoralised forces. The editor of the *Times of India* felt that the policy of Congress was almost openly violent and that they were determined to get rid of British power altogether in a year or two.[7]

The British government in India was faced with a situation of great difficulty and danger and sought help and guidance from England. The All-India Congress Committee held its session from 21-23 September, 1945. Since the above session, the Congress leaders were reported to have been making statements and speeches which were intended to provoke mass disorder. Special mention of the names of Patel in Bombay and Nehru and Pant in the United Provinces was made in this context. Actions of the INA men were glorified and officials who took part in the suppression of the 1942 movement were threatened to be tried and punished as war criminals. Patel made it clear that "Congress was not going to sit quiet after the election and wait on the convenience and pleasure of the British government. The Congress would demand an immediate and final solution...If such a solution was not forthcoming...sure as day follows night there would follow another struggle...when the time for action comes and the time for action may come soon. We must be able to act as one man...Nehru said a day earlier that revolution was inevitable."[8]

2. *Threat of serious disturbance all over the country*

Nehru had made the inevitability of revolution in India quite clear during the course of his interview with the Viceroy, who recorded: 'I believe that the Congress are counting on the INA as the spearhead of their revolt. They would suborn the Indian Army if they could and they hoped that their threats would impair the loyalty and efficiency of the police. They have been encouraged by events in French Indo-China and Indonesia which they are watching carefully; and a good deal may depend upon what happened there and in Syria and Palestine.'[9]

It was reported that the Congress leaders were organising attacks on the railways and public buildings, treasuries were to be looted and records destroyed; the whole administration was to be paralysed as was done in 1942. They were also planning to attack and murder any officials, British and Indian, on whom they could lay hands. Nehru praised people of Ballia, in which the rioters paralysed the administration during 1942 movement.

The Viceroy warned the Government in England to be prepared for a serious attempt by the Congress, probably next spring and even earlier to subvert by force the administration in India. He wrote that half measures would be of no use in dealing with such a movement. The Congress demanded immediate independence of India. The Viceroy considered that its suppression would involve the use of a considerable force of British troops. The situation was that the British members of the ICS and IFS were disspirited and discontented. The Indian members of these services were uneasy about the future and under strong political and social pressure, while the Indian subordinates on whom the administration so largely depended were reluctant to make enemies of the future masters of India. Wavell wrote on 6 November, 1945 that 'the dangers of inaction are grave, since the capacity of the administration in rural districts to stand up to serious disturbances is largely a matter of morale and service; morale is now bad in many districts and is being steadily undermined.'[10]

Besides this the officials in India agreed that INA problem was the most difficult problem that the British had faced in India. The INA trials afforded Congress leaders a splendid opportunity of mobilising the popular opinion against the government which they no doubt exploited. The Congress established a strong defence committee under Bhulabhai Desai with Nehru and Tej Bahadur Sapru. The Muslim League also associated itself with the defence of the INA officers.

As a last resort Wavell met Gandhi and convinced him about the violence of Congress speeches. Gandhi promised to get their tone lowered. At the same time he asserted that he had always tried for a settlement but was frustrated by the British policy of divide and rule. Wavell persuaded Gandhi not to antagonise them because independent India would want Britain's co-operation in defence and in commercial development. But Gandhi firmly replied that India needed no help from Britain in trade or defence. He said she would develop her trade in her own way and her defence would be the moral force of non-violence which would eventually conquer the whole world and bring about universal peace. Moreover, Gandhi had no trust of the British who broke their word.

On 27 December, 1945 Lord Wavell sent the political assessment of the Cabinet to the Secretary of State with a programme for political action. He explained the whole situation in this way that the object of the Congress was to seize power even by most violent means. He felt that Indian business magnates who were pro-Congress were anxious for a solution without conflict and disorder. He wrote that big landowners disliked and feared the Congress. The scheduled castes were divided and many of them supported the Congress. The League, though strongly anti-Congress, was not pro-government. As time went on the loyalty of the Indian officials, the Indian Army and the police was becoming difficult. A large number of British officials would seek the first opportunity to retire. The attitude of the Princes was that they would like to be rid of the British if it were not for the fear of the Congress. War with Japan and change of government in Britain had considerable effect on the Indian situation.[11]

'The whole country is in the throes of serious discontent. We are sitting on the edge of volcano which may erupt at any moment. A spark set ablaze Bombay, Calcutta and Karachi. These pre-storn conditions are not limited to big cities but are found even in the remotest villages. The truth is people are tired of foreign domination and want to end it immediately.'[12]

India in 1945-46 was a smouldering volcano which might erupt. The British administration in India could no longer 'rely on the Indian Armed Forces and it was impossible to hold India any longer by force of arms'.[13]

An examination of the contemporary press and intelligence reports reveals the revolutionary potential of the situation. When the British delegation was about to start for India Attlee said in the British

Parliament: 'The temperature of 1946 is not the temperature of 1920, 1930 or even 1942. I am quite certain that at the present time the tide of nationalism is running very high in India and indeed all over'.[14] India was passing through turmoil. The British Government could no longer hold India but no colonical power ever quits on its own.

The Government of India and the British Government in England were taken aback. Gravely disturbed by the event, the Prime Minister of England and the Secretary of State for India demanded a detailed report from the Viceroy.[15] English newspapers gave wide coverage of the event. The Commander-in-Chief of the armed forces in India wrote to the British Cabinet that 'if and when trouble comes, it may be on a greater scale than 1942, and is likely to be a combination of the wrecking of communication and widespread disorder in the rural districts'.[16] The authorities of Port Blair (Andamans) in a confidential urgent wire to New Delhi expressed their grave concern because the seven mine-sweepers there had stopped duty and all ships hoisted the Congress flag.[17] RIN ratings attached to Bahrein Naval Base refused duty out of sympathy with the RIN ratings in India. The Political Officer in Bahrein expressed similar concern.[18] The Air Force men expressed solidarity with RIN ratings.

3. The RIN Challenge

The history of the RIN uprising of 1946 is shrouded in controversy and needs proper examination. While some believe this event to be 'untimely and irresponsible' or 'a nail in the coffin of Swaraj', others describe it as the most serious revolt of the Indian armed forces against the British rule after 1857 which shook the foundations of the British Empire in India and hence the last glorious landmark in the struggle for India's freedom.

The events were as swift as stirring. On 18 February, 1946 the ratings in the Signals Training Establishment *Talwar* lent on hunger-strike in protest against bad food and racial discrimination. On the next day the strike spread to Castle and Fort Barracks and the tricolour, Crescent and hammer-and-sickle were flown on the mastheads of 22 ships in Bombay harbour. The ratings set up a Central Strike Committee and formulated certain demands of a specific nature. These related to abolition of discrimination in pay, release of INA undertrials and evacuation of Indian troops from Indonesia, among others. On

20 February the ratings were surrounded by the army guards. Fighting ensued on the following day at Castle Barracks when the ratings attempted to break through their forced encirclement. Within the next couple of days the mutiny spread to naval bases all over the country, 'involving at its height 78 ships, 20 shore establishments and 20,000 ratings.' In Bombay, in particular, a wave of sympathy swept the working class people who came out on the streets in support of the ratings. British troops were called in, as the Indian soldiers refused to open fire on their fellow-men. According to official figures casualties were 228 civilians killed and 1046 injured. On 23 February the ratings surrendered on the advice of the Congress leaders. "We surrender," they declared, "to India and not to Britain."

RIN Strike Enquiry Commission felt that food and bad service conditions were some of the important factors leading to the RIN strike. But the course of inquiry revealed facts which added new dimensions to the study of the RIN uprising.

Contact with INA personnel, diary of L/Tel.B.C. Dutt, a probe into the demands of the ratings and their slogans and actions compel a proper examination for a proper understanding of the events leading to the RIN revolt.

Reports for the quarter ending 1 December, 1945 concede that some ratings were influenced by INA propaganda and were sympathetic to INA.[19] The Inquiry Commission report further explains that majority of the ratings were politically conscious. The ratings' contact with INA and Azad Hind literature in Singapore, Malaya and Burma, free access to political meetings and inflammatory articles in press were some of the facts responsible for the revolt in RIN.[20]

Reviewing the whole situation after the war, the inquiry report gave interesting details as under:

"At the end of the war the world was in a state of unrest both political and economic. The transition from war time to peace time economy was inevitably attended by strained and unsettled relations between the employers and the employees owing to troubles over retrenchment, wages and costs and a sense of general disillusionment with the fruits of victory.

"The political situation was equally tense particularly in India where the effect of demand for freedom and the withdrawal of British control was reinforced by an insistent demand from all parties for withdrawal of Indian troops from Indonesia and later by general sympathy with I.N.A. and agitation for their release.

"Men of the Royal Indian Navy who had become politically conscious through the influences of the Press, the Radio, contact with Royal Navy and other Navies of the Empire, while serving abroad in foreign waters and experience of colour bar in South Africa, were particularly affected by the prevailing political unrest.

"Other factors which helped in undermining the discipline of the Service were the history of previous mutinies in the Royal Indian Navy, and the mutiny in the R.A.F. and R.I. A.F. misleadingly described as 'strike', and the apparent leniency of authorities in handling it".[21]

Dutt was one of the leaders of the ratings. The evidence of his diary and other papers shows that he was in touch with some outside organisations. One of his papers set out the necessity of a revolution in the forces.[22]

Between March 1942 and February 1946 there were at least nine uprisings in the RIN. There is ample evidence to prove that the RIN ratings were in touch with the INA people. Some of them kept Netaji's photographs and celebrated his birthday. They often shouted slogans like 'Jai Hind' and 'Subbas Ki Jai'. They sang INA songs. They hoisted Congress, Muslim League and Jai Hind flags on their ships. Some of their major demands were to set free political prisoners, to release all INA personnel unconditionally and to recall the armed forces from Indonesia. When they were asked to surrender they surrendered to the Indian people and not to the British authorities. Dutt in a letter to a fellow rating pathetically wrote, "you know, Souren, that day on 22nd February, 1946 at 5.00 P.M. when we were forced to surrender to the British who were aided and abetted by the national leaders I wept in despair".[23]

A probe into the contemporary newspapers reveals that the Naval Uprising was widely acclaimed by the general public. Common men and students in Bombay, Calcutta, Madras, Trivandrum, Karachi, Cochin and Delhi were reported to have supported this struggle. Bandhs and strikes were observed in their support throughout the country.[24] Indian soldiers stationed at Jabalpore went on strike on 28 February, 1946. They came out of their barracks and demonstrated on the city streets, shouting 'Jai Hind' and 'Quit India'. The people of the city observed hartal and fraternized with the soldiers.[25] People in the streets of Karachi shouted the slogan, 'Long live brave men of Navy',[26] on hearing of their gallant fight from H.M.I.S. *Hindustan,* which was stationed at Karachi.

The cooperation of the masses was acknowledged by the Naval Central Strike Committee:

"Our strike has been a historic event in the life of our nation. For the first time the blood of the men in services and in the streets flowed together for a common cause. We in the services will never forget this. We know also that our brothers and sisters will not forget, 'Long live our people,' 'Jai Hind'."[27]

Nehru felt that the RIN strike had demonstrated how the mind of the Indian armed forces was working and had shown that the iron wall which the British had created between the Indian army and the Indian people had collapsed.[28]

The Indian National Congress, the Muslim League and the Communist Party of India were the major parties in the politics of the period. The British Government in India had been very skilfully maintaining a balance between demands of the national leaders and imperial imperatives. As long as armed forces remained loyal the Government of India succeeded in maintaining the balance. The Commander-in-Chief observed in December 1945, "If there is a widespread revolt against the British, everything will depend upon the reliability of the Indian armed forces".[29]

This balance being disturbed by revolts in the armed forces, the Government now depended upon the political parties as a last resort. Wavell wired Attlee that although the top leaders of the Congress had nothing to do with the RIN event, the smaller Congress fry had a good deal to do with it and probably also the Communist agitators. In a subsequent despateh to the Prime Minister, the Viceroy explained that the disturbances in India followed the much usual pattern 'wherein Indian political leaders use these mobs for their own ends and are then surprised and alarmed that they break out on their own. They are probably being incited at present by left wing Congressmen and Communists against the intention of more responsible leaders.'[30]

All the political parties organised a mammoth rally in the Idgah ground of Karachi in support of the Naval revolt.[31] Nehru thundered at Chowpatty, Bombay, that the army should be fully politically conscious because besides being soldiers they had to be citizens and must know that as citizens of the country they had to discharge certain responsibilities to their people.[32] Sardar Patel denounced the revolt as sheer anarchy which must be stopped at once.[33] Jinnah declared it as untimely and irresponsible.[43] Gandhi considered the revolt as a nail in the coffin of Swaraj and denounced the combination of Hindus, Muslims and others for the purpose of violent actions as unholy and bad for India.[35] He said that Aruna Asaf Ali and her comrades had to ask every time whether non-violence had or had not raised India from her slumber of ages and created in them a yearning for Swaraj. In his opinion there was only one answer.[36]

The ratings felt that no political leaders of any party came forward to help them who, they explained, were perhaps too busy in jockeying for position in the new set-up that was in the offing.[37] Imperialism obtained a much needed reprieve, cunningly counter-attacked with the divisive weapon and succeeded in pushing partition down the throat of the compromising leadership.[38]

There was no place in the minds of the national leaders for any violent outbreak or upsurge that was likely to endanger or delay the imminent achievement of political freedom. Thus both the Congress and the Muslim League, the two main political parties, viewed the Naval revolt as unwelcome.[39]

The Governor of Sind wrote, 'there is little doubt that the communists were at the bottom of the trouble...but the ultimate responsibility must be borne by Nehru, Aruna Asaf Ali and all those who have preached violence and glorified the INA.'[40]

4. Conclusion

An examination of the available material in the subject reveals that the British Government—Conservative, Liberal or Labour—in spite of shaken economic conditions would like to hang on to India. But it was their fear that mass unrest had reached a level which could not be controlled by any help from the Army, Police, and Civil Service, Even the British officials were longing for catching the first available means of transport to leave India. The Viceroy had already made it clear that any uprising in India at that time could not be managed with the available resources in India. Under the circumstances the Royal Indian Navy revolt proved one of the most important events in the Indian freedom, struggle In its last message the Naval Central Strike Committee rightly claims: "Our strike has been a historic event in the life of our nation. For the first time the blood of the men in the services and the people flowed together in a common cause. We in the services will never forget."[41]

—Raj Kumar

References

1. Subrata Bannerjee, *The RIN Strike* (New Delhi: People's Publishing House, 1981), p. 3.
2. *Ibid.*
3. *Ibid.*
4. Penderel Moon, *Wavell The Viceroy's Journal*, 1977, p. 179.
5. *Ibid.*
6. *Ibid.*, p. 180.
7. *Ibid.*
8. *Ibid.*, p. 182.
9. *Ibid.*
10. *Ibid.*, p. 184.
11. *Ibid.*, p. 196.
12. Jawaharlal Nehru, while speaking at Jhansi on 2 March, 1946. *The Statesman* (New Delhi), 4 [illegible]arch, 1946.
13. Francis Tuker was the GOC of the Eastern Command in India in 1946. Francis Tuker, *While Memory Serves* (London, 1949), p. 89.
14. Mr. Attlee, British Prime Minister in Parliament, on 15 March, 1946.
15. Nicholas Mansergh (en-in-chief), *The Transfer of Power* 1942-47, Vol. VI., pp. 1044-47.
16. *Ibid.*, p. 578.
17. Cypher Telegram Secret 1368, Home, Poll. F. No. 115/46(a)/NAI.
18. *Ibid.*
19. *RIN* Strike Enquiry Commission Report, p. 25.
20. *Ibid.*, p. 26
21. *Ibid.*, p. 25
22. *Ibid.*,
23. Proceedings 37 RIN Uprising Seminar, Calcutta, 1983.
24. *Ibid.*
25. *Amrita Bazar Patrika* (Calcutta), 1 March, 1946.
26. Proceedings 37 RIN Uprising Seminar, Calcutta, 1933.
27. *Ibid.*
28. *The Statesman* (New Delhi), 4 March, 1946.
29. *Transfer of Power*, Vol. VI, p. 1055.
30. *Ibid.*, pp. 1055-56.
31. Proceedings 37 RIN Uprising Seminar, Calcutta, 1933.

32. *Free Press Journal,* 26 February, 1946.
33. *Amrita Bazar Patrika,* 25 February, 1946.
34. *Ibid.*
35. *The Statesman* (Calcutta), 24 February, 1946.
36. Proceedings 37 RIN Uprising Seminar, Calcutta, 1983.
37. *Ibid.*
38. *Ibid.*
39. *Ibid.*
40. F. Mudie Governor of Sind, in a wire to Wavell.
41. *The RIN Strike,* p. 75.

Appendix I

Annie Besant and Her Nationalism

Between the years 1910 and 1917, when the Extremist Party had temporarily broken down, and yet the spirit of extremism was more and more pervading the public mind, there stepped into the breach thus created, a very versatile, astute, and brilliant personality of Mrs. Annie Besant who made herself an Indian political leader of the very front rank during those years.

As a leader of the Theosophical Movement, she was closely studying the psychology of the Indian people and had already made a name for herself in India, especially among the Hindus. She started as a constructive educationist and founded the Central Hindu College in Benares which subsequently developed into the Hindu University. She had her machinery of religious propaganda – the press, and a number of local organisations all over India and a body of local leaders—ready, which she could convert at any moment into a machinery for political propaganda. She pleased the authorities by criticising the excesses of the Bengal Nationalists and created a faourable impression in the Government and pro-government circles.

She thus wrote on the Swadeshi movement in 1906:—

"So much confusion exists in so many minds just now as to the real meaning and objects of Swadeshi movement, and so many attempts are being made to turn it to a temporary political purpose, that it is the duty of those who have been working in it for many years, and who realise its permanent value, to do their utmost to keep it on its proper lines and to preserve it for its proper purposes...

"No country can escape severe poverty, if it has but one industry and that industry agriculture, and even the agriculture of a too narrow kind. Slowly and steadily, India has been losing the arts, crafts, and industries, which once enriched her people. Her handicraftsmen, perfected by hundreds of generations, are being starved out, for lack of customers to buy their products. Driven out of their own crafts by lack of customers, the craftsmen have betaken themselves to the only possible industry open to them—agriculture. Already overcrowded, it becomes more over-crowded still. The balance of industries is disturbed, ryot and craftsman no longer support each other, and when a bad year comes, the impoverished ryot and the artisan turned into cultivators, are all engulfed in the yawning abyss of famine.

"For all this, Swadeshism is the only remedy; and hence we cannot afford to renounce it because some people are trying to use it for local instead of national, for political instead of economic purposes."

Mrs. Besant had a very shrewd perception of the essential needs of the Indian situation. She first made a bold bid of social and religious leadership. She knew that nothing appeals more to the Indian mind than her past culture and glory and consequently she developed a scheme of national education independently of politics. This was a fundamental difference between her scheme and the scheme of Bengali nationalists. She very wisely avoided all political interference between her scheme on the moral and spiritual needs of India. "The needs of India," she wrote in 1905, "are, among others, the development of a national spirit, an education founded on Indian ideals, and enriched, not dominated, by the thought and culture of the West." Here was a real insight : and Mr. Besant never lacked energy to convert an insight into a reality.

Mrs. Besant, following Swami Vivekananda, perceived that the present system of education is a failure because it is dominated by everything foreign. "Nothing can more swiftly emasculate national life, nothing can more surely weaken national character, than allowing the education of the young to be controlled by foreign influences, to be dominated by foreign ideals. From 1896 onwards, I have ventured to urge on the Indian people that the education which was given to their sons was denationalising and despiritualising. Foreign habits, foreign manners, foreign dress, foreign ways are all enforced in a foreign language with, in missionary schools, a foreign religion to boot, sterilizing the boy's heart, and despiritualising his whole nature. Is it any wonder that the national spirit decayed?''

She then proceeds to lay down her ideal of a true system of national education:—

(1) It must be controlled by Indians, shaped by Indians, carried on by Indians... It must hold up Indian ideals of devotion, wisdom, and morality, and must be permeated by the Indian religious spirit rather than fed on the letter of the creeds. That spirit is spacious, tolerant, all-embracing and recognises that man goes to God along many roads and that all the prophets came from Him.

(2) National education must live in an atmosphere of proud and glorious patriotism, and this atmosphere must be kept sweet, fresh, and bracing by the study of Indian literature, Indian history, Indian triumphs in science, in art, in politics, in war, in colonization, in manufactures, in trade, in commerce. The Arthashastra must be studied as well as the Dharmashastra, science and politics as well as religion.

(3) National education must not be separated from the homes of the nation. The ideals, the interests, the principles, the emotions of the one must be those of the other. For the nation is built out of families, and the present opposition between the home and the school must cease.

(4) National education must meet the national temperament at every point and develop the national character. India is not to become a lesser– nor even a greater—England, but to evolve into a mightier India. British ideals are good for Britain but it is India's ideals that are good for India. We do not want echoes nor monotones; we want a choral melody of nations, mirroring the varied qualities of Nature and of God. Shall nature show but a single colour, and trees and flowers, and mountains and sky wear but a single hue? Harmonious variety and not monotony is the mark of perfection.

Away from all apologies for India, with all deprecatory explanations of India's ways and customs and traditions, India is herself and needs not to be justified; for verily God has evolved no greater, no more exquisite nationality than India's among all the broken reflections of His own perfect beauty.

Mrs. Besant here combines an extraordinary enthusiasm for India and her ideals, a strong sense of reality by making ample provision for the Western science and technology and by insisting that a widespread propaganda should be undertaken insisting on Indian princes, merchants, and employers of every kind, giving the preference in employment to the graduates of these national universities. But cautious as she was and fully alive to the dangers of the Indian situation, she insisted that *students* should not take part in politics. She wrote in 1905, "I hold that students should not be permitted to enter the arena of party politics while pursuing their studies. The excitement of party struggles indisposes the lads for steady application, and youth runs into wild excesses where mature men remain staid. Political struggles are for men, not for boys, and the hot blood of youth is not to be utilised by politicians to create public ferment and put pressure upon Government." An attitude like this served to remove all doubts and misapprehensions in the mind of the Government about the political sanity of Mrs. Besant in those days and enabled her to avoid certain rocks which proved the undoing of many a project of national education.

But Mrs. Annie Besant became bolder in course of time and cast aside all this conservatism in favour of a more radical national policy. She could not give a lead to the nation as long as she allowed herself to be dominated by the cautious ideology of the Indian Liberals. She knew that she could not placate both the Government and the people : and she chose to cast her lot among the Indian nationalists. She wrote: "The boys should grow up, through their school and college life in an atmosphere of pure and passionate patriotism, full of pride in their country, full of aspiration for her service. The high spirit of the boys must be trained and disciplined but never broken, love and not fear must be the root of their obedience, and trust not terror must characteriese their attitude to their teachers.

"The present generation of lads is splendid material but is mostly uncared for out of the class-hour, and un-loved by their teachers in the Government and missionary schools; their budding patriotism is treated as sedition, their self-respect is insubordination, their high spirits as rebellion; their national heroes must be worshipped in secret and the national portraits which should hang in their class-rooms must be hidden away in their boxes. We have to train our boys for freedom, and the very qualities now repressed, are national assets, to be utilised, not eradicated. We need not fear their high spirits, their daring, their pride, their sensitive dignity, these are the jewels of a free nation, though dreaded by the authorities over a subject people. Our boys must be as free in India as English boys are in England."

Mrs. Besant felt that the revolutionary movement was not a school-boy affair which could be suppressed by a little repression. The Reforms of 1909 had done nothing to placate the politically serious Indian mind. She knew that the stern policy adopted by the Government would drive young boys to the camp of anarchy more and more or would convert them into slaves. Here demand for National Education was a reply to this policy of the Government. But she realised that unless the people were given a bold and statesman-like lead for freedom, a lead which was not forthcoming from the Moderates—there would be no end to Indian unrest. The Extremist party had been temporarily broken: but the country required a lead on the lines of extremist agitation. This conviction seized her in 1913, when she returned from England, and she started the Home Rule Movement in 1914.

Mrs. Besant was very keen on the imperial connection. To her the Empire stood for all that it stood for in the eyes of the Liberal leaders; she was further proud of it because she hailed from Great Britain; and above all, the Empire was to her "a larger instrument and symbol of the evolving universal brotherhood of man, which it was the dream of Theosophy to realise on earth." She set herself out, therefore, with her characteristic shrewdness to bring back the faith of the Indian intelligentsia to the ideal of the Empire. But this could only be if the ideal of nationality be reconciled with the empire-ideal. This was the inner significance of the fight for Home Rule which she launched in 1914.

The sad experiences of the Indian Extremists had also taught them the need of imperial connection. The Moderates were adopting now a bolder attitude and were reconciled to the ideal of colonial self-government completely. Thus there was growing moderation among the Extremists and there was growing radicalism among the Moderates. The men's minds were thus prepared for a great reconcilation and a forward movement in Indian politics. The Government, too, showed considerable sympathy with the reasonable aspirations of the people, repealed the Partition of Bengal, and foretold the adoption of a new policy in Lord Harding's Despatch of August, 1911. A new cry of "Equal Partnership or Co-partnership in the Empire", began to supplant the old cry of "Colonial Self-Government", allegiance to the British connection was emphasised more than loyalty to British rule.

Mrs. Besant pushed herself forward as the champion of this new cry of Nationalist Imperialism. She thus hearalded the re-entry of the Extremist elements of the country into organised and constitutional politics with slight modification in their creed and programme. She appeared in the Congress of 1914 and said, "India claims the right, as a nation, to justice among the peoples of the Empire... India is growing in the sense of her dignity. She is not content to be a child any longer in the nursery of the empire. She is showing the responsibility of the man in Europe. Give her the freedom of the man in India."

During 1914-1916, her Home Rule League continued its vigorous propaganda preparing the nation's mind for new ideals. Tilak too started a similar Home Rule League in Maharashtra and joined forces with Mrs. Besant. The country was thus roused once more by the inspiring cry of Home Rule under the able leadership of Mrs. Besant and Tilak.

In 1916, Mrs. Besant said at the Lucknow Congress, "England at her peril calls on Indian soldiers to fight the liberty of Belgium and the sacredness of treaties, and then sends those soldiers back home to find their people still in bondage and treaties disregarded, torn in pieces, and thrown aside...There is only one thing which makes a nation fit for freedom, and that is the heart to aspire after it, and the will which is determined to have it".

Her internment threw a halo of martyrdom round her; and in 1917 she had the honour to preside over the Indian National Congress. Her presidentship marked the signal for the end of the dominance of the Liberal Party in the country. She trenchantly exposed the contradictions of the Imperialist's logic in her Presidential speech. The Imperialist was praying for victory over autocracy in Europe but wanted to maintain it in India. India was forced to see a further of perpetual subordination before her. "The Briton rules in Great Britain, the Frenchman in France, the American in America, each dominion in its own area; alone among the peoples of the world, he was not to feel his own country as his own. 'Britain for the British' was right and natural, 'India for the Indian' was wrong, was seditious. It must be 'India for the Empire' or not even for the Empire but, 'for the rest of the world.

Appendix II

Salutation to Bharat

This, this is the land that saw
father and mother live and thrive.
This is the land where countless ancestors
lived their hoary lives and died.
Thoughts a thousand grew
and flourished in this land.
In remembrance of it all
may I not praise my land?
Let me sing time and again

Mother, I bow to you.
Mother, I bow to you.

This, this is the land that gave us
birth and suck and the light of knowledge.
This is the land where our mothers
lisped their first words and grew in wisdom.
Here in their pure virgin girlhood
they danced and sang in abandon.
Here too in river or tank
they cooled their lustrous bodies.
In their memory I sing:

Mother, I bow to you.
Mother, I how to you.

This, this is the land where, as young women,
    our mothers married and reared their hearths.
'twas here, here they knew the rapture
    of motherhood, the pride of children.
Here the people's greatness soared high above
    in a prodigal spread of temples;
and when they ceased to be, the gentle dust
    mingled with the holy mother earth.
In commemoration may I sing:

Mother, I bow to you.
Mother, I bow to you.

— Subramaniam Bharti

Appendix III

Statement of Madan Lal Dhingra

I attempted to shed English blood intentionally and of purpose, as an humble protest against the inhuman transportation and hangings of Indian youth.

In this attempt I consulted none but my own conscience; conspired with none but my own duty.

I believe that a nation unwillingly held down by foreign bayonets is in a perpetual state of war. Since open battle in rendered impossible I attacked by surprise—since cannon could not be had I drew forth and fired a revolver.

As a Hindu I feel that the slavery of my nation is an insult to my God. Her cause is the cause of freedom. Her service is the service of Sri Krishna. Neither rich nor able, a poor son like myself can offer nothing but his blood on the altar of Mother's deliverance and so I rejoice at the prospect of my martyrdom.

The only lesson required in India is to learn how to die and the only way to teach it is by dying alone.

The soul is immortal and if everyone of my countrymen takes at least two lives of Englishmen before his body falls the Mother's salvation is a day's work.

This war ceases not only with the independence of India alone, it shall continue as long as the English and Hindu races exist in this world.

Until our country is free Sri Krishna stands exhorting 'if killed you attain Heaven; if successful you win the earth'.

It is my fervent prayer, "May I be reborn of the same mother and may I redie in the same sacred cause till my mission is done and she stands free for the good of humanity and to the glory of God."

Foreign Department, General B, Confidential, 1909, No. 13.

Appendix IV

Correspondence with Mahatma Gandhi August 1942– April 1944

1.—The 1942 Letters.

(1)

August 14th, 1942.

Dear Lord Linlithgow,

The Government of India were wrong in precipitating the crisis. The Government resolution justifying this step is full of distortions and misrepresentations. That you have the approval of your Indian "colleagues" can have no significance, except this, that in India you can always command such services. That co-operation is an additional justification for the demand of withdrawal irrespective of what people and parties may say.

The Government of India should have waited at least till the time I inaugurated mass action. I had publicly stated that I fully contemplated sending you a letter before taking concrete action. It was to be an appeal to you for an impartial examination of the Congress case. As you know, the Congress has readily filled in every omission that has been discovered in the conception of its demand. So could I have dealt with every difficulty if you had given me the opportunity. The precipitate action of the Government leads one to think that they were afraid that the extreme caution and gradualness with which the Congress was moving towards direct action might make world opinion veer round to the Congress, as it had already begun doing, and expose the hollowness of the grounds for the government's rejection of the Congress demand. They should surely have waited for an authentic report of my speeches on Friday and on Saturday night after the passing of the resoution by the All-India Congress Committee. You would have found in them that I would not hastily begin action. You should have taken advantage of the interval foreshadowed in them, and explored every possibility of satisfying the Congress demand.

The resolution says : "The Government of India have waited patiently in the hope that wiser counsels might prevail. They have been disappointed in that hope". I suppose wiser counsels here means abandonment of its demand by the Congress. Why should the abandonment of the demand legitimate at all times be hoped for by a Government pledged to guarantee independence to India? Is it a challenge that could only be met by immediate repression instead of patient reasoning with the demanding party? I venture to suggest that it is a long draft upon the credulity of mankind to say that the acceptance of the demand "would plunge India into confusion." Anyway the summary rejection of demand *has* plunged the nation and the Government into confusion. The Congress was making every effort to identify India with the Allied cause.

The Government resolution says : "The Governor-General in Council has been aware too for some days past of dangerous preparations by the Congress Party for unlawful and in some cases violent activities directed among other things to interruption of communications and public utility seryices, the organisation of strikes, tampering with the loyalty of Government servants, and interference with defence measures including recruitment". This is a gross distortion of the reality. Violence was never contemplated at any stage. A definition of what could be included in non-violent action has been interpreted in a sinister and subtle manner, as if the Congress was preparing for violent action. Everything was openly discussed among Congress circles, for nothing was to be done secretly. And why is it tampering with your loyalty if I ask you to give up a job which is harming the British people?

Instead of publishing behind the backs of principal Congressmen the misleading paragraph the Government immediately they came to know of the "preparations", should have brought to book the parties concerned with the preparations. That would have been the appropriate course. By their unsupported allegations in the resolution they have laid themselves open to the charge of unfair dealing.

The Congress movement was intended to evoke in the people the measure of sacrifice sufficient to compel attention. It was intended to demonstrate what measure of popular support it had. Was it wise at this time of the day to seek to suppress a popular movement avowedly non-violent?

The Government resolution further says : "The Congress is not India's mouthpiece. Yet in the interests of securing their own dominance and in pursuit of the totalitarian policy its leaders have consistently impeded the efforts made to bring India to full nationhood". It is a gross libel thus to accuse the oldest national organisation of India. This language lies ill in the mouth of a Government which has, as can be proved from published records consistently thwarted every national effort for attaining freedom, and sought to suppress the Congress by hook or by crook.

The Government of India have not condescended to consider the Congress offer that if simultaneously with the declaration of the independence of India they could not trust the Congress to form a stable provisional government they should ask the Muslim League to do so, and that any national government formed by the League would be loyally accepted by the Congress. Such an offer is hardly consistent with the charge of totalitarianism against the Congress.

Let me examine the Government offer. "It is that as soon as hostilities cease, India shall devise for herself, with full freedom of decision and on the basis embracing all and not only a single party, the form of government which she regards as most suited to her conditions." Has this offer any reality about it? All parties have not agreed now. Will it be any more possible after the War? And if the parties have to act before independence is in their hands. Parties grow up like mushrooms, for without proving their representative character, the Government will welcome them as they have done in the past and if they, the parities, oppose the Congress and its activities, though they may do lip homage to independence, frustration is inherent in the Government offer. Hence the logical cry of withdrawal first. Only after the end of British power and a fundamental change in the political status of India from bondage to freedom, will the formation of a truly representative government, whether provisional or permanent, be possible. The living burial of the author of the demand has not resolved the deadlock, it has aggravated it.

Then the resolution proceeds "The suggestion put forward by the Congress Party that the millions of India uncertain as to the future are ready, despite the sad lessons of so many martyr countries, to throw themselves into the arms of the invaders is one that the Government of India cannot accept as a true representation of the feeling of the people of this great country". I do not know about the millions, but I can give my own evidence in support of the Congress statement. It is open to the Government not to believe the Congress evidence. No imperial power likes to be told that it is in peril. It is because the Congress is anxious for Great Britain to avoid the fate that has overtaken other imperial powers that it asks her to shed imperialism voluntarily by declaring India independent. The Congress has not approached the movement with any but the friendliest motives. Congress seeks to kill imperialism as much for the sake of the British people and humanity as for India. Notwithstanding assertions to the contrary, I maintain that the congress has no interests of its own, apart from that of the whole of India and the world.

The following passage from the peroration in the resolution is interesting. "But on them lies the task of defending India, of maintaining India's capacity to wage war, of safeguarding India's interests, of holding the balance between the different sections of her people without fear or favour". All I can say is that is a mockery of truth after the experience of Malaya Singapore and Burma. It is sad to find the Government of India claiming to hold the "balance" between the parties for which it is itself demonstrably responsible.

One thing more. The declared cause is common between the Government of India and us. To put it in the most concrete terms it is the protection of the freedom of China and Russia. The Government of India think that the freedom of India is not necessary for winning the cause. I think exactly the opposite. I have taken. Jawaharlal Nehru as my measuring rod. His personal contacts make him feel much more the misery of the impending ruin of China and Russia than I can—and may I say than even you can. In that misery he tried to forget his old quarrel with imperialism. He dreads much more than I do the success of Fascism and Nazism. I have argued with him of days together. He fought against my position with a passion which I have no words to describe. But the logic of facts overwhelmed him. He yielded when he saw clearly that without the freedom of India that of the other two was in great jeopardy. Surely you are wrong in having imprisoned such a powerful friend and ally. If notwithstanding the common cause the Government's answer to the Congress demand is hasty repression, they will not wonder if I draw the inference that it was not so much the Allied cause that weighed with the British Government, as the unexpressed determination to cling to the possession of India as an indispensable part of the imperial policy. This determination led to the rejection of the Congress demand and precipitated repression. The present mutual slaughter on a scale never before known to history is suffocating enough. But the slaughter of truth accompanying the butchery and enforced by the falsity of which the resolution is reeking adds strength to the Congress position.

It causes me deep pain to have to send you this long letter. But however much I dislike your action. I remain the same friend you have known me. I would still plead for reconsideration of the Government of India's whole policy. Do not disregard the pleading of one who claims to be a sincere friend of the British people. Heaven guide you!

I am,
Yours sincerely,
M. K. Gandhi.

2

August 22nd, 1942.

Dear Mr. Gandhi,

Thank you very much for your letter, dated the 14th August, which reached me only a day or two ago.

2. I have read, I need not say, what you have been good enough to say in your letter with very close attention, and I have given full weight to your views. But I fear in the result that it would not be possible for me either to accept the criticisms which you advance of the resolution of the Governor-General in Council, or your request that the whole policy of the Government of India should be reconsidered.

Yours sincerely,
Linlithgow.

II.— The "Fast" Correspondence.

(3)

New Year's Eve, 1942.

[Personal.]
Dear Lord Linlithgow,

This is a very personal letter. Contrary to the biblical injunction. I have allowed many suns to set on a quarrel I have harboured against you, but I must not allow the old year to expire without disburdening myself of what is rankling in my breast against you. I had thought we were friends and should still love to think so. However that has happened since the 9th of August last makes me wonder whether you still regard me as a friend. I have perhaps not come in such close touch with any other occupant of your *Gadi* as with you.

Your arrest of me, the communiqué you issued thereafter, your reply to Rajaji and the reasons given therefor, Mr. Amery's attack on me and much else I can catalogue go to show that at some stage or other you must have suspected my *bona fides.* Mention of other Congressmen in the same connection is by the way. I seem to be the *fons et origo* of all the evil imputed to the Congress. If I have not ceased to be you friend. Why did you not, before taking drastic action, send for me, tell me of your suspicions and make yourself sure of your facts? I am quite capable of seeing myself as others see me, but in this case I have failed hopelessly. I find that all the statements made about me in Government quarters in this connection contain palpable departures from truth, I have so much fallen from grace that I could not establish contact with a dying friend; I mean Prof. Bhansali who is fasting in regard to the Chimur affair; and I am expected to condemn the so-called violence of some people reputed to be Congressmen, although I have no data for such condemnation save the heavily censored reports of newspapers. I must own that I thoroughly distrust these reports. I could write much more but I must not lengthen my tale of woe. I am sure that what I have said is enough to enable you to fill in details.

You know I returned to India from South Africa at the end of 1914 with a mission which came to me in 1906, namely, to spread truth and non-violence among mankind in the place of violence and falsehood in all walks of life. The law of *Satyagraha* knows no defeat. Prison is one of the many ways of spreading the message, but it has its limits. You have placed me in a palace where every reasonable creature comfort is ensured. I have freely partaken of the fatter purely as a matter of duty, never as a pleasure, in the hope that some day those that have the power will realise that they have wronged innocent men. I had given myself six months. The period is drawing to a close, so is my patience. The law of *Satyagraha* as I know it prescribes a remedy in such moments of trial. In a sentence its "crucify the flesh by fasting". That same law forbids its use except as a last resort. I do not want to use it if I can avoid it. This is the way to avoid it, convince me of my error or errors and I shall make ample amends. You can send for me or send someone who knows your mind and can carry conviction. There are many other ways if you have the will. May I expect an early reply? May the New Year bring peace to us all.

I am,
Your sincere friend,
M. K. Gandhi.

(4)

January 13th, 1943.

[Personal.]
Dear Mr. Gandhi,

Thank you for your personal letter of December 31st, which I have just received.' I fully accept its personal character, and I welcome its frankness....

2. I was glad to have your letter, for, to be as open with you as our previous relations justify, If have been profoundly depressed during recent months first by the policy that was adopted by the Congress in August, secondly, because while that policy gave rise, as it was obvious it must, throughout the country to violence and crime (I say nothing of the risks to India from outside aggression) no word of condemnation for that violence and crime should have come from you, of from the Working Committee. When you were first at Poona I knew that you were not receiving newspapers, and I accepted that as explaining your silence. When arrangements were made that you and the Working Committee should have such newspapers as you desired I felt certain that the details those newspapers contained of what was happening would shock and distress you as much as it has as all, and that you would be anxious to make your condemnation of it categorical and widely known. But that was not the case; and it has been a real disappointment to me, all the more when I think of these murders, the burning alive of police officials, the wrecking of trains, the destruction of property, the misleading of these young students, which has done so much harm to India's good name, and to the Congress Party. Your many take it from me that the newspaper accounts you mention are well founded—I only wish they were not, for the story is a bad one. I well know the immense weight of your great authority in the Congress movement and with the Party and those who follow its lead, and I wish I could feel, again speaking very frankly, that a heavy responsibility did not rest on you. (And unhappily, while the initial responsibility rests with the leaders, others have to bear the consequences, whether as lawbreakers, with the results that involves, or as the victims).

3. But if I am right in reading your letter to mean that in the light of what has happened you wish now to retrace your steps and dissociate yourself from the policy of last summer, you have only to let me know and I will at once consider the matter further. And if I have failed to understand your object, you must not hesitate to let me know without delay in what respect I have done so, and tell me what positive suggestion you wish to put to me. You know me well enough after these many years to believe that I shall be only too concerned to

read with the same close attention as ever any message which I receive from you, to give it the fullest weight, and to approach it with the deepest anxiety to understand you feeling and your motives.

Yours sicerely
Linlithgow.

(5)

January 29th, 1943.

Dear Lord Linlithgow,

I must thank you warmly for your prompt reply to my letter of 19th instant. I wish I could agree with you that your letter is clear. I am sure you do not wish to imply by clearness simply that you hold a particular opinion strongly. I have pleaded and would continue to plead till the last breath, that you should at least make an attempt to convince me of the validity of the opinion you hold that the August resolution of the Congress is responsible for the popular violence that broke out on 9th August last and after, even though it broke out after the wholesale arrest of principal Congress workers. Was not the drastic and unwarranted action of the government responsible for the reported violence?

You have not even said what part of the August resolution is bad or offensive in your opinion. That resolution is in no way a retraction by the Congress of its policy of non-violence. It is definitely against Fascism in every shape or form. It tenders co-operation in war effort under circumstances which alone can make effective and nation-wide co-operation possible. Is all this open to reproach? Objection may be raised to that clause of the resolution which contemplated civil disobedience. But that by itself cannot constitute an objection since the principle of civil disobedience is impliedly conceded in what is known as the "Gandhi-Irwin pact". Even that civil disobedience was not to be started before knowing the result of the meeting for which I was to seek from you an appointment:

Then, take the unproved and in my opinion unprovable charges hurled against the Congress and me by so responsible a Minister as the Secretary of State for India.

Surely I can say with safety that it is for the Government to justify their action by solid evidence not by mere *ipse dixit.*

But you throw in my face the facts of murders by persons reputed to be Congressmen. I see the fact of the murders as clearly, I hope, as you do. They started leonine violence in the shape of the arrests already referred to. That violence is not any the less so, because it is organised on a scale so gigantic that it displaces the Mosaic law of tooth for tooth by that of ten thousand for one—not to mention the corollary of the Mosaic law, *i.e.,* of non-resistance as enunciated by Jesus Christ. I cannot interpret in any other manner the repressive measures of the all-powerful Government of India.

Add to this tale of woe the privations of the poor millions due to India-wide scarcity which I cannot help thinking might have been largely mitigated, if not altogether prevented, had there been a *bona fide* national government responsible to a popularly elected assembly.

If then I cannot get soothing balm for my pain, I must resort to the law prescribed for satyagrahis, namely, a fast according to capacity. I must commence after the early morning breakfast of the 9th February a fast for 21 days ending on the morning of the 2nd March. Usually, during my fasts, I take water with the addition of salts. But nowadays my system refuses water. This time therefore, I propose to add juices of citrus fruit to make water drinkable. For my wish is not to fast unto death, but to survive the ordeal, if god so wills. This fast can be ended sooner by the government giving the needed relief.

I am not marking this letter personal as I did the two previous ones. They were in no way confidential. They were a mere personal appeal.

I am,
Your sincere friend,
M. K. Gandhi.

P.S.—The following was inadvertently omitted.

The Government have evidently ignored or overlooked the very material fact that the Congress by its August resolution asked nothing for itself. All its demands were for the whole people. As you should be aware, the Congress was willing and prepared for the Government inviting Q.-A. -Jinnah to form a national government subject to such agreed adjustments as may be necessary for the duration of the war, such government being responsible to a duly elected assembly. Being isolated from the Working Committee except Shrimati Sarojini Devi, I do not know its present mind. But the committee is not likely to have changed its mind.

(6)

February, 5th, 1943.

Dear Mr. Gandhi,

Many thanks for your letter of 29th January which I have just received. I have read it, as always, with great care and with every anxiety to follow your mind and to do full justice to your argument. But I fear that my view of the responsibility of Congress and of yourself personally for the lamentable disorders of last autumn remains unchanged.

2. In my last letter I said that my knowledge of the facts left me no choice but to regard the Congress movement, and you as its authorised and fully empowered leader at the time of the decision of last August as responsible for the campaign of violence and crime that subsequently broke out. In reply you have reiterated your request that I should attempt to convince you that my opinion is correct. I would readily have responded earlier to that request were it not that your letters have no indication, such as I should have been entitled to expect, that you sought the information with an open mind. In each of them you have expressed profound distrust of the published reports of the recent happenings, although in your last letter, on the basis of the same information, you have not hesitated to lay the whole blame for them on the Government of India. In the same letter you have stated that I cannot expect you to accept the accuracy of the official reports on which I rely.... since the Congress Resolution of the 8th August declared a "mass struggle" in support of its demands, appointed you as its leader and authorised all Congressmen to act for themselves in the event of interference with the leadership of the movement. A body which passes a resolution in such terms is hardly entitled to

disclaim responsibility for any events that followed it. There is evidence that you and your friends expected this policy to lead to violence; and that you were prepared to condone it, and that the violence that ensued formed part of a concerted plan, conceived long before the arrest of Congress leaders. The general nature of the case against the Congress has been publicly stated b/ the Home Member in his speech in the Central Legislative Assembly on the 15th September last, and if you need further information I would refer you to it. I enclose a complete copy in case the press versions that you must have seen were not sufficient. I need only add that all the mass of evidence that has since come to light has confirmed the conclusions then reached. I have ample information that the campaign of sabotage has been conducted under secret instructions, circulated in the name of the All-India Congress Committee, that well-known Congressmen have organised and freely taken part in acts of violence and murder; and that even now an underground Congress organisation exists in which, among others, the wife of a member of the Congress Working Committee plays a prominent part, and which is actively engaged in planning the bomb outrages and other acts of terrorism that have disgusted the whole country. If we do not act on all this information or make it publicly known, it is because the time is not yet ripe; but you may rest assured that the charges against the Congress will have to be met sooner or later and it will then be for you and your colleagues to clear yourselves before the world if you can. And if in the meanwhile you yourself, by any action such as you now appear to be contemplating, attempt to find an easy way out, the judgement will go against you by default.

3. I have read with some surprise your statement that the principle of civil disobedience is implicitly conceded in the Delhi Settlement of the 5th March 1931, which you refer to as the "Gandhi-Irwin Pact". I have again looked at that document. Its basis was that civil disobedience would be "effectively discontinued" and that certain "reciprocal action" would be taken by Government. It was inherent in such a document that it should take notice of the existence of civil disobedience. But I can find nothing in it to suggest that civil disobedience was recognised as being in any circumstances legitimate.

And I cannot make it too plain that it is not so regarded by my Government.

4. To accept the point of view which you put forward would be to concede that the authorised government of the country, on which lies the responsibility for maintaining peace and good order, should allow subversive and revolutionary movements described by you yourself as open rebellion, to take place unchallenged; that they should allow preparations for violence, for the interruption of communications, for attacks on innocent persons, for the murder of police officers and others to proceed unchecked. My government and I are open indeed to the charge that we should have taken drastic action at an earlier stage against you and against the Congress leaders. But my anxiety and that of my Government has throughout been to give you, and to give the Congress organisation, every possible opportunity to withdraw from the position which you have decided to take up. Your statements of last June and July, the original resolution of the Working Committee of the 14th July, and your declaration on the same day that there was no room left for negotiation and that after all it was an open rebellion, are all of them grave and significant, even without your final exhortation to "do or die". But with a patience that was perhaps misplaced, it was decided to wait until the resolution of the All India Congress Committee made it clear that there could be no further toleration of the Congress attitude if Government was to discharge its responsibility to the people of India.

5. Let me in conclusion say how greatly I regret, having regard to your vieus... I hope and pray that wiser counsels may yet prevail with you. But the decision whether or not to undertake a fast with its attendant risks is clearly one that must be taken by you alone, and the responsibility for which and for its consequences must rest on you alone. I trust sincerely that in the light of what I have said you may think better of your resolution; and I would welcome a decision on your part to think better of it, not only because of my own natural reluctance to see you wilfully risk your life, but because I regard the use of a fast for political purposes as a form of political blackmail (*himsa*) for which there can be no moral justification, and

understood from your own previous writings that this was also your view.

Yours sincerely,
Linlithgow.

(7)

February 7th, 1943.

Dear Lord Linlithgow,

I have to thank you for your long reply, dated the 5th instant, to my letter of 29th January last. I would take your last point first, namely, the contemplated fast which begins on 9th instant. Your letter, form a *Satyagrahi's* standpoint, is an invitation to fast. No doubt the responsibility for the step and its consequences will be solely mine. You have allowed an expression to slip from your pen for which I was unprepared. In the concluding sentence of the second paragraph you describe the step as an attempt "to find an easy way out". That you, as a friend, can impute such a base and cowardly motive to me passes comprehension. You have also described it as "a form of political blackmail". Any you quote my previous writings on the subject against me. I abide by my writings. I hold that there is nothing inconsistent in them with the contemplated step. I wonder whether you have yourself read those writings.

I do claim that I have approached you with an open mind when I asked you to convince me of my error. "Profound distrust" of the published reports is in no way inconsistent with my having an open mind.

You say that there is evidence that I—I leave my friends out for the moment—"expected this policy to lead to violence", that I was "prepared to condone it", and that "the violence that ensused formed part of a concerted plan conceived long before the arrest of Congress leaders". I have seen no evidence in support of such a serious charge. You admit that part of the evidence has yet to be published. The speech of the Home Member, of which you have favoured me with a copy, may be taken as the opening speech of the prosecution counsel and nothing more. It contains unsupported imputations against

Congressmen. Of course he has described the violent outburst in graphic language. But he has not said why it took place when it did. You have condemned men and women before trying them and hearing their defence. Surely there is nothing wrong in my asking you to show me the evidence on which you hold them guilty. What you say in your letter carries no conviction. Proof should correspond to the canons of English jurisprudence.

If the wife of a member of the Working Committee is actively engaged in "planning the bomb outrages and other acts of terrorism", she should be tried before a court of law and punished if found guilty. The lady you refer to could only have done the things attributed to her after the wholesale arrests of 9th August last, which I have dared to describe as leonine violence.

You say that the time is not yet ripe to publish the charges against the Congress. Have you ever thought of the possibility of their being found baseless when they are put before an impartial Tribunal? Or that some of the condemned persons might have died in the meanwhile, or that some of the evidence that the living can produce might become unavailable?

I reiterate the statement that the principle of civil disobedience is implicitly conceded in the Settlement of 5th March 1931 arrived at between the then Viceroy on behalf of the Government of India and myself on behalf of the Congress. I hope you know that the principal Congressmen were discharged.... Civil disobedience was discontinued only on conditions being fulfilled by the Government. That by itself was, in my opinion, an acknowledgment of its legitimacy, of course under given circum-stances. It therefore seems somewhat strange to find you maintain that civil disobedience "cannot be recognised as being in any circumstances legitimate" by your government. You ignore the practice of the British government which has recognised this legitimacy under the name of "passive resistance".

Lastly you read into my letters a meaning which is wholly inconsistent with my declaration, in one of them, of adherence to unadulterated non-violence. For, you say in your letter under reply that "acceptance of my point of view would be to concede that the authorised government of the country on which lies the responsibility for maintaining peace and good order, should allow movements to take place that would admit preparations for violence, interruption of communications, for attacks on innocent persons, for murders of police officers and others to proceed unchecked''. I must be a strange friend of yours whom you believe to be capable of asking for recognition of such things as lawful.

I have not attempted an exhaustive reply to the views and statements attributed to me. This is not the place nor the time for such a reply. I have only picked out those things which in my opinion demanded an immediate answer. You have left me no loophole for escaping the ordeal I have set before myself. I begin it on the 9th instant with the clearest possible conscience. Despite your description of it as ''a form of political blackmail'', it is on my part meant to be an appeal to the Higest Tribunal for justice which I have failed to secure from you. If I do not survive the ordeal, I shall go to the Judgment Seat with the fullest faith in my innocence, Posterity will judge between you as representative of an all-powerful government and me as a humble man who has tried to serve his country and humanity through it.

My last letter was written against time, and therefore a material paragraph went in as postscript. I now send herewith a fair copy typed by Pearay Lal who has taken Mahadeo Desai's place. You will find the postscript paragraph restored to the place where it should have been.

I am,
Your sincere friend,
M. K. Gandhi.

(8)

Home Department,
February 7th, 1943.

Dear Mr. Gandhi,

The Government of India have been informed by His Excellency the Viceroy of your intentions as communicated to him of undertaking a fast for 21 days in certain circumstances. They have carefully considered the position, and the conclusions that they have reached in the light of such consideration are set out in the statement of which a copy is enclosed, which they would propose, in the event of your maintaining your present intention, to release in due course to the press.

2. The Government of India, as you will see from their statement, would be very reluctant to see you fast, and I am instructed to inform you that, as the statement makes clear, they would propose that, should you persist in your intention, you will be set at liberty for the purpose, and for the duration, of your fast as from the time of its commencement. During the period of your fast there will be no objection to your proceeding where you wish, though the Government of India trust that you will be able to arrange for your accommodation away from the Aga Khan's Palace.

3. Should you for any reason find yourself unable to take advantage of these arrangements, a decision which the Government of India would greatly regret, they will of course suitably amend the statement of which a copy is now enclosed before it issues. But they wish me to repeat, with all earnestness, their anxiety and their hope that the considerations which have carried so much weight with them will equally carry weight with you, and that you will not pursue your present tentative proposal. In that event, no occasion, will of course arise for the issue of any statement of any kind.

Yours sincerely,
R. Tottenham.

Additional Secretary to the Government of India.

(9)

February 8th, 1943.

Dear Sir Richard,

I have very carefully studied your letter. I am sorry to say that there is nothing in the correspondence which has taken place between His Excellency and myself or your letter, to warrant a recalling of my intention to fast. I have mentioned in my letters to His Excellency the conditions which can induce prevention or suspension of the step.

If the temporary release is offered for my convenience I do not need it. I shall be quite content to take my fast as a detenu or prisoner. If it is for the convenience of the Government, I am sorry I am unable to suit them, much as I should like to do so. I can say this much, that I, as a prisoner, shall avoid, as far as is humanly possible, every cause of inconvenience to the Government save what is inherent in the fast itself. The impending fast has not been conceived to be taken as a free man. Circumstances may arise, as they have done before now, when I may have to fast as a free man. If therefore I am released, there will be no fast in terms of my correspondence above-mentioned. I shall have to survey the situation *de novo* and decide what I should do. I have no desire to be released under false pretences. In spite of all that has been said against me, I hope not to belie the vow of truth and non-violence which alone makes life liveable for me. I say this, if it is only for my own satisfaction. It does me good to reiterate openly my faith, when outer darkness surrounds me, as it does just now.

I must not hustle the Government into a decision on this letter. I understand that your letter has been dictated through the telephone. In order to give the government enough time, I shall suspend the fast, if necessary, to Wednesday next, 10th instant.

So far as the statement proposed to be issued by the Government is concerned, and of which you have favoured me with a copy, I can have no opinion. But if I might have, I must say that it does me an injustice. The proper course would be to publish the full correspondence and let the public judge for themselves.

Yours sincerely,
M. K. Gandhi

(10)

Home Department,
February 9th, 1943.

Dear Mr. Gandhi

I am instructed to acknowledge the receipt of your letter of 8th February 1943, which has been laid before the Governor-General in Council. The Government of India note your decision with great regret. Their position remains the same, that is to say they are ready to set you at liberty for the purpose and duration of your fast. But if your are not prepared to take advantage of that fact, and if you fast while in detention, you will do no solely on your own responsibility and at your own risk. In that event you will be at liberty to have your own medical attendants, and also to receive visits from friends with the permission of government during its period. Suitable drafting alterations will be made in the statement which the Government of India would, in that event, issue to the press.

Yours sincerely,
R. Tottenham.

III. The Mr. Jinnah Correspondence.

(11)

May 4th, 1943.

To

The Secretary,

Government of India, Home Department.

Sir,

Will you please forward the enclosed to Quaid-e-Azam Jinnah?

I am,
Yours faithfully,
M. K. Gandhi.

(12)

May 4th, 1943.

Dear Quaid-e-Azam,

When some time after my incarceration, the Government asked me for a list of newspapers I would like to have, I included the *Dawn* in my list. I have been receiving it with more or less regularity. Whenever it comes to me, I read it carefully. I have followed the proceedings of the League as reported in the *Dawn* columns. I noted your invitation to me to write to you. Hence this letter.

I welcome your invitation. I suggest our meeting face to face rather than talking through correspondence. But I am in your hands.

I hope that this letter will be sent to you and, if you agree to my proposal, that the Government will let you visit me.

One thing I had better mention. There seems to be an "if" about your invitation. Do you say I should write only if I have changed my heart? God alone knows men's hearts. I would like you to take me as I am.

Why should not both you and I approach the great question of communal unity as men determined of finding a common solution and work together to make our solution acceptable to all who are concerned with it or are interested in it?

Yours sincerely,
M. K. Gandhi.

(13)

To

Quaid-e-Azam M. A. Jinnah,
Mount Pleasant Road, Bombay.

Home Department,
May 24th, 1943.

Dear Mr. Gandhi,

In reply to your letter of the 4th May in which you have requested the Government of India to forward a letter of the same date addressed by you to Mr. Jinnah, I am to inform you that the Government of India have decided that your letter cannot be forwarded. This decision is in accordance with the restrictions which as you are aware have been placed on your correspondence and interviews while you are under detention. Government propose shortly to issue a communique, of which I enclose an advance copy, stating the fact that the letter has been withheld and the reasons therefor.

Yours sincerely,
R. Tottenham.

Press Communiquè

The Government of India have received a request from Mr. Gandhi to forward a short letter from himself to Mr. Jinnah expressing a wish to meet him.

In accordance with their known policy in regard to correspondence or interviews with Mr. Gandhi the Government of India have decided that this letter cannot be forwarded and have so informed Mr. Gandhi and Mr. Jinnah. They are not prepared to give facilities for political correspondence or contact to a person detained for promoting an illegal mass movement which he has not disavowed and thus gravely embarrassing India's war effort at a critical time. It rests with Mr. Gandhi to satisfy the Government of India that he can safely be allowed once more to participate in the public affairs of the country, and until he does so, the disabilities from which he suffers are of his own choice.

(14)

May 27th, 1943.

Dear Sir Richard Tottenham,

I received last evening your letter of the 24th instant refusing my request to forward my letter addressed to Quaid-e-Azam Jinnah. I wrote only yesterday to the Superintendent of this camp asking him knidly to inquire whether my letter to Quaid-e-Azam Jinnah, and later, one dated the 15th instant, to Right Honourable Lord Samuel had been forwarded to the respective addresses.

I am sorry for the Government's decision. For my letter to the Quaid-e-Azam was sent in reply to his public invitation to me to write to him and I was especially encouraged to do so because his language had led me to think that, if I wrote to him, my letter would be forwarded to him. The public too are anxious that the Quaid-e-Azam and I should meet or at least establish contact. I have always been anxious to meet the Quaid-e-Azam, if per chance we could devise some solution of the communal tangle which might be generally acceptable. Therefore the disability in the present instance is much more that of the public than mine. As a *Satyagrahi* I may not regard as disabilities the restrictions which the Government have imposed upon me. As the Government are aware, I have denied myself even the pleasure of writing to my relatives as I am not allowed to perform the service of writing to my co-workers who are in a sense more to me than my relatives.

The advance copy of the contemplated communique with which you have considerately favoured me requires emendation in more places than one. For, as it stands, it does not square with facts.

As to the disavowal referred to in the proposed communiquè, the Government are aware that I regard the non-violent mass movement, for the launching of which the Congress gave me authority on the 8th of August last, as perfectly legitimate and in the interest both of the Government and the public. As it is, the Government left me no time to start the movement. Therefore how could a movement, which was never started, embarrass "India's" war effort? If then, there was any embarrassment by reason of the popular resentment of the government's action in resorting to the wholesale arrests of principal Congressmen, the responsibility was solely that of the government. The mass movement, as the resolution sanctioning it said in so many words, was sanctioned in order to promote India-wide efforts on behalf of the Allied cause, including the causes of Russia and China, whose danger was very great in August last and from which, in my opinion, they are by no means free even now. I hope the government will not feel offended when I say that all the war effort that is being put forth in India is not India's but the alien Government's. I submit that if the Government had complied with the request of the Congress as embodied in its August resolution, there would have been a mass effort without parallel for winning the battle for human freedom and ridding the world of the menace that Fascism, Nazism, Japanism and Imperalism are. I may be wholly wrong; anyway this is my deliberate and honest opinion.

In order to make the communiquè accord with facts, I suggest the following alteration in the first paragraph: after "Mr. Jinnah" add "in response to his public invitation to Mr. Gandhi to write to him, stating that he (Mr. Gandhi) would be willing to correspond with or meet him according as he wished".

I hope that the remaining portion of the communiquè too will be suitably amended in the light of my submission.

I am,
Yours sincerely,
M. K. Gandhi.

(15)

May 28th, 1943,

Dear Sir Richard Tottenham,

I handed my reply to your letter of the 24th instant, at about one o'clock yesterday, to the Superintendent. I hurried the writing and the despatch in the hope of my letter reaching you before the publication of the communiquè. I was therefore astonished and grieved to find the communique in the paper received in the afternoon, and

Reuter's report of the reactions upon it in London. Evidently there was no meaning in an advance copy of the communiquè being sent to me. I regard the communiquè not only to be inconsistent with facts but unfair to me. The only way partial redress can be given to me is the publication of the correspondence between us. I therefore request that it may be published.

I am,
Yours sincerely,
M. K. Gandhi.

(16)

Home Department,
June 4th, 1943.

Dear Mr. Gandhi,

I am directed to acknowledge your letter to Sir Richard Tottenham, dated 27th May 1943, and to say that the Government of India have considered it but see no reason to modify their communiquè already published.

Yours sincerely,
E. Conran-Smith,
Secretary to the Government of India.

(17)

Home Department,
June 8th, 1943.

Dear Mr. Gandhi,

In reply to your letter to Sir Richard Tottenham, dated 28th May 1943, I am directed to say that the advance copy of the communiquè stating government's reason for not forwarding your letter to Mr. Jinnah was furnished to you for your personal information and that government regret they see no reason to publish the Correspondence.

Yours sincerely,
E. Conran-Smith.

❑❑❑